SANTA  P9-EJI-348

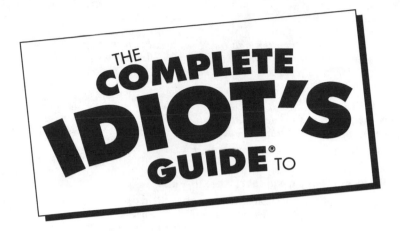

THE COMPLETE IDIOT'S GUIDE® TO

Coaching Youth Basketball

by Bill Gutman and Tom Finnegan, Ph.D.

A member of Penguin Group (USA) Inc.

*To every kid, down through the years, who has picked up a
basketball and looked for someone to teach him. And to my old friend
Al Levine, who could always hit a one-hander from the outside.*

Bill Gutman

*I would like to dedicate this book to my wife, Rosemary, whose love and
encouragement inspires me daily, and to all the basketball teams that I have
had the privilege to coach throughout my career. Thanks for the memories.*

Tom Finnegan, Ph.D.

Publisher: *Marie Butler-Knight*
Product Manager: *Phil Kitchel*
Senior Managing Editor: *Jennifer Chisholm*
Senior Acquisitions Editor: *Mike Sanders*
Development Editor: *Ginny Bess Munroe*
Production Editor: *Billy Fields*
Copy Editor: *Krista Hansing*
Illustrator: *Chris Eliopoulos*
Cover/Book Designer: *Trina Wurst*
Indexer: *Aamir Burki*
Layout/Proofreading: *Angela Calvert, John Etchison*

Contents at a Glance

Contents

Introduction

It's the first day of basketball practice, and you are standing face to face with your new team. Regardless of whether they are boys or girls, or 8- or 14-year-olds, they look to you to set the tone and the approach to both learning and playing the game, to get everyone involved equally, and to make practice and games fun.

To do this and to do it well, a coach today needs many different tools at his or her disposal. Not only do you need an in-depth knowledge of the game, but you must also be capable of teaching the fundamentals and individual skills of the game while creating a cohesive, smooth-working team. At the same time, you need to impart a positive attitude, one that says that while it's fun to win, a team playing hard and to the best of its ability shouldn't be ashamed if it loses.

The Complete Idiot's Guide to Coaching Youth Basketball has something for every coach working with youngsters today. Not only does this book provide a complete offensive scheme (with variations) that we feel is the perfect way to help your players learn the total offensive game, but it also covers the various forms of defense. The strategies set forth in this book will enable your team to cope with any basic basketball situation that might arise, both offensively and defensively.

Just as important, this book deals with important issues facing youngsters who compete in team sports today. Unfortunately, this is an era in which bad sportsmanship abounds in both collegiate and professional sports, in which parents often have unrealistic expectations of their children, and in which win-at-all-costs has become the dictate of the day. We address these issues to prepare you in case they permeate your team.

Use this book as the basic blueprint for the entire season, to organize your practices and games, to employ practical teaching techniques to use on both sides of the ball, and to show those in your charge the value of coming together as a team in which players and coach work together for a common goal.

How to Use This Book

For your ease of use, this book is organized into two different parts and a glossary.

Part 1, "What a Coach Needs to Know," discusses issues that extend beyond the court, including the value of good sportsmanship, the health and safety of your players, and dealing with problems from parents, players, and fans. Part 1 also advises coaches on how to make their players into a true team.

Part 2, "Teaching the Game," gets into the nuts and bolts of basketball, advising coaches on everything from teaching the basic fundamentals, to offensive and defensive tips and strategies, special plays and maneuvers, and finally coaching a game itself. It's a complete guide to coaching the youth game.

Additional Features

You'll notice notes that we've inserted in the margins and throughout the pages of this book. These extras take the following forms:

Quick Tips

These notes are pieces of coaching advice that can help your team with a particular phase of the game.

Hoop Lingo

These notes define some of the terms that are unique to basketball or have different meanings in different sports.

Coaching Corner

These notes advise you about various coaching strategies that will help your players and your team.

Fact of the Game

These notes offer some facts from the game of basketball, both past and present, which can help you with your coaching.

Did You Know?

These notes are some of the little-known facts of the game that you might find interesting and helpful.

Trademarks

All terms mentioned in this book that are known to be or are suspected of being trademarks or service marks have been appropriately capitalized. Alpha Books and Penguin Group (USA) Inc. cannot attest to the accuracy of this information. Use of a term in this book should not be regarded as affecting the validity of any trademark or service mark.

Part 1

What a Coach Needs to Know

There is a great deal more to coaching youth basketball today than just drawing X's and O's on a blackboard and teaching your players how to dribble, pass, and shoot. This first part of the book deals with a variety of issues that extend beyond the court itself. For example, it's up to you as a coach to set the parameters of good sportsmanship. It's also your responsibility to keep your players healthy and know when they are physically unable to play.

In today's world of youth sports, you may also have to deal with aggressive parents, kids who want to be stars, and fans who criticize you. Knowing how to deal with these potential problems will make you a better coach.

Finally, you must know how to take a group of diverse individuals with different skill levels and forge them into a team that pulls together, plays to its best ability every game, and doesn't feel it's the end of the world if they don't win them all.

You Are Coaching an Evolving Game

In This Chapter

- ◆ A game invented by request
- ◆ The wild and crazy rules of basketball in the early days
- ◆ Meet the players of yesteryear's teams
- ◆ Learn why the coach is more important now

Basketball wasn't always a game played by tall, chiseled athletes who leap high in the air to slam-dunk the ball through the hoop. In fact, this game, which celebrated its one hundredth birthday in 1991, is unique among all the team sports: It is the only sport that was actually invented by request. In reality, you'll be coaching a game that hasn't changed a great deal in the past half-century. But before that, basketball was often a helter-skelter game of now archaic and strange rules, of barnstorming teams, and of players who were very different from today's best. Because having an understanding of the past can always teach you something about the present, let's start by taking a brief look at the way the sport evolved into the game it is today.

The Inventor, James Naismith

In the winter of 1891, Luther Gillick, the head of the physical training department of the International Training School of the Young Men's Christian Association in Springfield, Massachusetts, had a problem. Dr. Gillick was concerned because he felt that the young men at the school were tired of the physical activities available in the winter months. What they needed, he felt, was a new and exciting game to pique their interest. That's when he asked James Naismith, a 29-year-old teacher at the school (which would later become Springfield College), to try to devise a new sport.

Naismith decided he wanted to create a game played with a large, light ball that would be handled with the hands. Because the game would be played indoors, he didn't want players running with the ball. He also wanted to create a goal into which the ball could be thrown, a goal that was located above the floor. To achieve this, he attached a wooden peach basket to the balcony at each end of the gym, 10 feet high. Because a goal was scored by throwing the ball into the basket, the logical thing was to call the new sport basketball. There were nine players on each side or team during those first games. This rule would obviously change, but James Naismith seemed to envision the kind of sport he wanted. Of the game he invented, Naismith said, "I had in mind the tall, agile, graceful, and expert athlete, one who could reach, jump, and act quickly and easily."

> **Did You Know?**
>
> James Naismith was born in 1861, the same year the American Civil War began. When he invented basketball thirty years later, he saw a game that could be played by women as well as men. In fact, he attended one of the first women's games in 1892 in Springfield, Massachusetts, and ultimately married one of the players, Maude Sherman.

What Kind of Rules Were These?

When James Naismith invented the game of basketball, he outlined thirteen basic rules for the game. The following are those 13 rules exactly as Naismith wrote them. Only a few are still applicable to today's game. Here are the rules:

1. The ball may be thrown in any direction with one or both hands.

2. The ball may be batted in any direction with one or both hands (never with the fist).

3. A player cannot run with the ball. The players must throw it from the spot on which he catches it, allowance to be made for a man who catches the ball when running if he tries to stop.

4. The ball must be held in or between the hands: the arms or body must not be used for holding it.

5. No shouldering, holding, pushing, tripping or striking in any way the person of any opponent shall be allowed: the first infringement of this rule by any person shall count as a foul, the second shall disqualify him until the next goal is made, or if there was evident intent to injure the person, for the whole of the game, no substitute allowed.

6. A foul is striking at the ball with the fist, violations of Rules 3, 4, and such as described in Rule 5.

7. If either side makes three consecutive fouls, it shall count as a goal for the opponents (consecutive fouls means without the opponents in the mean time making a foul.

8. A goal shall be made when the ball is thrown or batted from the ground into the basket and stays there, providing those defending the goal do not touch or disturb the goal. If the ball rests on the edges, and an opponent moves the basket, it shall count as a goal.

9. When the ball goes out of bounds, it shall be thrown into the field and played by the person first touching it. He has a right to hold it unmolested for five seconds. In case of a dispute the umpire shall throw it straight into the field. The thrower-in is allowed five seconds; if he holds it longer it shall go to the opponent. If any side persists in delaying the game the umpire shall call a foul on that side.

10. The umpire shall be the judge of the men and shall note the fouls and notify the referee when three consecutive fouls have been made. He shall have the power to disqualify men according to Rule 5.

11. The referee shall be the judge of the ball and shall decide when the ball is in play, in bounds, to which side it belongs, and shall keep the time. He shall decide when a goal has been made and keep account of the goals, with any other duties that are usually performed by a referee.

12. The time shall be two fifteen minute halves, with five minutes rest in between.

13. The side making the most goals in that time shall be declared the winners. In the case of a draw the game may, by agreement of the captains, be continued until another goal is made.

The first rules make no mention of dribbling, a center jump, or other soon-to-be-important aspects of play. Interestingly, there were some who wanted to call the new sport Naismith-ball. James Naismith wouldn't have that. Rather, he opted for the logical name, basketball, since the object was to put the ball in the basket.

Gives Kids Some History

Kids often think of basketball as what it is today—a game that involves athletes like Magic Johnson, Michael Jordan, Kobe Bryant, and Shaquille O'Neal, or even WNBA players like Chamique Holdsclaw and Lisa Leslie. That's how they see the sport. But basketball didn't evolve into the game it is today overnight. The rules in the early days often made it look like something completely different. A perfect example is the early rule which stated that the first player to touch the ball when it went out of bounds got to throw it in for his team. That often resulted in four or five players charging off the court after the ball. It looked more like a fumble in a football game than a ball going out of bounds in one of today's basketball games.

Basketball courts were also very different in the early days. Some baskets had backboards. They could be made of wood, glass, or even wire. But players sometimes came onto a court to find that the basket was attached to the end of a long pole with no backboard at all.

In addition, the ball was often oversized and lost its shape. It had a rubber bladder inside a leather cover and was laced together. If a player tried to dribble and the laces hit the floor, the ball often bounced away.

Did You Know?
The early pros often played in dance halls or in basements with pillars right out on the court. Dances at halftime made the courts slippery and dangerous. Players would sometimes put Vasoline on their shoes to prevent them from slipping on the dusty floors, a trick that didn't make the owners of the halls happy.

Because of the shape of the ball, dribbling wasn't easy, so most players didn't attempt it often. One of the early professional stars, a man named Elmer Ripley, described the game then as one in which "you moved the basketball and you moved yourself." It was a game filled with crisp passing. There was a center jump after each basket and, not surprisingly, the scores were always low. In a YMCA tournament held in 1896, with the winner to be named Champion of America, two teams from Brooklyn, New York, battled it out for 30 minutes. In the end, the East District defeated Brooklyn Central by the unlikely score of 4–0. You might ask whether it was basketball or baseball!

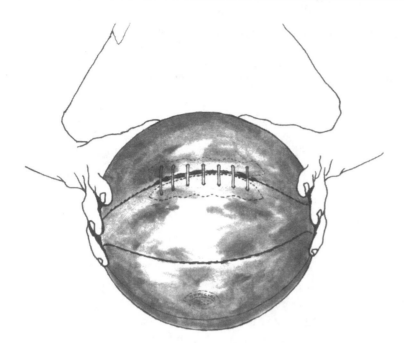

The early basketball was oversized, often misshapen; if the raised laces hit the floor, it bounced away.

The College Rules Were Different

The college rules were the first to become standardized. Here is a brief chronology of how the game slowly evolved at the college level into what it is today. Remember, James Naismith wrote the original 13 rules in 1891, so the changes began coming rather quickly:

- ◆ **1896:** A field goal was changed from three points to two points. Free throws now counted as one point instead of three.

- ◆ **1901:** A dribbler could not shoot the ball and could dribble only one time, using both hands.

- ◆ **1909:** A dribbler was finally allowed to shoot, and the two-hand dribble and double-dribble were made illegal.

- ◆ **1914:** The bottom of the net was cut away, allowing the ball to fall through to the floor.

- ◆ **1924:** A player who was fouled had to shoot his own free throws. Before that, one player shot all of his team's free throws.

- ◆ **1933:** A midcourt line was introduced to cut down on stalling. The team with the ball now had 10 seconds to advance it from the backcourt over the midcourt line.

- ◆ **1938:** The center jump after every basket scored was eliminated, leading to more continuous play.

- ◆ **1949:** Coaches were finally allowed to speak to players during a timeout.

Since 1949 the game has been fine-tuned with additional changes, such as the shot clock, wider foul lanes, and the three-point shot, just to name a few. But by 1949, all the old, archaic rules were gone, the NBA had started, and basketball finally resembled the sport that it is today.

The Similarities: Then and Now

As you can see, basketball rules have changed greatly over the last half-century. By 1949, the National Basketball Association was in its infancy and the college game was thriving. It's difficult now to even imagine the game with some of the old rules, such as a center jump after each basket and coaches prohibited from speaking with their teams during a timeout. How could they really coach under those circumstances? Today the role of the coach has evolved so that the coach is often the focal point of the team. This is even more evident in youth basketball, where the coach is often teaching the game, in addition to teaching the qualities that go into developing a well-rounded player who fully enjoys the sport.

Hoop Lingo

One of the more common slang terms used to describe basketball players is the word **cagers.** At first glance, it would seem that it might have derived from the hoop or the net, which can be seen as resembling a cage. Not in this case. When the game was still in its infancy in the early days of the twentieth century, a number of courts were surrounded either by high netting or a stiff wire cage. With both the net and cage games, the ball couldn't go out of bounds. This type of setup also made for some interesting basketball. In the rigid cage, the game sometimes resembled hockey, with players being slammed into the cage and often emerging bruised and bloodied. To counteract this, players wore hip pads, elbow and knee guards, and an aluminum cup. The cage didn't move when you hit it, but the net did. Players could bounce off the net to give themselves momentum when trying to lose a defender. Defensive players sometimes trapped the ball handler in the corner by pulling both ends of the net around him. Jump ball. And one player once leaped up, grabbed the net and held on near the basket, and then caught a pass and threw it in the hoop while his defender looked up helplessly. Now largely forgotten, the one result of the cage and net games remaining today is the still-used nickname of cagers.

The Women's Game

As mentioned earlier, James Naismith invented a game for both men and women. Women, indeed, began playing as early as the men—only it took a much longer period of time before women played a game that resembled the men's.

The women's game began with nine players on a side. However, each player was confined to a certain area of the court and the ball had to be passed to each area before a shot could be taken. While the ball moved, the players didn't. Even when the women's game evolved to six players on the side, there were restrictions. Three guards stayed at one end of the court for defense, while three forwards were at the other end to take the shots. As late at the 1950s, women's collegiate basketball permitted only two bounces and no sustained dribbling. And in the 1960s, when the men's game was flourishing, women were allowed just three bounces. It was felt that women just couldn't run up and down the court in sustained action.

Finally, in 1970, women began playing five to a side and were allowed the full dribble. Several years later a rule was passed providing money for women's athletic programs at the collegiate level, and from that point on women's basketball flourished on its own, producing great all-around players with the same basic skills as the men.

When girls played basketball in the early days, their uniforms consisted of long dresses.

Player Characteristics: Then and Now

Players in the early days of the sport had to be as tough as nails to endure some of the court conditions, but by and large players were typically small, quick men. A player who stood six feet tall was considered a very big man in those days. And the game back then emphasized speed and ball movement. As noted previously, there wasn't a lot of dribbling in early games; quick and crisp passes, as well as player movement, were the important strategies of the day. Players tried to help each other lose their defender by setting screens. The object was to get free under the basket for an easy shot, with the only other option being a long, two-hand set shot.

One of the first real plays to develop was the pivot play, in which the center set up around the area of the foul line with his back to the basket. A player passed the ball to the center, and then he tried to cut around him in order to get open for a return pass underneath the basket. It took timing and speed, as well as a great deal of teamwork, to perfect this basic play. In this respect, the early game isn't all that much different from what you will be teaching young players today.

Youth teams these days are often made up of players of similar height, just as in the early days of the game. There often won't be a dominant big man and an obvious small, quick point guard. Coaches can interchange positions and give players a chance to try both the forward and guard positions and, in some cases, even the center spot. Thus, a coach can teach the complete game, and, as the players grow and become older, they may assume more natural positions on the court. But a youth team that emphasizes speed, ball handling, and teamwork might look surprisingly similar to some of the teams playing nearly 100 years ago. So, in a sense, the more things change, the more they remain the same.

Coaching Styles: Then and Now

It really doesn't matter whether you are coaching boys, girls, or a mixed team, you will be teaching each group the same fundamental style of game—body and ball movement, crisp passing, and solid defense. The early coaches didn't have the same kind of responsibilities as coaches do today. That was because the players then were largely self-taught and were the ones bringing innovation and new plays to the sport. In fact, James Naismith once said flat out, "You can't coach basketball. You just play it." Some early coaches simply set up the schedules and practice times, and made sure the players were there. A few began to teach early basic plays and help the players run a tight practice.

Today, the coach has become a very important part of the team. This is especially true with kids who are just learning the game. It is the coach who will make the greatest impact. How well that coach does the job can well determine whether a boy or girl continues playing the sport in years to come.

Coaching Corner

Coaching kids today is a tremendous responsibility. Some of the things a coach must do include the following:

- Teaching all kids the basic fundamentals of the game.
- Taking a group of diverse individuals and making them into a TEAM.
- Showing the virtues of good sportsmanship before, during, and after games. Teammates and opponents alike should be treated with respect.
- Making sure your players know both how to win and how to lose well. It's more important for everyone to play, learn, and enjoy the experience than to win every game.

As with other sports, basketball has a long and interesting history. Just as this is a short chapter, a coach certainly shouldn't dwell on the history of the game for too long. But coaches should be aware of the game's history and impart some of it to their teams, just enough that each young player has a sense of the sport he is learning, how it evolved, and why basketball has a long and continuing tradition that should be shared among young people and old.

The Least You Need to Know

- Basketball was the only major sport invented by request. It was designed to fill a void during the cold winters when young athletes could not go outside very often.

- The inventor of the game, Dr. James Naismith, was a forward-thinking individual who intended basketball to be played by both boys and girls, men and women.

- The early rules of the game made basketball look nothing like it does today. It took more than 50 years for the men's game to resemble today's sport, more than 70 years for the women's game to come of age.

- The early coaches had very little to do with teaching the game and providing strategy for their teams. Today, the youth coach is often the single most important person in determining whether a young player will enjoy and continue in the game.

◆ Today's youth games are not that different from the very early game, in that the players are often pretty much the same size, with every player learning about each position on the court.

2

Coaching Responsibilities: Knowledge, Communication, and Fun

In This Chapter

- ◆ Know the game well, including offensive and defensive rules
- ◆ Communicating with young players is an important part of coaching
- ◆ Be flexible, enthusiastic, and positive
- ◆ Enjoying a serious and responsible job

Once you have made the decision and commitment to coach youth basketball, you must be aware of the acute responsibility that goes with the job. No matter what age level you are coaching, and whether you lead a boys' or girls' team, you should know that you now have the chance to play an important role in the development of young people as athletes. In addition, your attitude toward other elements of the game can help make the kids you coach much more solid citizens in other walks of life. Can a coach have that much influence? You bet! Thus, a good coach not only has to know, understand, and have the ability to teach basketball, but he must also know how to communicate with his players, teach positive values, show great enthusiasm for his job, keep winning and losing in perspective, and totally enjoy what he is doing.

Of course, you are first and foremost a coach, and that means you should have a very thorough knowledge of basketball before you blow the whistle for the first time. Some coaches have acquired the necessary knowledge by playing the game for years. Others, however, may have little or no playing experience. In that case, they must learn in other ways—by watching, reading, attending basketball clinics, and talking to established coaches at various levels. There is an awful lot to learn.

Rules and Fundamentals

You simply cannot teach a sport correctly without knowing the basic rules. Basketball is not an overtly complex sport, and even the youngest of players should be able to grasp the rules quickly, especially if they are presented in a clear and concise manner. Once a young player has a grasp of these basic rules, she can begin playing almost immediately because she then can learn the fundamental skills of the game. However, the rules should be learned first so that players apply the skills in the right context.

You should begin by familiarizing your players with the court. All basketball courts today are essentially the same. A standard court is rectangular in shape, measuring 94 feet long by 50 feet wide. Some are smaller, however, due to space constraints.

The basic basketball court hasn't changed much over the years. Here's what it looks like today.

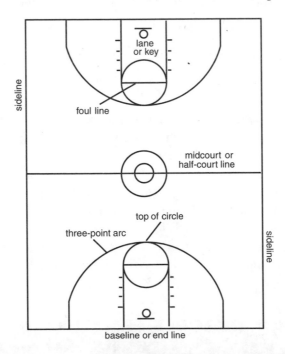

A number of basic rules are defined by the court itself, so the players should know this right away. They include the following:

◆ The court is divided by a halfcourt or midcourt line. The offensive team has 10 seconds to advance the ball over this line after taking possession in what is called the *backcourt*. Once the ball is advanced over the line to the *frontcourt*, it cannot be passed or dribbled behind the line (in the backcourt) or the team loses possession. That's called a backcourt violation.

◆ The foul line is located 15 feet from the backboard, which is 4 feet out from the *end line* or *baseline*. Two lines, 12 feet apart, extend on each side from the baseline to the foul line. This area is called the *key* or *lane*. An offensive player cannot stand in this area for more than three seconds, or it is a violation and the team loses the ball (possession).

◆ Many courts today have a symmetrical arc painted on the court, extending from a spot on the baseline and in from the corner, around the back of the foul circle and to the other baseline. This is called the *three-point arc*. A shot made with both feet beyond this circle counts three points instead of two. In high school and college ball, the arc is 19 feet, 9 inches from the basket. In the NBA, it is 22 feet away. Some courts used for very young players may not have the arc, since the players can't be expected to shoot from that far out yet.

Did You Know?

In the early days of basketball, the foul lane was just six feet wide, then opening to the twelve-foot wide foul circle. Because of the look, the area was referred to as the "key." That look, however, is long gone. By the late 1950s, the lane had been widened to 12 feet, due to the increased size of the players. The NBA soon went the college game one step further when it widened its lane to 16 feet. Yet despite these changes and some occasional debate, the size of the overall court has always remained the same.

Even if you are coaching eight- and nine-year-olds, the basic layout of the court remains the same. The only differences might be the smaller dimensions, the lack of the three-point arc, and baskets set at 8 feet instead of the standard 10 feet high. But the 10-second rule and 3-second rule always apply, and they begin as soon as your team walks onto the court for the first time.

The area inside the foul lane is sometimes called the **paint.** That's because on some courts, the area was painted a different color than the rest of the court. The top of the lane is still often referred to as the **key.** This goes back to the days when the foul lane was only 6 feet wide instead of the present 12 feet. The 6-foot lane opened up to the 12-foot-wide foul circle and gave the appearance of an actual key. The basket is often referred to as the **hoop** because of the round metal hoop that the net is attached to, while the backboards are often simply called the **glass.** That, of course, is a reference to the clear Plexiglas backboards present in so many gyms. But even where there are still wooden backboards, don't be surprised if someone says a banked shot "kissed the glass." And in a bit of modern terminology, someone hitting a three-point shot from behind the arc is often said to have "sunk a trey."

Additional Basic Rules

Here is a quick rundown of the basic rules of the game, rules that the coach should review with his new team soon after they meet and begin practicing. These are not, by any means, all the rules of the game—only those that young players should know when they begin. The others can be taught as a season unfolds and as the players become more familiar with the ebb and flow of the game itself.

Rules on Offense

A number of basic rules on offense will quickly become second nature to even young players. These are things players should know as soon as they begin practicing the offensive phase of the game. Some are connected to the fundamentals that will be described later, but we are talking about them now because they apply from the first time a young player steps on the court. These basics are as follows:

♦ **Dribbling.** The basketball can be advanced by bouncing or dribbling it down the court. A player must, of course, dribble with just one hand at a time, although he can switch hands any time he wants. What he cannot do, however, is stop the dribble and then begin dribbling again. This is a violation called a *double dribble.* The team whose player double dribbles loses possession of the ball, which is called a turnover. Once a player stops dribbling, he must either pass or shoot the ball. If he passes and then catches a quick return pass, he may resume dribbling.

◆ **Watch those steps.** One of the most common violations a young player makes on offense is *traveling* with the ball. The slang term for traveling is *steps*. A player must stop moving as soon as he stops his dribbling. If he takes a full step without dribbling, he is traveling. In addition, once he stops his dribble, he can move only one foot. The foot that stays on the court is called the *pivot foot*. The player can turn left, right, or completely around as long as the pivot foot doesn't move forward, sideways, or backward, or lose contact with the court. Otherwise, it's a traveling violation that also results in a turnover. Think of the pivot foot as being hooked to a swivel. It can turn on its axis, but otherwise it cannot move.

◆ **Passing.** The ball can be passed from one teammate to another in a variety of ways. We will discuss the types of passes later. There is one place, however, where the ball cannot be passed. Once the ball has been moved across the mid-court line, it cannot be passed to a teammate who is still behind the midcourt line. As noted previously, this is a backcourt violation and the team violating this rule will lose possession of the ball.

◆ **That three-second rule again.** Offensive players are free to move about the court any way they choose. Usually, however, their movements are dictated by the offensive scheme the coach wants to run. Players can also stop and not move if there is a reason, except for one place on the court. No player on the offensive team can stay in the foul lane or *paint* for more than three seconds. This is a violation that results in the offensive team losing possession of the basketball.

Rules on Defense

The goal of the offense is to move the basketball into a position where a player is free to take a good shot at the basket and score. Conversely, defensive players try to stop the offense from getting that good shot. They have to do this, however, within a set of rules. Coaches must know that a good defense is as important to winning a game as a good offense. However, if any defensive player violates the rules, a foul is called and the offensive player might receive one or two free throws from the foul line, depending on the foul. Thus, too many fouls can cause a team to lose a game. In addition, fouling isn't the proper way to play defense.

Let's take a look at some of the basic defensive rules. Then we will check out some of the most common fouls. These are the basic things you should tell your players that they *can* do on defense:

◆ **Defending the dribble.** A defensive player should try to disrupt the offensive player as he dribbles the ball. To do this, he must stay close to him and can try to deflect the ball away without making physical contact with the player. If he sees the dribbler moving left or right, he can try to move into his path, forcing the dribbler to change direction. He should also be ready to try to slap a pass away before the ball heads for its destination. Once the dribbler stops, the defensive player can get up very close to try to block, steal, or disrupt a pass. But it should be emphasized that the rules prohibit any physical contact with the offensive player if it is initiated by the defender.

◆ **Defending the pass.** A quick defensive player should always try to anticipate when and where a pass will be thrown. He can disrupt the offensive flow by deflecting the pass away, or if he's quick enough, he can sometimes intercept the pass to put his team on offense. Every defensive player on the floor should look to intercept or disrupt a pass, not just the person defending the player with the ball. Once again, a defensive player cannot make contact with an offensive player while trying to intercept a pass. Doing so is a foul. The rules also prohibit a defender from blocking a pass with his feet. If he does that, the offensive team gets the ball back.

◆ **Blocking a shot.** Defensive players can also block a shot as the offensive player releases it. This takes practice and great timing. But once again, there are rules. The player blocking or trying to block a shot cannot make body contact with the shooter. And the block is good only if the defender touches just the ball. If he also touches the hand or arm of the shooter, it is considered a foul.

Fact of the Game
If two players grab a loose ball simultaneously, the ref will whistle the play dead and call a held ball. Depending on the rules of your league, there is a jump ball to determine possession, or possession is decided by the possession arrow. With the possession arrow, each team alternates taking possession whenever play is stopped for a held ball.

◆ **Getting that loose ball.** Defensive players should always be ready to retrieve a loose ball, which can be the result of a slapped pass, blocked shot, or lost dribble. Once again, speed and timing are key. Players sometimes dive on the floor to try to get a loose ball. Remember to tell your team early on that this is basketball, not football. Any unnecessary roughness will result in a foul.

A typical reach-in foul occurs when a player hits the opponent's arm instead of the ball.

What Is and Isn't a Foul

Basketball is supposed to be a noncontact sport, but when you have 10 players going full speed in a confined area, it doesn't always work that way. Even in the early days of basketball, there was a penalty for contact on the court. The player making the contact was called for a foul. Today fouls are called for various reasons. Depending on the circumstances, the player who is fouled can be awarded one or two free throws from the foul line. A free throw, of course, counts one point. Most, but not all, fouls are called on defensive players. In some cases, a foul results in lost or gained possession of the ball.

The following are the most common types of fouls called in a game. Make sure your players are aware of them before they even start to practice, or things can quickly get out of hand.

- ◆ **Hand contact or checking.** A defensive player who slaps, pushes, holds, or blocks the offensive player with his hands will be called for a foul. Conversely, any offensive

Hoop Lingo

When a player is disqualified for committing too many personal fouls, he must leave the game. It doesn't matter whether it's the first quarter or the fourth. A player committing a fifth or sixth foul (depending on the league) is said to have **fouled out**.

player who uses his hand to push or ward off a defensive player can also be called for a foul.

- ◆ **Over the back.** If a player going for a rebound makes contact with the back of the player in front of him, a foul will be called.

- ◆ **Pick or screen.** A pick or screen is set by an offensive player by stopping and standing still on the court in order to allow a teammate to cut behind him and hopefully gain a step or two on his defender. If the defensive player runs into the player setting the pick, a foul is called on him. However, if the player setting the pick moves his body into the defender, pushes him, or initiates contact in any way to slow his progress, an offensive foul can be called on the player setting the pick.

- ◆ **Charging.** This is a foul committed by an offensive player who runs into a defender who has reached a spot on the floor and has stopped moving. It often occurs when an offensive player is *driving* to the basket. The defender sees the offensive player coming and sets himself in his path before the offensive player arrives.

- ◆ **Blocking.** If the defensive player is still in the process of moving into position when the offensive player hits him, a blocking foul is called on the defender. Also, if the defender moves just a little bit to initiate the contact, a blocking foul is called. Most officials, coaches, and players agree that the charge versus the block is often the most difficult call for an official to make.

These are the most common fouls that will be called on your players during a game, and you should be able to identify them in practice so that your players become familiar with them.

Those Nastier Fouls

Your players should be well aware of a couple additional fouls as well. For instance, a player who initiates very hard or violent contact with an opposing player to perhaps stop a sure basket or to get a rebound can be called for a *flagrant foul*. In this case, the player who is fouled is awarded an extra free throw. Depending on league rules, a player who commits two flagrant fouls in the same game can be disqualified and thrown out of the game.

In certain game situations, a coach will instruct his players to commit an *intentional foul*. This is usually a strategy used in the closing seconds of a tight game. The purpose is to give up a point on a single free throw instead of possibly two or three points if the offensive teams scores a basket. The team committing the intentional foul would then get the ball back with a chance for a two- or three-point basket of its own. To prevent an overuse of intentional fouls, most leagues award a bonus free throw if a team commits more than a certain number of fouls in one half.

Finally, there is the *technical foul.* A referee can call a technical foul on a player or coach, although it usually doesn't involve contact. A technical foul can be called for various types of unsportsmanlike conduct, such as using profanity, arguing a call excessively, fighting, or committing a technical violation, such as calling a timeout when there are no more remaining timeouts or for having six men on the court.

Coaching Corner

Technical fouls are sometimes called on a coach, usually for unsportsmanlike conduct or for violating a rule. Occasionally, a coach might do this to fire up his team. But this kind of coaching behavior has no place in youth basketball, because it sets a poor example for your players. Coaches who get technicals for arguing with the refs, running out onto the court during play, taunting opposing players or coaches, or even for throwing an object onto the court shouldn't be coaching at the youth level. In addition, technical fouls result in free throws for the opposing team and can result in losing a game.

How About the Penalties?

As a coach, you should always be sure to check league rules regarding the penalties for fouls, since they can vary somewhat at different levels. For instance, in most leagues right through the college level, a player is disqualified after committing five personal fouls in a game. In the NBA, however, a player is allowed six fouls.

As for free throws, the rule of thumb is that a player who is fouled gets a single free throw, or foul shot. If he is fouled while in the act of shooting the ball, he gets two free throws. If he makes the basket while being fouled, the basket counts and he is awarded an additional free throw, with a chance to make it a three-point play. Occasionally, a player is fouled while trying to launch a three-point field goal from behind the arc. In this case, the shooter is awarded three free throws. If he makes the shot and is fouled, he has a chance for a rare four-point play.

However, in some instances a foul does not result in a free throw. For example, when a foul is charged against an offensive player, his team simply loses possession of the ball, although the foul counts against the player's total. To speed up the game in some leagues, defensive fouls not committed in the act of shooting just result in the offensive team getting the ball out of bounds near where the foul was committed. The foul, however, counts against the player and his team; once the team reaches seven fouls in the half, free throws are awarded. In some levels, this results in a *one-and-one* situation. This means that if the player makes the first free throw, he is awarded a second one. If he misses the free throw, play resumes with one team rebounding the ball. Since rules can vary, you should be sure to check on all the free throw situations in your league before your team begins play.

Coaching Corner

Basketball games can be won or lost by 20 points or by just a single point. That's why it is important to make sure that every player practices free throws continually. No one is defending the foul shooter, so he can relax, take his time, and hopefully make the majority of his shots from the foul line. Wilt Chamberlain, arguably the best center who ever played basketball in the pros, was a notoriously poor foul shooter. Wilt tried everything—shooting overhand, shooting underhand, and standing off-center on the foul line. He barely made 50 percent of his free throws during his career. In one game during his second season of 1960–1961, Wilt hit rock bottom against the Detroit Pistons. He went to the foul line 10 times and missed all 10 free throws, the worst game from the foul line any NBA player ever had. It can happen to the very best, but with practice, hopefully it won't happen to your players.

Although it is important for a coach to fully inform his team about why fouls are called and how to try to avoid them, he should also understand that some forms of contact are allowed. There is simply no way basketball can be a completely noncontact sport. *Incidental contact* can occur as a player makes an effort to play an opponent, reach a loose ball, or perform what are considered normal offensive or defensive movements. The referee determines which type of contact is incidental and which results in a foul. But in a clean, fast-paced game, there will always be some contact and you should tell your players it isn't their place to argue with the official or claim they have been fouled. They should always continue to play until they hear the whistle. Then, if there is a dispute, you can handle it as the coach.

Communication Is Always the Key

When you meet a new team for the first time, whether they are 8- or 14-year-olds, and boys or girls, your job is to teach and coach them. It doesn't matter whether you are teaching individual skills, such as dribbling, or describing how you want them to play a zone defense. You've got to be able to communicate. If you are explaining the meaning of good sportsmanship, how to win and lose well, and what it means to be part of a team, you've got to communicate. You are the leader of the team, and you must set the standard for your players. You can't do that if you don't communicate in a direct, easy, and understandable manner.

Most young players look up to authority and respect leadership. In fact, they seem to crave some leadership in today's world. So the opportunity to communicate and display leadership skills is readily available. It's up to you to take it.

When communicating, look players in the eye, learn their names quickly so they feel that you know and care about them, and decide how you want to be addressed. Being addressed as "Coach" is fine. "Miss Jefferies," "Mr. Nolan," or something more formal is fine. "Bob" or "Janet" is not appropriate. Coaches should not be called by their first names because the implication for young people is that you want to be their friend. You can be a friend to your players, but you aren't one of their peers. It also sets up a casual environment, which doesn't necessarily imply a respectful environment. Feel free to call players by their first names, or even by a nickname if they prefer it. If a nickname seems even remotely negative, however, or you sense that the player doesn't like it, don't use it. Certainly don't use nicknames that players have dubbed another player if the so-named person isn't comfortable with the name. And don't tolerate name calling or nicknaming among players if it makes players uncomfortable. In other words, maintain a professional, respectful environment.

Coaching Corner

It doesn't matter whether you think you are going to have a very good team or a team that will struggle to learn the game: It is up to you as the coach to build confidence among your players. A confident player will learn faster, will play up to his potential, and won't be afraid to fail. If he knows he has played his best, he can better accept those games his team doesn't win. Thus, he will enjoy his entire basketball experience all the more. The coach has the job of building confidence in his players. That can happen only if you, as coach, approach your job and your team with the same kind of confidence. Bill Belichick, coach of the 2001 Super Bowl champion New England Patriots, has said that he expects the entire team, from the assistant coaches to the last man on the bench, to be an extension of him. He is the leader, and he wants his confidence to be felt by the entire team. That is something you, as a coach, should strive for as well. When you talk to your players, always sound positive so that they feel you are giving them the correct advice. If you sound hesitant and unsure, your players won't get the feeling that you are confident in your ability to coach and lead them.

Organizational Skills and Communication

In addition to speaking clearly and with a purpose, a coach should be well organized and always know just what she is going to do at each practice. That, too, is part of communicating. If you stumble from one thing to another, without a plan, and have to stop and think about what you are going to do next, you will lose the attention of your team. But if you are well prepared at each practice, know what you are going to say at team meetings, and show your players that you are always in control, they tend to listen and respond.

Explain, Explain, Explain

Players are individuals. Some are better basketball players than others, and some can understand the concepts you are teaching more quickly. It's important to take each player into consideration. If a player doesn't understand something, take the extra time to explain it to him. If a player questions one of your rules, explain to him why you made that rule and why it has to be followed. If there is any kind of dissension among players, speak to those players and explain the importance of being a team and working together. The more you communicate with your team, the more success you will have as a coach. But don't keep your players guessing why you are doing things a certain way. Always explain everything thoroughly—and explain it twice, if necessary. Also ask questions. Never assume that a player understands everything. Part of communicating is making sure players understand.

Part of successful communication can be summed up by the old adage that says to show and tell. It's one thing for coaches to explain things in theory, but they must also show them in action. In other words, if you are explaining to your players the correct way to set a screen, you can describe it and even draw the X's and O's on a blackboard. But to complete the communication of setting the screen, it is necessary to take the players on the court and *show* them how to do it. By combining show and tell, you will be communicating an athletic maneuver or play in the most thorough way possible. After that, if players still have questions, they can be addressed directly right out on the court.

A Winning Attitude

Still another part of communication will help make you successful. You can explain things all day, but it won't help if you appear bored, tired, or disinterested, as if you're just going through the motions. Always approach your team with an enthusiastic, positive attitude. Just as confidence is contagious, so is enthusiasm. If your players sense that you are coaching them because you love basketball, want to teach it, and want to make them better players, they will respond with a similar attitude. Young players often come in with an open mind. Even those who aren't sure whether they really want to play the game will look to see how you view the sport. So keep it positive. The glass must always be half full. Sure, there will be problems, but with a positive, enthusiastic attitude, you'll be better prepared to deal with them.

Coaching Corner

Most young players come into the game with an open mind. Like other things they are learning, they tend to want routine, they want leadership, and they want some discipline. You are responsible for providing that kind of environment, and that means setting the rules the players will follow. But don't be so rigid that nothing ever changes. If something isn't working the way you felt it would, try something new. If the players don't seem to be responding to certain practice routines, you might want to alter them or introduce something new and fresh. By being flexible, you can keep things from becoming stale and boring. A big part of your responsibility as a coach is to keep your players interested. They should look forward to practice and to games, and to spending time with you and with each other.

Above All, Let It Be Fun

As you can see, coaching youth basketball entails many responsibilities. Obviously, all of them are important parts of the equation for a successful coach. However, one element is, in a sense, perhaps more important than all the others combined. It is a small, three-letter word—f-u-n.

The kids you'll be coaching are not NBA players, and youth basketball is not a business. You are not in a race for Coach of the Year honors. No, you are there to teach kids a sport that has for years been a source of healthful enjoyment for so many individuals. Therefore, you should remember not to lose sight of a rather ominous statistic. At the beginning of the twenty-first century, some 75 percent of the kids who begin playing organized team sports early in life quit completely by the time they are 13.

There is no single reason for kids leaving organized sports. It's a rather complex issue. However, no matter what the reason is for kids turning their backs on sports, there seems to be a single overriding factor: The kids who decide they don't want to play anymore are not having fun. Knowing this, perhaps the single most important priority you have as a coach is to make sure the game remains fun for all of your players. That means that both the best player on the team and the one who is really struggling to master the individual skills of the game should still enjoy their time on the court. They should be having fun working, learning, and playing. As their leader and mentor, you've got to be aware of this at every stage of the season. Not only should your entire team be happy to take the court, but each individual player should also be enjoying the experience. If you can achieve that, you have really earned the right to be called "Coach."

Although we will be talking about coaching in much greater detail in the ensuing chapters, the basic responsibilities of a youth basketball coach will never change.

If you do all the things outlined in this chapter, you will find success as a coach. Once you get into the swing of things, you should organize practices that incorporate the learning and reinforcement of individual skills and potential game situations to get your team and players ready to compete and feel good about themselves, while also thoroughly enjoying the entire basketball experience.

The Least You Need to Know

- Make sure you know the game thoroughly before you blow your whistle for the first time. This includes knowing offensive and defensive rules, the fundamental skills of passing and dribbling, and how fouls occur and whether they result in turnovers or free throws.

- Make communication a priority. Explain things clearly to your team and to the individual players. Give them your reasons for whatever decisions you make regarding team and individual play. Answer all questions with patience and sincerity, and never ignore a player who wants to talk with you.

- Show confidence and enthusiasm at all times. If the players are to be an extension of you, you want them to mirror a positive attitude. If you are moody and uneven, a young player will see it immediately.

- Don't be rigid and unbending. Sure, you have to set rules, but always keep your options open and be flexible. Individual players sometimes require individual attention, and change is often good for the entire team.

- Don't forget the little three-letter word *fun*. Make the game fun, for both you and your players. And once you do that, be sure to keep it that way. In the end, this is the most important part of coaching.

Chapter **3**

Coaching and Sportsmanship

In This Chapter

- Good sportsmanship on the court
- How to win and lose well
- Where to draw the toughness line
- Structure and discipline

As a coach, you must set a number of other important parameters as soon as you begin working with a new team. All of your players should be totally aware of what you expect from them, both on and off the court. It is definitely in your best interest to set these rules as soon as you meet your new team.

In your early meetings with the players, you should obviously talk about the game itself, but coaching is more than a matter of X's and O's on the hardwood. For openers, you want a team that practices good sportsmanship and fully realizes that there is much more to the game than just winning. A team has to learn to both win and lose well. In fact, losing well is an acquired skill, one not always in tune with human nature. Therefore, as a coach you also have to know yourself very well—how tough a coach you want to be and how much structure and discipline you expect to have within the framework of your team. Be aware that coaching young kids today is not a walk in the park. Instead, it is a balancing act to which you hold the key.

This chapter discusses the best way to approach the overall challenge of coaching a team and how to go about reaching that balance in today's world, where players and teams that don't win are quickly labeled "losers." There is also a mentality in sports that espouses an in-your-face attitude: Taunting and showboating are accepted qualities, and people are often too anxious to throw a punch first and ask questions afterward. This includes the fans of the sport. These are hard realities that have trickled down from the world of professional athletics to the kids just starting to play. Kids have always idolized star athletes. But good, solid role models in today's sports world are often lacking. So you see, the job is not going to be an easy one. Hopefully, you will have your ducks in a row shortly after you begin working with your team.

Good Sports Are Good for Everyone

Sports and sportsmanship should go hand in hand. Unfortunately, that isn't always the case today. In a sense, good sportsmanship equals good manners. A player who is not a good sport on the basketball court will be more likely to also be ill-mannered toward others, even perhaps his own family. If you don't understand the importance of insisting upon good sportsmanship on your team, then you probably should not be coaching kids. Once again, your leadership will reflect on your team. Consider, then, the following scenarios:

- ◆ During a game, every time one of your players commits a foul, he either argues the call, throws his hands in the air, or continually shakes his head as if he can't believe it.

- ◆ A player who is fouled hard while driving to the basket gets right in the face of the player who committed the foul, and maybe even shoves him a bit.

- ◆ The players on your bench continually taunt players on the other team, calling them names and laughing when one of them makes a bad play.

- ◆ In practice, the better players on your team are constantly criticizing those who aren't as good, telling them they are holding the entire team back.

- ◆ After a tough loss, some of your players trash the locker room, knocking over benches and garbage cans.

- ◆ Players either taunt or challenge fans who are rooting for the opposing team.

- ◆ While you are talking to your team, several players are whispering and giggling among themselves.

◆ Your team wins a close, hard-fought game and has played very well. When it's over, several players refuse to shake their opponents' hands and instead begin to showboat and do a victory dance.

All of the previously described situations are examples of poor sportsmanship, much of which is based on disrespect—disrespect for authority figures, opposing players, teammates, the referees, coaches, and other adults. Players allowed or even encouraged to be this way are, in effect, being given a mandate by their coach to do similar things at school, at home, and in their interactions outside basketball. As a coach, not only do you have to be sure to talk about the value of good sportsmanship and detail the kind of behavior you expect, but you must also take immediate action whenever one of your players crosses the line.

If you are coaching at the youngest levels, the eight- and nine-year-olds, your players will be almost like a dry sponge, ready to soak up the knowledge and advice you give to them. You may find a few players who are already showing signs of bad sportsmanship, but you should be able to correct the problem by explaining the way you feel and telling them directly what you expect. At the upper age levels, you may find that young teenagers are not only more competitive, but also already well defined as personalities. At this level, disrespectful behavior might be more difficult to change. Much will depend on how strongly you present your case, how badly the player wants to remain as part of the team, and to what lengths you are willing to go to make sure that poor sportsmanship simply isn't tolerated.

Coaching Corner

Getting your team to exhibit good sportsmanship and character throughout the season might well be a season-long chore. There always will be some players who naturally have short fuses and bad tempers. Others may take a long time to accept losing, while still others, bursting with energy, have to let off steam. However, coaches are also not immune to these kinds of behaviors. For every Dean Smith or John Wooden (winning coaches who were always calm and laid-back), there can also be a Bobby Knight or Lefty Dreisell (winning coaches who were always volatile and explosive). As the leader of your team, most players will look to you to set the tone. If you are constantly screaming at officials, raving after a loss, answering fans who are heckling you, or berating a team member for a bonehead play, you will be showing the same kind of poor sportsmanship that you are trying to curb. You can't say one thing and do another. As a coach, you also may have to keep some of your emotions in check and practice what you preach. Just as you'll tell your players, it's all for the good of the team. Remember the old adage that says character is caught, not taught. As a coach, you should always be the number-one example of what you expect from your players.

The Best Route to Take

Obviously, you have to set the ground rules early. Tell your team that learning to be good sports is just as important as learning the game. Then post a set of rules involving sportsmanship that you want followed at all times. The rules should be in effect as soon as the players walk in the gym for practice. In fact, they should apply every time the team gets together, whether for practice, a team meeting, or a game. Make it clear that anyone breaking the rules of good sportsmanship will be penalized. This can be anything from asking a poor sport to leave practice, to taking him out of a game, even perhaps suspending him for one or more games, depending on the infraction. As with everything else, be sure to explain fully and carefully why it is important to you, to the team, and to each player to practice good sportsmanship at all times. Let them know you won't accept anything less.

After setting these rules, make sure you are consistent. If you sit one player for arguing with an official or showing up an opponent, make sure you do the same thing with another player. Once again, you are the leader who will set the tone. Even young kids are very observant. If you are inconsistent and don't apply the same standards to all players, you will begin to lose the respect of the entire team.

Win or lose, good sports always shake hands with their opponents after a game.

The following is a suggestion for some of the rules you might want to set for your team. If you feel strongly that something is missing, feel free to add it to the list.

- Always be polite and courteous to your coach, your teammates, your opponents, and league officials.

- Refrain from using profanity or bad language toward a teammate, opponent, or league official.

- Never argue a foul call with an official. You may ask what you did to commit the foul, but don't protest, raise your voice, or show up the official in any way.

- Don't let your temper get the best of you. Never shove a teammate in practice or an opponent in a game. Never slam or kick the basketball in anger. Don't pound your fists into walls or lockers. And, obviously, absolutely no fighting—with opponents on the court or among teammates at practice or in the locker room.

- No showboating, taunting, or gloating over a victory. If you want to make it policy, insist that your team always cheer an opponent after a game and offer to shake hands. If the opponent won't shake, have your players simply walk away.

- There should be no criticizing of teammates, either during practice or during games. If a player is trying his best but still makes a mistake, the others should accept it. If a player isn't trying, the coach will see it and handle it.

Coaching Corner

When former National Football League head coach Bill Parcells was in high school, he was a star in three sports. His basketball coach, Mickey Corcoran, remembered a night when his team was winning a game by 17 points. Suddenly, sophomore Parcells was called for a technical foul by arguing too loudly and too long with an official over a call. Coach Corcoran immediately pulled Parcells out of the game. Then the lead began to evaporate and Corcoran knew he had a big decision to make. "If I put him back," he said, "we would undoubtedly win. But he's also going to think, 'The coach really needs me.' So I'm fighting with myself about what to do. The more I thought about it, the more I knew I couldn't put him back in. So I sat him and we lost the game in overtime."

By being consistent and not putting the end result of the game ahead of his rules of sportsmanship and discipline, Corcoran got the respect of his team and its players. Parcells played another two years and never again repeated his actions. Though he later became a volatile head coach in the NFL, as a young player he had enough respect for Coach Corcoran to learn his lesson and do things the way the coach expected. And that is what you, too, should strive for with your players.

If all your players follow these basic rules, you will have a team you can be proud of, no matter what its win-loss record is. Getting players to show respect for each other and for authority can only help them at home, in school, and in any other group endeavors that they undertake.

Can Anything Be Better Than Winning?

No one wins them all, but in America everyone seems to want to win at all costs. There is a huge emphasis on winning everywhere in sports, from the pros on down. Many high school coaches use winning to go after college jobs. Collegiate coaches have to win to keep their jobs, and if they win enough, they will usually get the chance to move to a bigger school, make more money, and have better players to coach. Winning and losing are now associated with more than sports. If you make a big business deal, you're a winner. If another guy gets the deal, you become a loser. A young politician winning an election becomes a rising star in his party. An aspiring politician who loses badly may not get another chance. He's already got a label—he's a loser.

With this kind of prevalent mentality, it shouldn't be surprising that winning is often overemphasized in youth sports. Coaches of certain elite traveling teams in some cities and towns are actually hired by parents to help the team win, make winners of the kids, and maybe help the more talented ones get on the road to a possible college athletic scholarship and even a professional career. If kids are told long enough that winning is the only thing that matters, they are going to start believing it. Some kids as young as 10 want to play only on a winning team. Unfortunately, many of these kids are in for a big letdown, and the pressure to win is one of the reasons they'll leave team sports. As we said, no one wins them all, not even those who are considered the very best.

It's extremely important for a basketball coach to make it very clear from the beginning that he wants his team members to play hard and play to the best of their ability, but that he doesn't expect them to win every game. If you're coaching kids at the lower age levels, you'll have a better chance to start them off in the right direction. It's a known fact that most 9- and 10-year-olds are more interested in simply playing and having fun. Many of them don't even keep track of the score. With the older kids, the teenagers, you might find that they look at winning differently. They are beginning to hear it from parents and see it on television. Many of them won't be very happy at first if their team loses.

> **Quick Tips**
>
> No one wins them all. This not only applies to sports, but to other aspects of growing up. A youngster may fail a test at school, not do a chore correctly at home, or not sing well enough to be in the church choir. These can all be difficult setbacks for youngsters. If these same kids are already playing basketball and you have taught them how to accept losses—to put it behind them, practice more, and try harder—they will be better equipped to deal with setbacks in other phases of their lives. As long as a youngster knows she has tried her best, she should be able to accept the result and move on. If she knows she can approach you for extra help on a jump shot, she can also approach her math teacher for extra help with long division. That is why you, as a coach, can have so much influence with the players on your team.

Evaluating a Win and a Loss

As a coach, you must be aware of the factors that determine the difference between winning and losing that apply at all levels of coaching. You may have some control of these factors, but not all of them. When you evaluate an upcoming opponent or a recently completed game, you should incorporate the following into your evaluation. Remember, this evaluation is so you can properly evaluate your team as well as game situations. Never feel that you have to win all the time or give your team the feeling that winning is the only thing that matters.

- **Superior personnel.** Which team had the better talent? The team with the better talent will win most of the time. If the talent is equal and both teams are equally competitive, you move to the next point.

- **Superior conditioning.** This is a major factor in close contests. Teams that physically make it over the long haul tend to come out on top. If personnel and conditioning are equal, look further.

- **Superior teaching.** This is a factor especially in the area of fundamental skills because the winning team will commit fewer mental mistakes and physical turnovers in the course of the game. If all these factors balance each other, move to the next factor.

- **Superior mental attitude.** This is the team that tries harder, always looks to *tough it out*, and finds a way to win. If there is equality here as well, the final factor comes into play.

♦ **Superior coaching strategy.** Now you are hands-on. The use and placement of personnel during a game, your coaching strategy, and the execution of your game plan could give your team its final advantage.

If you are able to understand and be aware of this overview, you will mature as a coach and be more capable of developing your team's abilities and setting realistic goals for each player and for the team as a whole.

How Do You Strike the Proper Balance?

To strike a balance between winning and losing, you have to make your position clear from the beginning. You are there to teach and coach basketball. Your objective is to make everyone learn to appreciate the game, to fully enjoy playing it, and to play to the best of their ability. Playing their best obviously translates into trying to win. *Trying.* That is the optimum word here. As long as your team works and plays clean and hard, that should be what satisfies you most as a coach. If they do that, improvement will come, both for the individuals and the team. Winning should be incidental. If it happens, fine. If it doesn't, well, that is also acceptable as long as the team doesn't stop trying.

To create the proper atmosphere, you have to explain to your players right from the start that you, as a coach, are not overly concerned with winning. You are more concerned with the effort they make and their overall approach to the game. That includes showing good sportsmanship, playing hard, and supporting each other as a team. It's all right to admit to them that you, like them, would prefer to win. But a loss is not the end of the world. In fact, a loss in the so-called big game is not the end of the world. Even the loss in the championship game is something everyone can live with. Athletes have to do it all the time. Also tell your team that if each player knows she is trying hard and playing to the best of her ability, losing a game—or losing several games—is nothing to be ashamed of; it does not make them *losers.*

Deep down inside, every coach wants to win. He wants it for his players and, perhaps to some degree, for himself. Yet as a youth coach, your primary job is not to win at all costs, but to build a cohesive, unified team made up of players who work hard and pull for each other. Watch your players carefully. If they do their best and lose, they can be somewhat disappointed, but they should still be satisfied with their effort. If they don't play well and lose badly, then they have a right to be down. It's your job, however, to point out the areas that need improvement and promise to work with them to achieve it. Keep the team together, keep them working, and always emphasize the positive. If you do that, winning and losing will become secondary, just where they belong.

> ### Coaching Corner
>
> Chances are, all your players will not have equal ability. In fact, you may have several who are much better than the rest. As a coach, you have to decide where you are going with your team. Do you allow those best players to dominate? Or do you ask them to share time and maybe shots with players of lesser ability? This is a decision you will have to make. At the lower age group levels, the answer is pretty obvious: Everyone should play. There shouldn't be a star system, or a set rotation, as they call it in the pros. With the older players, the decision might be a bit more difficult. Again, everyone should get playing time. However, in the final minutes of a close game, you might want to have your top players on the court. This will approximate what happens with players who go on to play in high school and beyond. So, in a sense, you're getting them ready, and you're also preparing those who are not quite good enough to be in there at the end. Of course, if others improve greatly as the season progresses, you should feel free to make any changes you see fit. And above all, every player should have the feeling that he contributed in some way to the team effort.

Where to Draw the Toughness Line

The legend of the tough and successful coach is an old story. Football's Vince Lombardi and college basketball's Bobby Knight are just two examples. Lombardi was tough but fair with his players, while Knight let his temper flare off as well as on the court—and it ultimately cost him his job at Indiana University (although he was subsequently hired by Texas Tech). Both coaches, however, produced winning teams—and, to many, that's always the bottom line. The only reason this is being mentioned here is that there are numerous examples of youth coaches in various sports who also feel that they have to be tough. However, there is a difference between being tough and being firm, and defining the difference is something all youth coaches should know.

The one thing young basketball players don't need is a drill sergeant, a coach who insists on strict discipline fortified by a voice always several decibels above the normal range. Children usually don't react well to screaming and yelling at home. If they hear it at home, they certainly don't want to hear more of the same-ole, same-ole from the coach. And if they don't hear screaming at home, they won't react well in a sports atmosphere that they expect to be fun. So before you even start, make up your mind that you will never berate your team in a loud and threatening voice. Even though it may initially get their attention, it won't work in the long run. Kids just don't react well to threats, and they can't enjoy themselves if they are frightened of the coach standing before them.

Did You Know?

Back in the early 1970s, when Larry Csonka was a bone-crunching fullback for the world champion Miami Dolphins, he came across a scene at a local park that he found terribly upsetting. During a Pop Warner League football game in progress among very young boys, one of the players was injured. The boy lay on the ground, and within seconds his coach was standing over him—screaming. Csonka remembered the coach yelling at the boy to get up, to be a man, to stop crying and return to the game. Though he was one of the toughest players of his time, Csonka knew that this kind of toughness in a youth coach was completely wrong. In fact, he went so far as to say that the man he saw screaming at the fallen child should not have been coaching youth sports, period. Csonka was right. Who knows what damage that kind of coach might have done to the young boys who looked up to and trusted him?

No one can say how many youth coaches today shouldn't be out there. The important thing is that you don't become one of them. You must be aware from the time you start just which lines you won't cross. It's fine to set rules and regulations and then back them up with examples. Here are some do's and don'ts of coaching that every youth coach should follow without exception;

♦ If a player breaks the rules of good sportsmanship, it is necessary to discipline him. But never fly off the handle, rant and rave, threaten a player on your team, and begin to coach by intimidation.

♦ Under no circumstances whatsoever should you ever put a hand on a player in anger. That could not only cause you to lose your job, but it could land you in trouble with the law, as well. And it could be the end of your coaching career.

♦ Obviously, players must be accountable if they break the rules. That's why you must insist that players listen to your instructions carefully and play the way in which you direct them.

♦ If a player goes off on his own and is disrupting the team, bench him. Then explain to him why he was wrong and reiterate the importance of the team concept. Again, never lose your temper and begin to yell, either in front of others or when you are with him one on one.

♦ Patience is the keyword for a successful coach. If the kids don't understand your concepts at first, take the time to explain again. Do it as long as it takes.

♦ Walk your players through the concept you are teaching. Never, however, show them you are angry because they don't understand immediately. Remember, this may be completely new to them.

◆ Never discipline players for not understanding an offensive or defensive concept quickly enough. And never single out the kids who take longer to understand. Always be aware that you are a teacher, the same as if you were in a classroom, and you have to allow for individual differences.

Having a reputation as a tough coach is not something to brag about in youth basketball. Instead, you should strive to be a firm coach who tolerates no nonsense, one who is fair with his players and who always finds a way to inject some fun into each practice session. That is the best way, perhaps the only way, to earn the respect of your entire team.

Keep a Consistent Routine

It's no secret that most kids, especially the younger ones, crave discipline. They want to follow a leader or someone who will give them direction. At the same time, they also want structure and consistency. Kids will work hard, but they like to be in familiar territory. That's why they wouldn't do as well if they had a different coach at each practice session. You are the number-one constant at this time in their basketball lives. Though we will delve into the specifics of practice routines later, it is important that you know when starting off to keep things the same. That way, the players know when they come to practice just what they have to do to get ready. They know how you structure your practices, and because of this they know when to stop fooling around and be serious.

Don't forget, however, that you can also bend the rules occasionally. For example, if you end practices by having the players run a few wind sprints, you might suspend that if the team has just come off an especially good game or a great practice session. That's yet another way to earn respect and make the experience fun. If you are firm, fair, and consistent in the way you treat each of your players, you'll get results. Do that, and there simply is no reason that you have to play the role of the tough coach.

The Least You Need to Know

◆ Emphasize the importance of good sportsmanship with each and every member of your team from day one.

◆ Set a good example for your players. You are the leader and the teacher. If you show qualities of poor sportsmanship, your players will likely follow your example.

◆ Make sure your players know that winning at all costs is not what you are all about. Teach them how to both win and lose well. That means not gloating over a defeated opponent and not dwelling on a loss and looking to blame someone.

◆ Let your players know from the beginning that you have rules you expect them to follow. Anyone breaking those rules will be disciplined.

◆ Never scream at, humiliate, threaten, or touch a player in anger. These qualities simply won't work when coaching kids, and could ultimately cost you your job.

Chapter 4

Dealing with Problem Players and Problem Parents

In This Chapter

- ◆ Disruptive kids
- ◆ The Star Syndrome
- ◆ Your dealings with parents
- ◆ Problem parents at games

In a perfect world, this chapter would not have to be written. You could go out and coach the game, get your team in line, and then try to get the absolute best out of each and every player. In addition, you would have the total support of all the parents, who would go out of their way to give positive reinforcement to their children and the team. The players would bond together, pull for each other, and listen to your every word. You might not necessarily win a championship, but you would have a totally enjoyable, trouble-free coaching experience.

Unfortunately, it can never be this easy or this idyllic. Depending on the group you are coaching, you will more than likely run into problems with one or more of your players. This can occur for a variety of reasons. You may be able to deal with some of the problems quite easily, but others will be more difficult. They may not involve just the players. Youth sports today has sometimes found itself under a cloud of controversy as many parents have lost sight of the real reasons their son or daughter should be playing. They wittingly or unwittingly begin to apply pressures, which can not only sour their own child on sports, but can sometimes disrupt an entire team as well.

Let's Look at the Problems

Without mincing words, here is a list of potential problems you might have to confront during your tenure as a youth basketball coach:

- **The free spirit.** This is a generous and kind name given to a player who lacks discipline, doesn't listen, and tends to do his own thing at practice and at games.

- **The complainer.** This is a player who isn't happy about anything. He tends to complain about his teammates, his playing time, not getting enough shots, or having to run wind sprints at practice.

- **The rule breaker.** This can be a player who lets his emotions get the best of him and doesn't follow your rules for sportsmanship, for not criticizing teammates, and for showing respect for opponents and officials.

- **The star.** This can be a tough one because the star is usually your most talented player and wants to be treated that way. He carps about your team concept because he's more about showcasing his talents and keeping his scoring average up.

- **The kid who doesn't want to be there**. This may not happen too often, but once in a while you might find a player who just doesn't want to play. He's there only because his parents have urged him to find a sport and become more physically active.

- **The burnout**. This is a term that, years ago, would never be applied to a very young athlete. Not anymore. The burnout might be a player under tremendous pressure from parents to excel, one who is playing on two or three youth teams at the same time. He is tired and no longer having fun. Both of these last two problems are most likely to surface in the 12-to-14-year age group.

Just as the teacher in a classroom has to deal with a roomful of individuals with different personalities, you will run into the same situations with your basketball team. If you have already been coaching for a number of years, you have likely dealt with many of these problems. If you are a new coach, well, you have to be prepared. The problems won't be the same every season, but a few always come up in one form or another.

If a player isn't paying attention while you are talking, you've got to find out why.

Some problems are easier to deal with than others, but all must be addressed so that you can remain in charge and maintain harmony on your team. In many cases, you will be able to deal with the problems yourself, but occasionally you may have to involve the parents or take more drastic action. The solutions may not always make you comfortable.

How About the Solutions?

One player can bring a team down, so it's important to address issues that result from problem players. Let's take a look at some of the potential problems from players and the best ways to address them. Remember, you have responsibility to the entire team as well as to the player and to yourself as a coach. Always give a problem player the benefit of the doubt at first, and every chance to get his act straight.

Freeing the Free Spirit

The free spirit may be a very nice kid who just doesn't like rules. She is more or less someone who goes her own way and approaches her place on the team with that same kind of loose attitude. This person doesn't intentionally disrupt your team, but she simply doesn't set a good example for the other kids. She may fool around during drills, talk and giggle while you are addressing the team, and take some wild shots at the wrong time during games. Yet, often the free spirit is a happy person who enjoys being the center of attention or a sometimes rule breaker.

You've got to ascertain whether your free-spirited player really wants to play basketball and participate as a member of the team. To be frank, the free spirit who likes to go her own way is sometimes more comfortable in an individual sport, whether it be tennis, track and field, or snowboarding—a place where she can perform without worrying about blending in with a team. If after you talk to this person she still refuses to change and follow your rules, you may have to ask her to leave the team. Occasionally, the free-spirited player realizes that she has to follow the rules to remain with the team, and she will leave on her own. You may also speak to her parents. If she behaves the same way at home, it may be time for her to join an individually played sport. As a coach, you simply cannot allow one person to make her own rules while all the others follow yours. It won't work.

> **Quick Tips**
>
> One of the bywords for any successful sports team is *chemistry*. A team with good chemistry is often a winning team. It is a team with a mix of players who work together and whose talents complement each other. They blend and they click. Good chemistry is the ingredient that has helped teams with less talented players defeat teams made up of stars and superstars. Great professional teams such as the Bill Russell–Bob Cousy Boston Celtics and the Michael Jordan–led Chicago Bulls had team chemistry that complemented the talents of the players. Having good chemistry on your youth teams won't guarantee a championship, but it will guarantee a group of players who work together, learn the nuances of the game, and have fun. This is what you always strive to achieve as a coach. One bad apple, however, can poison the brew, and that's when you'll have to step in and get the chemistry working all over again.

Whiners and Complainers

The complainer is the player who is never satisfied. Instead of working to change themselves, complainers just complain. Nothing is right, and whatever you do won't make it right.

Once again, you may not be dealing with a bad kid; you are likely dealing with a kid who prefers to complain rather than work hard. Make an effort to point out to your complainer that most of the things he complains about he also has the power to change. If he complains about not getting enough playing time, tell him to work harder in practice. If he complains to the officials every time a foul is called, tell him to play better defense and stop being sloppy. If he complains that practices are too hard, explain to him what it feels like to run out of gas at the end of a game. You can emphasize this by having him run some wind sprints. If you instill a real work ethic, hopefully the complaining will stop.

Coaching Corner

As a coach, you might find a player who complains constantly difficult to deal with. Sometimes, however, you should try to dig a bit deeper before deciding he doesn't belong on the team. Speak to the parents to find out if he also complains at home. Tell them what he is doing at practice. See if there is a pattern. You might be dealing with a youngster who has some additional problems. He may want attention, especially if he isn't as good as some of the other players. He may also have low self-esteem, another reason to draw attention to himself. Also speak to the player in a one-on-one situation to see if he will open up to you. Another avenue to explore is to speak to his teacher at school, or perhaps a guidance counselor. In other words, try to get at the root of the problem and perhaps recruit some other people to help you. Any time you can salvage a player, and get at the root of a problem, you are also helping that player both on and off the court.

Breaking the Rules

The rule breaker is another who goes his own way, but unlike the free spirit, this person can be a real problem on the team. He doesn't like authority and will push you as hard and as far as he can. It may seem as if he rebels against every rule you make. This disdain for authority may result in bad sportsmanship, criticizing teammates, and showing nearly everyone a genuine lack of respect. The rule breaker might even smirk at you as you try to explain why he has to toe the line. In a worst-case scenario, the rule breaker may simply not belong on the team. But you should never quit on a kid until you cover all the bases, including a chat with his parents. However, if this player continues to flout the rules and break them, then he cannot continue being a part of the team.

Stellar Performers

Unlike the rule breaker, the star usually loves to play the game and wants to excel. That can be the problem. He often doesn't want to share the ball. There may not be a player like this among nine-year-olds, but once you coach older kids, visions of superstardom are often dancing in their heads.

One of the problems here is that you may be dealing with your best player. But he may also be the kind of player who is satisfied when he gets 25 points, even though the team loses. With this kid, you really have to convince him of the team concept—that by playing with and not against his teammates, he will ultimately be a better player. Use some examples of the well-known greats, like Magic Johnson, Larry Bird, and Michael Jordan, who were great players in their own right but never abandoned the team concept. If this doesn't work, then you may have to make him realize that he can't be the star while sitting on the bench. Let him know that you, as his coach, will work hard to make him the best player possible, but he must also help you if he wants to play on the best *team* possible.

Finally, you should emphasize to this player that no one can become a great player if he doesn't get off the bench and into the game. You, as the coach, hold the key to this opportunity for players to showcase their skills. If you use the power you have judiciously, you can exercise control over this and other delicate situations.

Quick Tips

While you may have to convince your best player that he can't take all the shots, and that he shouldn't be satisfied when he scores 30 points but the team loses, you must also give him a chance to use his talents. That's where striking a balance comes into play. This is especially true of the older group. If you have an outstanding player, designate short periods during the game when he can try to dominate the offense. This should be at a time when the team needs points badly and he is the best option. It may be at crunch time at the end of the game, or at the point when your team is starting to fall too far behind. But also emphasize to this player that he will only get a chance to dominate if he works at other phases of the game, such as passing, getting his teammates involved, and working as hard on defense as he does on offense.

The Most Serious of the Player Problems

A couple of the problems you may encounter may make it near impossible to salvage the player for your team, but you may still be able to help him as a person. The first is the kid who simply doesn't want to be there and doesn't like basketball, but is on the team because of parental or peer pressure. You can spot disinterest in a second. The player doesn't listen when you speak, goes through the motions on the court, doesn't interact with teammates, and shows absolutely no joy in playing the game.

Once again, you should first speak with the player. If you feel that the situation is hopeless, call his parents and tell them that he can no longer play for you and why. If they realize what they have done, the parents will agree. If not, they'll probably force him onto another team and pass the problem to the next coach.

When approaching parents with this or other problems, you should begin by explaining that you are trying to solve your problem in a way that is best for their child. You are not looking to have him punished or penalized. Rather, you would like to try to get to the root of the problem so he can continue playing with the team. Also explain that you can't have one or two players sabotaging your efforts to make your team into a cohesive unit. Always try to be accommodating with parents. Don't attack their son's or daughter's character or give the impression you don't like the player in question. Make sure they understand that you are trying to help their child become a viable member of your team.

Dismissing a player from the team should be a last resort. Once again, you should contact the parents first, explain that the problems are continuing, and let them know that the entire team is being affected. See if the parents might have a final suggestion. If they don't, hopefully they will agree with your decision.

Quick Tips

There is one other thing you might do with a player who doesn't want to be part of the team. Ask him if there is something else he might want to do instead of playing basketball. If he admits he always wanted to play tennis, or take piano lessons, or build model cars and airplanes, you may want to take this information to his parents. Explain to them what you were told and suggest politely that they consider allowing their son to try the alternative. If the time comes later when he wants to play basketball again, you will be happy to welcome him back as a part of the team. You yourself may love the sport, but don't expect every single player to share your views.

Burned-Out Players

The final problem player is the most serious of all: the burnout. This is a kid who has been pushed and pressured, has talent, and, as such, has very high and sometimes unrealistic expectations from his parents. This is a growing problem in today's world: Parents of talented young athletes begin to envision college scholarships, perhaps Olympic glory, and eventually multimillion-dollar professional contracts. Chances are, this kid will be playing on two or three teams at once, already sleeping and eating basketball—and he's had enough. Instead of enjoying his talent and his sport, he wants to end it. The joy is gone. At age 12 or 14, basketball has become almost like a job. It's no longer a game for him, and he has had enough.

A kid exhibiting these signs of burnout doesn't belong on the team. But he also needs help. If someone doesn't allow him to be a kid and enjoy basketball once again, he will become a part of the statistic that maintains that 75 percent of kids are quitting team sports by the age of 13. Speak to his parents. If you get nowhere and still want to try to help, you can perhaps speak with a teacher, counselor, or clergyman, someone who can possibly bring some reason to the situation. Otherwise, the kid will have to work it out on his own—but not with your team.

No coach has problem-free seasons all the time. You have to realize that some of these situations will arise—and the better prepared you are to face them, the less time it will take from the players who want to be there and really need you as their coach.

Time to Deal with the Parents

There was a time when parents, for the most part, were totally supportive of their son's or daughter's athletic endeavors. They did what good parents should do, helping their children to participate in healthful and fun activities that would allow their children to make new friends, improve their self-esteem, and have the experience of working with others in a team effort. They were all about positive reinforcement. They made sure their kids made it to practice and games on time, they rooted for them, and they told them to listen to and respect their coach. There are, of course, still parents like that, but there are also parents who see sports in an entirely different light from their children. Not only do these parents sometimes take the joy of sports from their children, but they can cause problems for the coach as well.

Some of the situations that can lead to parent-child-coach problems include the following:

- The parent with unrealistic expectations for his child

- The parent who looks at a sport as his child's free ticket to college, and perhaps a future lucrative career as a professional athlete

- The parent who looks at his child's athletic ability as a symbol of prestige for the entire family

- The parent who thinks he knows more about the sport than the coach

- The parent who is living vicariously through the athletic exploits of his children

- The parent who is himself a poor sport and thus is a disruptive presence at his child's games

This is quite a laundry list of potential problems. It certainly shouldn't scare you away from your desire to coach, but you definitely should be aware of things you may have to deal with from time to time. There are ways to prevent or stop some of these problems, such as keeping the lines of communication with your players' parents open. This section discusses the efforts you can make to prevent and resolve these issues.

Sending a Letter to Mom and Dad

The best way to open the doors of communication is to send a letter to the parents of each of your players. Do this at the beginning of the season or immediately before the season starts. Introduce yourself as the coach, and outline your plans for the season. You might also want to discuss your philosophy, telling them that your goal is to teach the fundamentals of the game and its strategies, and to let the players have fun. Let them know that you are not a win-at-all-costs coach and that everyone will get playing time.

You should also remind parents that everyone on the team should be at practices and games on time. Let parents know that you welcome their support at games and also for any special team activities (such as a team trip to a high school or college game, and perhaps a team dinner at season's end). Ask them to inform you of any health or injury problems their children may have and of any special circumstances, such as allergic reaction to a bee sting. Finally, let the parents know that you are always willing to discuss any aspects of the child's progress and development, as well as any problems that might arise.

Here's a sample letter you might use to communicate with your parents.

Dear Mr. and Mrs. Smith:

My name is Joe Hobson and I will be coaching your son's recreation league basketball team this year. I hope to meet you personally soon, but I wanted to take this opportunity to introduce myself and let you know what I hope to bring to all the players on the Rockets this year.

My job is to teach your son and the other players the game of basketball, including the fundamental individual skills of the game and basic strategies of team play. In addition to that, I plan to emphasize the importance of working together as a team, exhibiting good sportsmanship toward teammates, opponents, referees, and fans. We will emphasize competing and playing to the best of our ability, but winning will not be the end all. No one wins them all.

I am asking all parents to make sure their children arrive at games and practices on time, are dressed properly, have bottled water or a sports drink with them, and also have transportation home. I would also appreciate it if you inform me of any allergies your son may have, and to let me know whenever you feel he is not 100 percent physically healthy, or if you suspect he may be hiding an injury.

You are welcome to come and watch us practice as well as supporting us at our games. I would hope that you exhibit the same kind of good sportsmanship that I will be trying to instill in my players. Remember, the lines of communication are always open and I'm always willing to discuss any problems that might arise. Conversely, if I sense a problem, I hope I can come to you to discuss it, as well. If you have any additional questions, please don't hesitate to ask.

Yours truly,
Joe

By starting with a letter home, and then by meeting the parents of your players, you have a leg up on alleviating problems and perhaps even knowing where the problems might come from. For example, if you meet a parent who raves about how good a shot his son has and says that he expects the boy to average between 15 and 20 points a game, that parent is going to be disappointed if his child doesn't meet his expectations. You can explain immediately that that is unlikely to happen. Explain that all the players will be playing and that everyone has to learn how to shoot and how to make their shots.

At the same time, explain that you will not only work on the strengths of the players, but also will try to improve areas in which they are weak. Your goal is to make complete players who understand and enjoy the game. Even though a son may not have a chance to score as many points as his father envisions, tell the father that his son will emerge as a better player, something that will help him if he chooses to play at the next level.

Problems Arising During the Season

No coach can eliminate all problems with parents before the season starts. However, if you listen to your kids, you may be able to find out some negative things that are happening at home. For example, you are the coach. Kids really don't like it when a parent becomes a second coach and tells them things that may be different from what you have been telling them. If you are teaching a particular skill, such as a jump shot, and the next day one of your players says his Dad feels he should take the shot differently, that player is going to get confused. Who does he listen to, his coach or his father? Once again, it's time for a talk with the parents.

Kids may also be upset when parents take losses harder than they do. You, as a coach, are teaching your kids to play hard and not to let losses bother them. Yet, some parents act as if a loss is the end of the world and put part of the blame on their own child, other players, and maybe even you, as the coach. Once again, explain your philosophy to your players, emphasizing playing hard and working as a team to improve. If all the players do that, they will get better and the wins will come.

Perhaps the most overt of the problems are parents who act badly at games. Poor sportsmanship by parents has become one of the major drawbacks of all youth sports. This may include parents who berate their own child or some of her teammates. Sometimes this reverse sportsmanship takes the form of screaming at the referees on calls (good or bad calls), or even yelling at the coach, demanding that their children play more, or demanding other substitutions. The worst-case scenario involves parents who come to games acting under the influence of alcohol and those who resort to violence against other parents, coaches, or officials. It has happened too much in recent years to be ignored.

Did You Know?

Over the last few years the term *sports rage* has become almost as commonplace as *road rage*. It describes the extreme anger being brought to games by parents and spectators—and even some young players—that leads to violence. There have been numerous incidents of brawls between parents during youth games, of officials being attacked by parents and coaches. The most overt incident was the death of a volunteer coach at a youth hockey game when he got into a fight with the father of one of the players after an argument about rough play. The parent received a 6-10 year prison sentence for involuntary manslaughter. Today, the National Association of Sports Officials offer "assault insurance" to their 19,000 members because of the numerous reports of physical violence against officials. There are also programs in place to actually teach parents how to be good sports. It has become a major problem that every youth coach must be aware of and address. As Kathleen Avitt, national program director for the nonprofit Parents Alliance for Youth Sports said, "Too many angry adults are setting poor examples for children and they are totally destroying the concept of what youth sports is supposed to be." This is certainly much food for thought for every coach.

What You Can Do

The most important thing is to keep the lines of communication open. If one of your players indicates that he is having problems at home regarding his play or his place on the team, try to talk to his parent or parents. Once again, you can explain your philosophy of coaching, what you feel is important for maintaining balance on the team, and how you are trying to make each person on your team a better player. You can also remind the parent that you want to be sure that each player on your team is enjoying the basketball experience and having fun. Let parents know that many kids are leaving team sports early because of various pressures that are robbing the game of its fun. Hopefully this will help.

If you meet a parent who seems to be living vicariously through his child and won't be satisfied with his son or daughter being anything less than the star of the team, then you have a problem. This situation sometimes occurs with a parent who has limited athletic skills and thus experienced little, if any, athletic success as a youth. It can also happen with the parent who had a modestly successful athletic career at some level but "just missed" professional stardom and believes that his child is entitled to reach that goal.

You will have to explain that you don't believe in the star system and that, while some players are obviously better than others, everyone will get an equal chance to experience all phases of the game. If one particular player is outstanding, that ability will certainly show, but the player will not become the focal point and is not allowed to dominate the game to the detriment of the others. If the parent still refuses to understand and continues to demand that his child get more shots and playing time, you may have to ask him to find another team for his son or daughter.

A loud and abusive parent can hurt everyone and can be a difficult problem to solve.

The parent who is loud and disruptive during the game is obviously a major problem. Not only can this type of abusive behavior lead to more problems, but it is also setting a terrible example for all the players—not to mention that it is often a real embarrassment for the child of that parent. These kinds of parents sometimes don't understand the game or simply don't care. You might, for example, have a parent who actually implores his son to foul hard, to "make it count." That kind of thinking borders on dirty play, which is something you cannot tolerate. Another parent may be screaming at the officials every time a call goes against your team. Yet another parent may direct his abuse toward you, berating you for taking his child out of the game or for not constantly having your best players on the floor.

Try to approach these parents in a friendly but straightforward manner. Be honest. Explain that their behavior is not only embarrassing their child, but it is also disrupting the game. Tell them that it is taking some of the fun away from the player and the team as a whole. You may also explain that although you don't always agree with every call from the officials, you know they are doing the best job that they can and you always instruct your players not to argue a call. Also tell a difficult parent that your coaching philosophy is geared toward helping each player on your team and that you see no reason to change it. Having a parent yell at you or urge his child to complain is only going to hurt the child in the long run.

Basically, you have to be as firm with difficult parents as you are with your team. Make it clear that you cannot be intimidated into making changes you don't want to make. Obviously, you won't please everyone. Sometimes a parent pulls his child off your team for his own reasons. If you know that you are doing your job to the best of your ability, you can't let that bother you. You deal with parents the best you can. Never, however, sink to the level of a disruptive parent. Don't get into a shouting match with a parent, and never allow yourself to be goaded into a physical confrontation. If you are physically assaulted in any way, you must get the local authorities involved.

In any case, continue positive reinforcement with your players. Keep explaining why this kind of behavior is wrong, and try to keep the fun in the game. There always will be some problems, with the occasional one that is simply beyond your control. As long as you are straight with your team and have a solid support network among yourself, other coaches, league officials, and the parents who do it right, your overall coaching experience will remain a positive one.

The Least You Need to Know

◆ No matter what age level you are coaching, you have to anticipate having some problems with a few players and perhaps a few parents. You must be prepared to handle this.

◆ Be aware of the types of problems you may encounter with players before the season begins. Remember, always try to do what is in the best interest of the player and the team.

◆ Always write an introductory letter to the parents of all your players at the beginning of the season. Let them know your coaching philosophy and what you expect from both player and parents. Keep the lines of communication open.

◆ Be prepared to speak to parents who are giving their son or daughter advice that is contrary to yours, or are being a disruptive influence at practice or games.

◆ Coaches today should be aware of the rising incidence of *sports rage* and do everything they can to foster respect and good sportsmanship among their players and their parents.

Chapter 5

Keeping Your Team Healthy

In This Chapter

- ◆ Take precautions immediately
- ◆ Boys and girls are different
- ◆ Recognizing big and little hurts
- ◆ Keeping your team healthy

When you are coaching youth basketball, your responsibilities go a great deal further than just teaching the X's and O's of the game. Because you are dealing with young children and teenagers, you also have a responsibility for their health and well-being while they are members of your team. Because basketball is a physical game with a great deal of running, changing direction, stopping and starting, as well as jumping, there is always the potential for injury. That potential increases if the players are not in good physical condition and are not taking care of their health in general.

In this chapter, we discuss ways that you can be better prepared to keep your team healthy. This includes recognizing the players who don't seem to be thriving physically during the season, as well as keeping a careful eye out for injuries. Some kids will tell you when they are hurt, but many kids are not always truthful. Some might exaggerate their injuries, especially if they are not enjoying the basketball experience. Others, however, might try to hide their injuries so that they can continue playing. Still others may not realize the full extent of certain injuries, and it will be up to you to know when to call parents or even a doctor. The last thing you want to happen to any member of your team is to suffer a serious injury, or an injury that becomes serious because you didn't see it in time.

The Need for Some Training

Depending on the rules and regulations in the area in which you coach, you may be required to have some training in first aid and in recognizing injuries common to sports before you can coach. Some towns, cities, or counties even require their coaches to be certified in first aid and some form of emergency treatment. Therefore, know your local requirements and be sure to comply with them. However, even if there are no specialized requirements in medical aid, it would benefit you to know as much as you can about recognizing injuries, helping your players prevent them, and quickly aiding an injured player until the professionals arrive.

Quick Tips

Today, there are a variety of specialized sports medicine first-aid kits on the market. This is an important piece of equipment for every coach to have. One of the better kits on the market, costing upwards of $130.00, includes among many things the following: An emergency first aid manual, emergency guide, finger splint, butterfly bandages, antibiotic ointment, antiseptic towelettes, 5" x 9" trauma pads, triangle bandages, eye pads, gauze, elastic bandages, elastic tape, adhesive tape, many assorted bandages, cotton-tipped applicators, nitrile gloves, antimicrobial hand wipes, chemical ice packs, SAM splint, forceps, eye wash, sting relief pads, tweezers, a disposable penlight, and accident report forms.

There are smaller kits on the market, but this is a fine example of one that will allow the coach to treat a variety of ailments immediately.

As soon as you meet your players, you can take some immediate steps to help safeguard their health and ensure their safety at games and practices. The following tips come from the National Athletic Trainers' Association and National Youth Sports Safety Foundation, and are geared to protect young athletes:

◆ All safety equipment in your sport should be required and properly maintained. With basketball, this means that you should make sure your players have the proper shoes (sneakers) and perhaps a mouth guard to protect players' teeth.

◆ All facilities should be maintained and inspected regularly. Always be sure the gym floor is in good condition and that there are no objects on the sidelines that could cause players to trip and fall.

◆ There should be a first-aid kit at all practices and games.

Every coach should be sure to have a first-aid kit at all practices and at games.

◆ Plenty of fluids should be available for players to drink during practices and games. This is especially important if you're coaching in the summer or in a year-round hot-weather climate.

◆ A coach should have an emergency information card for each member of his team. It should have parents' phone numbers; any specific allergies, such as to foods or bee stings; any medical problems, such as asthma; a list of medications the player is taking; and any additional information that might help the coach watch for potential physical problems.

Quick Tips

Coaches should also be aware of emergency plans for the building in which they are practicing or playing. This includes the location of fire alarms, fire exits, and the safest place to go in case of a sudden weather event, such as a tornado. A coach must be prepared to direct and protect his players in any kind of emergency.

◆ Coach and players should all know the location of the nearest telephone (or make sure someone has a cell phone available), and should be able to give any emergency crew directions to the place where they are practicing or playing.

◆ This one may be difficult, but it is also recommended that a *first responder* who is certified in first aid and CPR attend at all practices and games. That being the case, no one should touch or move an injured player until the first responder examines him. This is why it is extremely helpful for any youth coach to be certified in first aid and CPR.

Watch for Changes and Signs of Trouble

A coach should always watch each player very carefully at every practice and at games. Watch for signs of change in the player's performance and attitude. This can be a sign of physical trouble. If a player who is always upbeat and energetic suddenly seems tired and lethargic, it can be a sign of trouble. If a player is suddenly losing stamina and gasping for breath in situations she usually breezes through with no trouble, it may indicate a medical or physical problem. If a player who is always the first one on the court and the last to leave suddenly seems disinterested in practicing and playing, there may be a physical problem or problems at home.

Did You Know?

It took many years for people to realize that girls and young women were capable of playing the same kind of full-court basketball as boys and men. But while the playing field is now equal, there are still differences in the physical makeup of boys and girls, something every coach should acknowledge. Although the injury rates for girls are no higher than those of boys, some injuries are more prevalent in girls. The most serious of these is a tear of the anterior cruciate ligament (ACL) in the knee. This is an injury that can occur in basketball, and some studies now show that female athletes are tearing knee ligaments at a rate of 6 to 10 times more often than that of men. This is something to watch carefully if you are coaching a girls' or mixed team.

It is not known for certain why girls tend to suffer knee ligament injuries more than boys, but most medical people feel it has to do with the physiology of the two sexes. One sports medicine specialist thinks that women's wider hips may put more strain on the knee joint, while another specialist thinks that the angle of the knee is a bit different in the female because of the pelvis. At any rate, the statistics don't lie. As a coach, you should always be certain to read the latest medical information on this and other medical subjects. The more knowledge you have, the better you can prepare your players and hopefully keep injuries to a minimum.

Never be reluctant to call parents to discuss any changes you observe in a player's physical condition or overall attitude. Sometimes the apparent problem may be nothing. Perhaps the player's priorities suddenly change. This can happen with kids. But if there is something wrong, parents should know about it.

Never hesitate to suggest that parents take their child to a doctor. It's better to be safe when it comes to the overall health and well-being of your players. Parents should appreciate the fact that you are an observant and concerned coach, and should not resent you suggesting that something might be bothering their child. That, too, is part of your overall coaching responsibilities.

Girls are more likely to tear the anterior cruciate ligament (ACL) in their knee than boys.

Gender Differences and Injury

Studies show that female athletes also tend to suffer more stress fractures, which usually occur in the weight-bearing bones of the lower leg and foot. Medical professionals aren't sure why, but some think that the eating disorders anorexia and bulimia, which are more prevalent in young girls, can be a contributing factor where stress fractures are concerned. If you are coaching a girls' team, look for any signs of sudden or continued weight loss among your players. It may be a sign of an eating disorder, which is a problem in itself, and it could also lead to a stress fracture.

Two physical problems arise in young athletes, both male and female, for the simple reason that they are still growing. The first, called Osgood-Schlatter disease, is fairly common in young athletes. It occurs more often among boys than girls. It is caused by repetitive stress during running and jumping, as well as activities involving motions of the knee. Basically, this condition is an inflammation and pain in the tendon of the knee that may result in an enlargement or swelling below the kneecap. Applying ice and stretching help, and if the pain isn't too severe, the athlete can continue to play. If the pain becomes too severe, rest is the solution. This is a condition that disappears once the athlete stops growing, but it is something you should watch for among members of your team.

Quick Tips

Stress fractures may be the least of the problem if a young girl has a serious eating disorder. Statistics show that these disorders are increasing at an accelerating rate and are becoming a major problem for young girls. The coach of a girls' team must watch her players carefully. If there is a sign of an eating disorder in any of her players, she should contact the parents immediately and strongly suggest that they consult a doctor and perhaps a psychologist. This is extremely important because an unchecked eating disorder can result in serious illness or even death.

The other condition a young player is prone to is a growth-plate injury. The growth plate is an area of developing tissue near the ends of the long bones. The growth plates determine the future length and shape of the mature bone. When the athlete stops growing, the growth plates are replaced by solid bone. These growth plates, however, are prone to fractures because they are simply the weakest points on a growing skeleton. The greatest incidents of these injuries occur in 11- to 12-year-old girls and in 14-year-old boys. Older girls have fewer of these fractures because of the higher rate at which their bodies mature compared to boys.

Growth-plate fractures can be caused by a fall or blow to the body, or even by overuse. If one of your players complains of a persistent pain in his arms or legs, and you see that it is affecting his ability to perform, or to put pressure on a limb, it could be a growth-plate injury and that player should be checked by a doctor immediately. There can be several degrees of fracture, but the treatment usually results in immobilizing the injured limb with a cast or split, which is left in place until the injury heals over a few weeks or several months. Any serious injury, such as one to the growth plate, should be rehabilitated under the direction of a doctor or athletic trainer. You should receive a note giving the player medical clearance to resume participation with the team.

The Little Hurts and the Big Hurts

Any coach who continues with his job long enough will see his share of injuries among his players. He certainly won't have the knowledge of an athletic trainer or doctor, but the more experience he accumulates during his career, the better he can recognize injuries and make the right recommendation to the injured player. Of course, you can't always tell the seriousness of an injury. Part of being a good coach is to make sure your players are always open and honest about anything that is bothering them, no matter how small.

No player, even a very young one, will go through an entire season without some kind of aches and pains, bumps and bruises. As a coach, you should make it your business to speak to each player individually before or after every practice just to see how everyone is feeling physically. If something hurts, check it out and then watch the player carefully. Make sure that your players are aware of their own bodies; they are going to have to tell you what hurts and how badly it hurts. Together, you'll have to decide which of their aches and pains need medical attention.

Coaching Corner

Although communication is an important part of the entire coaching experience, it is especially important when it comes to the health of your players. Each player must have the feeling that you genuinely care about him as an individual to the point where he trusts you completely. Make sure each player knows the importance of telling you about any ache or pain, any suspicion that he might have an injury, no matter how minor. At this level, there is absolutely no need for a kid to tough it out and play through an injury. The last thing any coach wants is to let a minor injury slide until it becomes a major injury. This should be a topic of conversation the first day of practice and every day thereafter. Even when most of the kids are being open with you, watch them carefully for signs of injury, such as a limp, a player wincing in pain when he jumps, or one rubbing an elbow or knee constantly during lulls in practice. And in cases where you feel the player is not being honest about a possible injury, contact his parents and recommend they take him to a doctor, or at least an athletic trainer.

Some of the small aches and pains that are part of the normal process of practicing and playing the game are as follows:

- ◆ Cramps occur when a muscle knots up in intense contractions. A cramp can occur when an athlete loses fluids through sweating or when he isn't in top shape. Though a cramp is painful, it is not serious and can be gently stretched out.

◆ Normal muscle soreness occurs when new muscles are used for the first time and become fatigued. Rest will generally take the soreness away or diminish it greatly, and the player can continue to practice without interruption.

◆ Bumps and bruises occur in any contact sport, and basketball is no exception. Most are minor, and the player can continue to practice as they heal. A more serious bruise, called a contusion, will cause some internal bleeding, swelling, pain, and stiffness. Yet in most cases, even a contusion is not a serious injury. However, a severe contusion should be looked at by a doctor.

◆ Blisters can be annoying and can linger if not treated quickly. Basketball players can get blisters from a new or ill-fitting pair of shoes, as well as by not smoothing out their socks on the bottom of the sneakers. Socks that are too large will cause additional friction in the heel area, while socks with holes can also be a cause of blisters. Cover the blister with a small adhesive bandage and give it time to heal. Larger blisters can be drained carefully without removing the protective skin. Untreated blisters can sometimes become infected, and then the injury is no longer minor.

◆ A sprain is a stretched or torn ligament, while a strain is a stretched or torn muscle or tendon. Both can vary from very mild to severe. With a mild sprain or strain, a player can usually continue to play. However, in some cases this can be a mistake. To be safe, if any player suffers what appears to be a sprain or strain, you should immediately direct her to stop playing and have the injury checked.

Quick Tips

Even the milder sprains and strains that don't need a doctor's care should be treated at home. Coaches can safely recommend a method called R.I.C.E. therapy to treat these injuries. R.I.C.E. stands for Rest, Ice, Compression, and Elevation. Rest simply means to stop using the sprained area immediately. Ice should then be applied within the first 24 hours after the injury. The ice pack can be kept on the injured area for up to 2 hours at a time, constantly or intermittently. This should be continued at 2-hour intervals for 24 hours. After 24 hours, you can use heat, but never use heat during the first 24 hours after the injury. It can increase bleeding and swelling, and can lengthen the healing time. The injury should also be wrapped with an elastic bandage or special sleeve to compress the joint. Compression helps reduce swelling. Finally, elevate the injured area whenever possible so that fluid can drain and reduce swelling. These are the four important steps to take in R.I.C.E. therapy. It is an accepted and universal treatment, and it works.

As a coach, you are the first line of defense against injuries. But in the course of a season, players will be hurt. Though you can't be expected to take the place of a doctor, the more you know about the most common sports injuries, the faster you can recommend or summon the proper help for the kids. You should also be aware that the most common of these injuries are often due to overexertion. If you work your team too hard so that the players are becoming exhausted toward the end of the practice, that's when many injuries can occur. As fatigue sets in and young muscles tire, both strength and coordination decrease. This is when a player is most vulnerable.

Signs of Serious Injury

When you talk to your players about injuries and instruct them to tell you about any kind of injury they have, you should make them aware of the warning signs that an injury may be serious. Let them know that if they begin to experience any of these signs, they should tell you immediately so you can summon help. Here is what they should look for:

- A sharp or burning pain that does not subside in a short time

- Any sharp, tearing pain in the leg area after a quick, explosive movement

- Intense pain in the ankle or knee after jumping and landing awkwardly

- Any pain or tightness in an arm, shoulder, wrist, hand, foot, knee, or leg that restricts movement or the ability to put pressure on that body part

- Any type of bruise or other apparent minor injury that doesn't heal in the time it should

- Any feeling of dizziness, lightheadedness, or nausea following a blow to the head or an intense workout in the heat

If a player reports any of these symptoms, sit that player down immediately and summon help. If there is an athletic trainer or first responder nearby, have that person give the initial examination and recommend follow-up. If the injury seems extremely serious or dangerous, call for an ambulance and an emergency medical technician (EMT) immediately. Remember, your players trust you and their parents trust you. Always make the health and physical well-being of your players your number-one consideration at all times.

Did You Know?

Any head injury, even one that is seemingly minor, should be taken seriously. It doesn't take an especially hard blow to the head to give a young player a concussion. Even mild concussions should be taken seriously, and players who fall to the court and hit their heads, or even take a hard elbow to the head, should be removed from practice or the game immediately. Let the player sit on the bench for a few minutes and constantly check on how he feels. If he reports any dizziness, lightheadedness, or nausea, he should be examined by a doctor immediately. If not, it still may be a good idea to call his parents, tell them what happened, and suggest they have their child examined by a doctor. If you feel strongly about this and the parents refuse, you can tell them you will not allow their child to return to the team without a note from their doctor. Repeated concussions can result in permanent neurological damage, and for that reason all blows to the head should be considered potentially dangerous to the player.

Keeping Your Team Healthy

As we said before, there is no way that any basketball team can avoid injuries completely. But there are steps that you, as the coach, can take to keep your players as healthy as possible. A good place to begin is to heartily suggest an overall healthful lifestyle. Explain once more that basketball is a very physical sport with a great deal of stop-and-go running, sudden sprints, quick stops, and much jumping. To practice and play the sport, young players must be sure to get enough sleep and to eat right. The sleep part is the easier of the two. Players will quickly find that if they come to practice already tired, they won't play well and will be even more tired when practice ends. In addition, they won't play their best in games.

Eating is a different story. Kids on the whole love fast foods, and fast foods simply aren't the most healthful way to eat. You can suggest a balanced diet with whole grains, fruits, and vegetables; however, if parents don't eat that way, their kids won't. And there will be times when kids won't eat what's best for them anyway. Perhaps all you can do, then, is tell them what you know, maybe give them literature on good nutrition, and hope for the best. One thing that you should always tell all your players from the start, however, is that anyone who is found to be using alcohol, tobacco, or drugs is off the team. Period. These abuses simply can't be tolerated.

Starting the Correct Way on the Court

You may not have total control over what your players eat and how much they sleep, but as soon as they step onto the court for the first time, you can take measures to try to keep them as healthy and injury-free as possible. Overall physical conditioning is extremely important. The nature of the sport itself will get players in condition because they will be running in practice and games. If you have a relatively easy practice because you are demonstrating drills and walking through plays, you can have them run some wind sprints at the end for general conditioning. Remember, if you work your players to exhaustion, they are much more likely to get injured. But once they are in game shape, their physical condition should help prevent some injuries.

One of the most important things for any athlete to know is the value of stretching. Stretching loosens both muscles and tendons, and gets players ready to absorb the impact of any explosive sport. When muscles aren't properly warmed up and stretched, they are much more prone to pull, strain, or tear. Since basketball is a sport that involves running, jumping, reaching, making quick starts and stops, and changing speeds, cold muscles are ripe for injury. Stretching is an aspect of basketball that is sometimes overlooked by coaches. Some feel that kids can warm up adequately by running layup drills and just moving around the court. In a sense, players do warm up this way, maybe breaking a light sweat and getting ready to play. But stretching is considered extremely important for young athletes in any sport. It is not a bad idea to give your players a 10-minute stretching routine to follow before they even take the court. In fact, it's also a good idea to repeat the routine after practice and before they shower.

The following stretching routine was developed for young athletes by the American Academy of Orthopedic Surgeons. It can be done in 10 minutes and should be followed even if the athlete is playing at the local park away from his coach and teammates. This type of routine has been shown to go a long way toward helping the athlete prevent minor injuries, and perhaps even some major ones as well.

Here is the routine. You should try it first and then teach it to your players.

1. **Seat straddle lotus.** Sit down on the floor. Place the soles of your feet together and drop your knees toward the floor. Place your forearms on the inside of your knees, and gently push your knees to the ground. Lean forward, bringing your chin to your feet. Hold this position for five seconds, and repeat it three to six times.

2. **Seat side straddle.** Sit with your legs spread and straight out. Place both your hands on the same ankle. Slowly bring your chin to your knee while keeping the legs straight. Hold for five seconds. Repeat three to six times. Alternate the exercise on opposite legs.

3. **Seat stretch.** Sit with your legs together, your feet flexed, and your hands on your ankles. Then bring your chin to your knees. Hold for five seconds, and repeat three to six times.

4. **Lying quad stretch.** Lie on your back with one leg straight and the other leg with hip turned in, with the foot facing out and the knee bent. Press the bent knee to the floor. Hold it five seconds, and repeat three to six times before switching to the other leg.

5. **Knees to chest.** Lie on your back with your knees bent. Grasp your knees and bring them out toward your armpits, rocking gently. Hold for five seconds. Repeat three to five times.

6. **Forward lunges.** Stand straight. Place your right leg forward until your knee is bent at a right angle. Lunge forward, keeping your back leg straight. The stretch should be felt on the left groin. Hold for five seconds. Repeat three to six times, then lunge forward with the other leg and repeat the stretching routine.

7. **Side lunges.** Stand with your legs apart. Bend the left knee while leaning toward the left. Keep your back straight and your right leg straight. Hold for five seconds. Repeat three to six times, and then do the opposite leg.

8. **Crossover.** Stand with legs crossed. Keep your feet close together and your legs straight. Bend at the waist and touch your toes. Hold for five seconds. Repeat three to six times before crossing over with the opposite leg.

9. **Standing quad stretch.** Stand using your left hand to support you. Reach down with your right hand and pull your right foot to your buttocks. Hold for five seconds. Repeat three to six times before switching to the other leg.

These stretches should be done one after the other. Tell your players to increase the tension gradually. If with any stretch they feel the muscle stretching to the point of pain, they should stop and decrease the tension. You may discover other stretching programs, including a few stretches for the upper body. Whatever routine you finally decide upon, have your players consistently stick with it. Stretching is just another way to get your team ready to play basketball and another way to keep injuries to a minimum.

Two Sets of Rules Apply Here

Players must follow two sets of rules to play the game in a clean and healthful way that will hopefully prevent some potential injuries. There are the rules of the sport, and then there are your rules. The game should be played the proper way with the correct form for all the individual skills. Obviously, this is something you must teach your players during practice and into the season.

You also have to teach additional rules of sportsmanship, because injuries sometimes occur as the result of dirty play on the court. No one on your team should ever try to hurt an opponent intentionally with an overly hard foul or by tripping, pushing, throwing an elbow, or committing a flagrant foul. You should be sure that every player on your team knows that this kind of thing will absolutely not be tolerated.

Dirty play can result in a variety of injuries. Tripping an opponent intentionally can cause a bad fall, a possible concussion, or a hand, wrist, elbow, or shoulder injury, or a bad contusion. An elbow thrown in anger can also cause a concussion, an eye injury, and possible broken nose, cut lip, or lost teeth. These are all serious injuries with potentially dire consequences to both players involved. If your opponents are playing dirty, let the referee know but instruct your players not to retaliate. Hopefully, the officials will put a halt to the problem.

> **Quick Tips**
>
> Healthy, injury-free players will always gain more from the sport than those who are tired, who are dragging, or who are nursing a pulled muscle or ankle sprain. Injuries cannot be avoided entirely, but a good coach knows the best ways to get his players ready and keep them as healthy as possible.

The Least You Need to Know

◆ It's up to you to keep your team as healthy and injury-free as possible.

◆ Make it your business to know about the physiology of young athletes and the differences between boys and girls.

◆ Always have an athletic first-aid kit at practices and at games.

◆ Learn the signs of different types of injury and check the health of each player before practice and games.

◆ Never allow a player to continue playing with an injury, and if you feel a visit to the doctor is in order, follow up to make sure it is done.

Chapter 6

Knowing Your Age Group

In This Chapter

◆ Different ages, different kids

◆ What you can and can't do

◆ Staying within limits

◆ Satisfaction at any age

Youth basketball encompasses a variety of age levels. At the lower end are the eight- and nine-year-olds. Next are the 10- to 12-year-olds and, finally, the 13- and 14-year-olds. Both on and off the basketball court, there is a huge difference between an 8-year-old and a 14-year-old. This goes for both boys and girls. You wouldn't match up a team of 8- and 9-year-olds against a team of 13- and 14-year-olds any more than you would put a team of NBA players against a high school JV team. As a coach, you might find yourself working with several different age levels and, as such, you will have to alter your approach to accommodate each group.

As a coach, you must always be well aware of both the physical and mental makeup of your team, and a great deal of that is determined by their ages. In today's world of youth sports, many young kids are being pushed too hard too soon, and that is one reason many of them are quitting. So it's your job to keep things in perspective and to make sure that the kids who really enjoy the sport at each level are more than willing to continue on to the next. In this chapter, we look at the differences among the younger kids you might be coaching, the older kids, and the group in between.

Decide Beforehand Where You Want to Be

Because there is a wide range of age levels coming under the heading of youth basketball, a coach must know at which level he will feel the most comfortable. Some coaches are equally at home with the nine-year-olds and the older kids. In most cases, these coaches have been working at it for some time and are very familiar with the differences in the kids. So, they know what to expect and what they can and cannot do. For example, if you feel as a coach that you want to direct a more competitive team, one that can learn the complex strategies of the game and go all-out on the court, then you will probably get more satisfaction coaching at the upper levels. If you feel you'll get more of a kick out of teaching the basic skills of the game, getting kids to learn about working together as a team but at a much slower pace, then perhaps you should stick to the younger group.

Did You Know?

As a general rule, the youngest age group is less competitive than the older kids. However, in today's world it doesn't always work that way. Nine-year-olds and 10-year-olds are quitting teams because they aren't winning often enough. These youngsters are already buying into the win-at-all-costs philosophy that trickles down from the professional levels. In most cases, they have been pushed and influenced by others, usually their parents. If you are coaching eight- and nine-year-olds and have one or two players who are already ferocious competitors who won't accept losing, they may not be right for your team. You simply cannot let an attitude like that spread to all of your players.

Some coaches enjoy the change of pace that goes with working at several levels. If you fit into that group and have the time, you can certainly coach more than one team and work with the different age groups. Or, you can vary it from year to year. But as a coach, there is one thing you should be completely certain about. You should know exactly what you can do at each age level. That means understanding kids of that particular age and knowing what they are capable of physically, mentally, and emotionally. The one thing you cannot do is push kids beyond their limits. That will only lead to major problems, as well as make you a bad coach—and being a bad coach is the last thing you want.

Players at each age level are very different physically, mentally, and emotionally.

The Youngest Players

At one time, the chronological age of a young athlete was pretty much the key to how that athlete would behave when it came to organized sports. There was a rule of thumb that young children of three and four years of age didn't have the attention span, the motor skills, or the ability to understand the rules of complex sports. For years, it was suggested that these very young children begin with individual sports that help develop hand-eye coordination.

Between the ages of five and seven, it was felt that kids didn't have the psychological development to take directions, to both play and concentrate on coaching instructions at the same time. It was pretty much agreed by those who studied this age group that the kids could safely begin playing sports such as soccer and T-ball, but they were not ready for other team sports.

Finally, between the ages of 8 and 10, kids are supposedly able to understand their role in a team sport as well as some of the basic complexities of the game. This is the time, experts suggested, that kids begin playing baseball and

> **Fact of the Game**
>
> Experts suggest that kids avoid contact sports until they are eight years old. Basketball comes under the heading of a contact sport. Football and hockey, however, are considered *collision* sports, and it has been suggested that kids not play these sports until they are at least 10 years old. Unfortunately, many parents are putting their kids in these sports at younger ages.

basketball. At this age they are also supposed to be ready to participate in contact sports. It was also considered a given that for many years children under the age of 10 were not really interested in competition, that they just wanted to go out, run around, and have fun. Through observation, it was felt that kids in this age group usually didn't tend to keep score and weren't even aware of the score most of the time. Playing, more than winning and losing, was the important thing. And, indeed, for many this will be their first competitive peer situation.

Coaching Corner

Because of the emphasis on sports success, winning and losing, and pressures put on by misguided parents and coaches with the wrong priorities, it isn't always possible to pigeon-hole kids into distinct age versus ability categories anymore. Hopefully, the majority of young athletes will still fit the classic mold for their age groups. But more kids are being pushed to excel and be ultracompetitive at an early age. Kids are also being pressured into striving to make what are called elite traveling teams, teams in towns and cities that take only the best players and then seek out top-flight competition in other towns, with the specific objective to win while pushing the kids to excel at the next level. This situation is often orchestrated by the unrealistic expectations of parents, many of whom envision their kids winning college scholarships and someday enriching the entire family through the multimillion-dollar contracts handed out in professional sports. In some cases, even toddlers are being put in organized programs already geared to make them competitive and start them on an athletic life. In a nutshell, there are simply too many kids who are no longer being allowed to be kids, especially where participation in team sports is concerned.

If you are coaching at the youngest age (eight- to nine-year-olds) of the spectrum and find a kid who already seems much more advanced than the others, one who is already talking about winning and having the best players on the court, and he doesn't seem to want to listen or follow your philosophy, you might suggest to his parents that he seek another team. He simply won't fit in with the rest of the kids, who are beginners and typically want to have fun. With the youngest players, it's very important to have players close to the same skill level and who enjoy learning the game. Winning and losing should be a very low priority.

At this age, your players should be using the women's regulation-size basketball, which is smaller than the men's, but they should be working with the standard-height basket.

Obviously, these kids are nowhere close to being fully developed physically, and they cannot be expected to have endless stamina. They should not be pushed too hard, something that can be alleviated by always alternating players and not leaving anyone out on the court for too long. Always watch younger children carefully so that they do not become too tired or approach exhaustion. Overexertion takes the fun out of the game and makes children vulnerable to possible injury.

Besides giving this age group the fundamentals of the game—both the individual skills and basic strategies—you will be teaching them to work together as a team. This may be something they haven't been exposed to before and it is extremely important that each and every one grasps the concept of teamwork and unselfishness. The old expression "There is no 'I' in *team*" is very important for them to learn. Remember, at this age level, the kids are in the process of developing their personality and establishing a sense of identity.

You also cannot expect kids at this age to be overly physical. In fact, many in this age group still have a genuine physical fear of pain and being injured. Put more of an emphasis on the purity of the game, teaching skills, speed, and quickness. There is no need at this level to push kids to be aggressive and tough. That will come as they grow into the game. For these eight- and nine-year-olds, basketball should be a totally fun and playful experience.

No matter what age level you are coaching, always remind your players that there is no "I" in team.

Moving to the Next Level

When you are dealing with kids in the 10- to 12-year-old range, you can begin to teach more of the complexities of the game, such as a basic offense and the different types of defense, as well as things such as setting screens and plays like the backdoor, pick-and-roll, and give-and-go. You will also probably begin to see more competitive kids who are always aware of the score and are beginning to play to win as well as to have fun. At this point, you will be working with the standard men's basketball and, of course, the 10-foot-high basket. Kids at this age are also becoming more aggressive, so you can now encourage some of the more physical aspects of the game, such as rebounding, boxing out, and driving hard to the basket.

Coaching Corner

While you can begin to encourage 10- to 12-year-olds to become more aggressive when rebounding, boxing out, and going hard to the basket, you also have to discourage overly aggressive and outright dirty play. Young players may try to push the envelope by pushing, elbowing, throwing a punch, or challenging another player. These things may happen on the playground or local park, and an overly aggressive player can try to bring it to your team. Continue to emphasize the importance of good sportsmanship and, at the same time, make it very clear that any form of dirty play will not be tolerated.

One thing you should be aware of when coaching this age group is that more girls than boys reach puberty during this time. As mentioned earlier, puberty is often a time of rapid growth, and some kids become more susceptible to the injuries mentioned in Chapter 5. This is something you should watch carefully at both this age level and the older age levels.

Show and teach this middle group more of the complexities and subtleties of the game, employ more strategies on both offense and defense, and allow your team to play to win—as long as you continue to emphasize that winning is not the most important thing to you as a coach. In other words, don't make it a priority.

Once again, you have to make *team* play your top priority. You must strive to forge a bond among your players and let them know that in basketball, as in other team sports, everyone is in it together and is working for a common end.

Each of your players should also be en route to building self-confidence. Sportsmanship is definitely part of being a team. Also remind them that there is no star system on your team. Everyone plays and learns the game together. You are doing this for two reasons. First, obviously, a star system is not what the game is about at this level (nor should it be at any level). Second, these players are still not physically mature enough to go all-out for an entire game. Though they will have more endurance than the younger groups, it is still necessary to alternate players in order to keep everyone fresh and strong, and to lower the possibility of injury through fatigue.

Coaching Corner

As a coach, you have the ability to wield a tremendous amount of influence over your players. Believe it or not, you may be the prime motivating factor in whether some of your players continue in the sport. Those who have studied youth sports have said flat out that coaches can either motivate a child to excel or crush a child with negative feedback and too-high expectations. A win-at-all-costs coach should not be in youth sports. A coach who allows the less talented players to sit the bench for most of the game should not be involved in youth sports. Most kids would rather get the chance to play even if the team loses than sit out even if the team wins. Your job is to give all players positive feedback and encouragement as well as playing time. You may even have to buck the philosophy of some parents who don't agree with your methods. Stick to your guns and give your community a positive foundation on which to build.

A coach can add another positive thing at this level. Instead of positioning yourself as a dictator and authoritarian figure, make meetings and practices something of an open forum. Yes, you are the teacher and make most of the decisions. But there is no harm in having question-and-answer sessions about the team and the game's strategies, and asking your players for their opinions on basketball-related matters. This will not only give them a better feeling of a *team* and being a part of the entire process, but it will also enable them to increase their knowledge of the game.

The Upper-Level Age Group

Players in the 13- and 14-year-old group are ready to acquire a real working knowledge of the game. You can teach them more of the complex strategies of offense and defense, as well as the best ways to meld their individual skills with those of their teammates.

An "everybody plays" scenario is still the best policy, but the best players will now tend to take charge more and try much harder to win. You may also notice more aggressiveness on the part of players. At this point, players are bigger and stronger and naturally more physical. They also tend to watch college and professional games and notice the contact among players they follow and idolize.

Therefore, it is still up to you to emphasize sportsmanship and caution against rough play. More so than ever, dirty play and fighting cannot be tolerated. The older kids are more likely to allow their tempers to get the best of them, so always remind your team that if they become angry, they should simply concentrate on playing better and playing harder. Fighting and rough play simply cannot be tolerated—ever. You can also have your team work harder at conditioning, which tends to ease some of the aggression. As mentioned earlier, you will see athletes reaching puberty at this age and going through growing spurts. Watch carefully for signs of the kinds of injuries described in the previous chapter.

Coaching the upper levels of youth basketball gives you something of a different kind of satisfaction. You'll have a hand in turning some of your kids into outstanding players who perhaps will go on to excel at the high school level and even beyond. However, never forget that you are there to help each and every member of your team, from the best player to the one who might enjoy the game but just doesn't have the same kind of natural ability and often struggles. You are everyone's coach.

Satisfaction at Any Age

Youth basketball coaches come from every walk of life. They are auto mechanics, insurance salesmen, dentists, stockbrokers, and so on. The majority played basketball at some level and thoroughly enjoyed the experience. Generally, they want to give something back. All kids, even the ones who don't go on to play at an organized level in school or beyond, remember their childhood sports experiences. A positive experience not only fosters an active and healthful lifestyle that can continue for years, but it can also be an influence on how players live their lives as adults. A young athlete can acquire a sense of sportsmanship and fair play, and will likely transfer the same qualities to his family and business life as he ages.

Do the right thing as a coach, and you'll feel a sense of satisfaction, no matter what age level you coach. For openers, you are teaching kids a game that you love. You get to see players learn the skills and fundamentals of the sport, and you get to see their improvements. In an age when many kids are being pushed too hard by both parents and coaches with skewed priorities, you can feel good if you know that you are providing your players with values, such as good sportsmanship, a solid work ethic, and a sense of working together, that extend beyond the basketball court. The enjoyment you have in coaching and the positive attitude you apply to your job are contagious. Hopefully, this gives your players that same kind of enthusiasm for all facets of the sport.

Now that we are ready to delve into the nuts and bolts of the game, you should be well aware of both the positive and negative aspects of coaching, and know which is the better road to travel—better and much more satisfying.

The Least You Need to Know

- ◆ Be sure you know the differences in the various age groups of youth basketball and decide which one you would feel most comfortable coaching.

- ◆ As the kids get older, they will become more competitive and more physically aggressive. Don't push the young ones too soon.

- ◆ Regardless of which age level you are coaching, always make it a point to let your players know that dirty play will not be tolerated.

- ◆ Positive reinforcement is one of the keys to keeping players from getting down. Sometimes the expectations at home are too great and a player feels he is letting his parents down.

- ◆ Coaching youth basketball, teaching skills, and watching players improve can give you tremendous satisfaction and a sense of accomplishment.

Chapter 7

The Making of a Team

In This Chapter

- ◆ Defining your concept of "team"
- ◆ An assist is as good as a hoop
- ◆ Working together has its rewards
- ◆ Ways to bring your team together

One of the definitions found in the dictionary for the word *team* is quite simple. It reads, a "set of players forming one side in a game." That is certainly true, but only in the strictest sense of the word. How many sets of players forming a side in a game simply don't work together? They may have the same uniform on their backs, but they play as if they are five different individuals. Some players are selfish and want to be stars. Others allow personal dislikes to cloud their judgment when it comes to their teammates. Still others simply don't get it. They would rather throw up a 20-foot jump shot than pass the ball to a teammate who is free under the basket. While they are obviously a set of players forming one side in a game, they are about as far from a real *team* as you can get.

The goal of all good coaches is to take a group of individual players and make them into a complete team. This chapter discusses the various ways a coach can go about accomplishing this. As you'll see, there is more to making a real team than sending five players onto the court to run a particular offense and defense. Even in the NBA, there have been groups of talented players who have failed to live up to expectations because they never fully meshed as a team. At the same time, there have been other clubs at all levels of play who have achieved more than anyone expected simply because they became a real team in every sense of the word. Because you are the coach, the teacher, and the leader, it is up to you to convince your individual players that the total team concept is the only way to go. In fact, it's what you plan to teach them and the only result you will accept.

Make the Concept of *Team* Clear Immediately

Depending on the age level you are coaching, you may have to approach the team concept a bit differently. To begin, it's best to limit your team to 10 to 12 players. That way, you are not going to be in a situation in which players have to sit and watch the others play. If you have upwards of 13 to 15 players, it simply isn't a manageable number because there are too many players to weave into a real team. In making your final decision, however, it is important that you always have at least 10 available players for teaching team offense and defense, as well as scrimmage situations. Remember, you are also going to be spending time with each player, which is another reason to keep the limit to 12.

With the youngest kids, the eight- and nine-year-olds, the experience of working with others and forming a team may be an entirely new concept. Since some of your players may be participating in a group sport for the first time, they will be learning from scratch. Most of them should be very receptive to the concept of working together as a team. As a rule, kids would rather be part of a group than feel like a fifth wheel. Once you explain the satisfactions they will gain from working together to achieve a common goal, adding that every single one of them can play an important part, they should begin to make an effort to come together. Of course, teaching kids the team concept doesn't work if the first thing you do is talk about the importance of winning. If winning becomes the priority, the best players may begin to resent those who aren't as good, feeling that they are going to drag the team down. That's yet another reason why you should always put an emphasis on working together as a team ahead of winning the game.

Quick Tips

From the very first day of practice you should make it a habit to always put an emphasis on the team.

Tell the players to always think team first. Then you can reinforce it before scrimmages and games, and during timeouts, by having the players gather in a circle, put their hands together and shout, "TEAM!" before taking the court.

If your players understand the team concept, they will work together the entire season.

The Older Kids Are Tougher to Convince

When you are dealing with both the middle and older age groups of kids, the "let's be a team" speech might be more difficult to sell. At these ages, players are more aware of the complete basketball picture. Many have probably seen "hot dog" types of players, superstars who take over a game and players who love to pump up 20 shots a night. In other words, a player who already feels he is going to be a star might not like sharing shots and playing time with the last guy on the bench. Or, at crunch time, he might want to be the hero by throwing up the long jumper rather than passing to a teammate cutting to the hoop. If too many of these incidents occur, the team concept will go down the drain.

Once again, the ball is back in your court. You have to convince your team that everyone will get more satisfaction from the game if it is played the right way, and this means playing by working together. Here are some guidelines to help players understand what you mean by "working together":

- ◆ **The open player gets the ball.** Whenever possible, the open man gets the ball. You work the ball around to get an open shot instead of having one player force a shot.

- ◆ **Play tight defense.** You play tight defense to stop the other team from scoring instead of loafing on defense and waiting to get a shot on offense.

With these maxims in place, you can then remind the player who doesn't pass but always shoots first that the time will come when he is open and won't get the ball because his teammates will remember that he never passes. It may take a while for all this to sink in, and the lessons may have to be learned on the court. Finally, if you have a player who just won't listen, then perhaps he has to learn his lesson from the bench.

Did You Know?

Some of the greatest all-around players in basketball history have not only espoused the team game, but also reveled in it. Oscar Robertson, known as the Big O, was a great scorer who always had a way to get free for a big shot, if it was needed. Yet when he retired, the Big O was the NBA's all-time leader in assists. He knew from the first that a good pass was as effective as a good shot. Earvin "Magic" Johnson, like Robertson, was an all-around player who could do everything on the court. His main mission, however, was to make all his teammates better players because of his presence on the court. He was part of five championship teams, and when he retired, he had passed Robertson as the career leader in assists. Point guard John Stockton is only 6 feet, 1 inch tall, small by today's NBA standards. But he has always been brilliant at knowing how to set up his teammates and run the game. Still playing in 2002, Stockton has always been an instinctive passer who has broken all the assist records in his career. These three players obviously all learned an important lesson early: You play for the team, and you look for your teammates on the court, not just the basket. By doing this, you make everyone around you better players.

There is nothing wrong with using familiar frames of reference to make a point about team play. In fact, kids often relate better when they are shown what you mean. Actions do speak louder than words.

Show your team tapes of players such as Robertson, Johnson, and Stockton, pointing out how they always play for the team first. You can also take your team to local high school or college games, if they are available in your area, and point out the advantages of playing as a team. Conversely, if there is a selfish player on the court who doesn't look for his teammates, you should point out that a forced shot that misses is worth nothing. A quick pass to an open teammate may well be worth two points. You can also point out examples from other walks of life. Firefighters, for example, must work together as a team to put out a dangerous fire, while even a good rock band must coordinate its music and work together if it is to succeed and be the best it can be.

Did You Know?

One way to convince your players that a good pass is worth more than a bad shot is to simply do the math. A player with 10 assists and no baskets will still have added at least 20 points to his team's total. This adds up to more if an assist or two leads to a three-point shot. If that same player had five baskets and two assists he will only have added 14 points to his team's total, a couple of more if a hoop or two was a trey. So scoring isn't always the end-all. Encourage players to pass to the open man and add to the overall team's score.

Creative Ways to Encourage Teamwork

Once your team is together, you should work to foster camaraderie and teamwork in as many ways as you can. For example, note these creative team exercises:

- ◆ Set up a routine in which everyone has a responsibility to the team at practices and games. A couple of players can bring the water and any post-practice refreshments. Others can be responsible for getting the basketballs onto the court.

- ◆ Have the players take turns in evaluating the last practice—not in the sense that they criticize teammates, but that they give their opinions on things that went well and areas where the team needs more work. In other words, allow your players to participate in everything that affects the team as a whole.

- ◆ During practices, be sure to give positive reinforcement to all things that the players do well. This certainly includes individual drills and improvement in skills and fundamentals. But when the players excel as a team in running an offense or defense, help each other on the court by setting picks, call out defensive switches, and work the ball smoothly and crisply, let them know they are playing the game the right way—as a team.

These ideas are not to say that you should discourage individuality, with a player occasionally freelancing when there is a breakdown, but the constant emphasis should be on the team.

It's impossible to make all the players on your team like each other. There always will be someone who rubs another player the wrong way. This is a workable situation, but only if it doesn't disrupt the team. As a coach, you can't demand that all your players be bosom buddies and hang out everywhere together. But you can insist that while the players are at practice or at a game, they put personal differences aside and become a team. Any player who cannot do this simply cannot remain part of the team because, in this case, one bad apple *can* spoil the bunch. If you detect a degree of enmity between two players, speak to both of them together. Once again, explain the importance of the team and of working together, and tell them that it takes real character for someone to put personal feelings aside for the sake of the team. Hopefully, this will defuse the situation—at least when they are at practice and playing in games.

Coaching Corner

One of the things a coach might consider to inspire teamwork is to get together with his players, and perhaps some of their parents, to watch a film such as *Hoosiers*. This is the true story of a small Indiana high school that defied all odds by winning the state championship in the early 1950s when it defeated a school many times its size. At the beginning of the film, the team's new coach meets with his small contingent of players and tells them immediately that they must always think in terms of the team. No matter what happens on or off the court, he says, everything is "team, team, team." The story is not only true, but also inspirational, and it shows that a real team that no one thought could defeat a big-school team has the ability to come together and succeed, no matter what the odds.

Never let personal feelings between two players affect team play. On the court, personal feelings must be forgotten.

Reward Team Play

As a rule, kids respond well to responsibility and reward. Let your players know from the start that you are counting on all of them to contribute to the team effort. Encourage them to air their differences and discuss problems in team meetings. Make the meetings an open forum and allow everyone to speak. Perhaps you can also set up a system of rotating captains so that each player has a chance to lead the team onto the court and act as team spokesman. Also encourage the players on the bench to cheer for their teammates on the court and, no matter what happens, to never criticize a teammate during practice or at games. Problems should be discussed at team meetings.

You should also be sure to make a note every time a player makes an unselfish play that helps the team. You might institute a system in which a player receives a gold star for a particularly good team play. Once the players decide they like getting the stars, they will work all the more to continue looking for ways to achieve them. This system will probably be more effective with younger kids who respond better to this type of reward. The same result may be achieved with the older players by simply singling them out for praise and pointing out that what the player just did is what you are looking for from everyone.

Another way to bring the team together is perhaps to take everyone out after a good practice or game (win or lose) for pizza or another snack. You might also have other types of *team* nights when you, the players, and some parents participate in other activities, such as a movie or bowling. You can also give the team an identity by perhaps having some caps or T-shirts made with the name or nickname of the team on them. Make the players feel special to be part of your team and everything it stands for, and they will respond.

Remember, there probably isn't a coach alive who is going to make every single player happy every time. Some players may not agree with the position you have assigned them. Some may not like their role. Some may want to score more. Others may want to play more. Still others may not be happy when the team loses. These are all things that you will have to deal with during your coaching career. Some of these problems will be addressed later in the book. Others you will have to figure out as you become more experienced and coach a wider variety of youngsters. But perhaps the best thing you can say when you meet new players for the first time is this:

> Hi, I'm Coach Smith. Before I tell you about myself and what I want us to accomplish together, remember this: Above everything else, basketball is a *team* game!

The Least You Need to Know

- ◆ Make the team concept a number-one priority beginning with the very first day of practice.

- ◆ Having 12 players on your team is the optimum number. With fewer, you won't have 10 for a scrimmage if 1 or 2 miss practice. With more, too many players will have to stand around while the others are working.

- ◆ Let your team know that working together is important at both ends of the floor. A player who loafs on defense to save himself for offense isn't a team player.

- ◆ A great way to show the value of teamwork is to point out that an assist is worth as much as a basket.

- ◆ Add to the sense of team by taking some trips together, having pizza after a game, or making caps and shirts with the team name or nickname. That way your players will take pride in being part of the team.

Part 2

Teaching the Game

This part of the book gives you a complete picture of teaching and coaching, beginning with advice on how to run a well-organized practice. We then delve into the basic fundamentals of the game—dribbling, passing, shooting, and rebounding—and the best ways to teach these skills.

Next, we describe the different positions on the court and why it is important for players to know how to play each position. There are valuable tips on how to run both the offense and defense, and then we move to more complex aspects of the game, including discussion of a motion offense that allows each player to become fully involved in all aspects of the offensive game, and both a man-to-man defense and several types of zone defense.

And finally, we close with a discussion of game day, suggesting ways for coaches to handle everything from setting up the bench to substituting players.

Running a Good Practice

In This Chapter

- ◆ Set a schedule
- ◆ Get to the most important stuff first
- ◆ Keep it flexible, not boring
- ◆ A typical practice session

Perhaps the single most important aspect of coaching youth basketball is the practice session. Going by the numbers, you will be involved in many more practices than games. Practice is where you not only teach the skills of the game, but also bring your players together into a cohesive, well-conditioned team. Productive practice sessions can only add to your overall effort on behalf of your players. Sloppy, poorly organized practices will not only result in bad habits that will carry over to games, but will also fail to give your players a positive basketball experience.

In this chapter, we talk about the importance of the practice session, concentrating on planning, structuring, and adjusting practices to keep them fresh, instructive, and also fun. Using the template presented in this chapter, you should have a better understanding of why it is imperative that the coach carefully choreograph and control all of his team's practices. The ensuing chapters provide more detailed information on specific drills and strategies that will undoubtedly be part of the practice session. This chapter, therefore, simply addresses the best ways to run practices, with a brief example showing how a particular practice might go. The general premises discussed here apply to all age levels as far as practice is concerned.

Make Practice Convenient for Everyone

Regardless of the number of players on your team, you need everyone to have a good practice. So the first step you must take is to secure a facility that is available when you decide to hold your practices. This is not always as easy as it sounds. Practice must be at a time that is convenient for all of your players. There are stories about hockey teams that can secure ice time only at 4 or 5 A.M., which makes it very inconvenient for parents and players alike. Fortunately, many basketball facilities are available, so off-hours scheduling isn't necessary.

Remember, practice not only has to be at a time when all the players can be there, but it also must be at a time when they can find transportation both to and from the facility. Part of this problem can perhaps be solved by the parents carpooling and bringing several players together. This isn't always as simple as it sounds, because it is not always convenient to have all your players and their parents available at the same time. Yet you simply cannot conduct a good practice with only five or six players. So finding that mutually acceptable time for practice is the first problem you have to solve. Once that time is firmed up and agreed upon, try not to change it. Any last-minute or even permanent change might result in missing players.

Quick Tips

If your team is affiliated with a school or town recreation program, there may be a facility already waiting for you. Then you simply have to set up a good time. But if you are coaching a group of youngsters from a neighborhood or from several different schools, you may have to look farther. The best way is to obtain a list of all the local basketball facilities, including nearby schools, recreation centers, local parks, and even perhaps colleges in the immediate area. Find out which ones make courts available to local youth teams. Some facilities charge a fee for practice time. If this is the case, you may have to get a sponsor for your team, either a local business or organization; in some cases, you might ask the parents to chip in. Hopefully, finding a facility won't be a problem, but sometimes a coach has to search a bit, especially when he is coaching a team not affiliated with a local organization or league.

A Routine That Has Purpose

As mentioned earlier, kids like routine. If they know what you expect them to do when they get to practice and how you are going to proceed, they can jump right in without wasting time and fooling around. Chances are, you will be on a tight schedule, either with the use of the gym or because of the time you are allotting for practice. So if you have only an hour, for example, you don't want it to take 15 minutes to get the players organized and ready to practice. Begin by setting a specific time for when your players are to be dressed and on the floor. After they are dressed, start the practice immediately.

If you want your team to warm up doing a series of stretching exercises, appoint a different player to lead the exercises at each session. That way, each player has the responsibility of getting his teammates out on the court, lining them up, and starting to stretch right away. With that done, you may also want to get them ready for basketball by just running a few simple layup drills that will get everyone moving. Some of the different drills you can run during practice are discussed in an upcoming chapter. Once the players are warmed up and in the basketball-playing mode, you're ready to begin the actual practice.

There should always be a specific order in which to proceed at practice, and it should always follow a similar pattern. For example, the following works well:

1. Do stretching and warm-up drills.

2. Next work on what you feel is the most important thing you want to accomplish during the practice session that day, such as the crossover dribble.

3. Then work on an aspect of the game that is secondary to that particular practice but still important.

4. Depending on the time, let the players do something they enjoy, something that is fun but also improves a skill.

5. Try to find time to talk about the practice, what went well, what didn't, and why. Solicit input from the players.

There is, of course, a good reason to continually work on the part of the game you feel is most important at the beginning of practice.

Quick Tips

Divide your team into two lines. The first player in each line dribbles the length of the court, turns around, and dribbles back. Each player then hands off the ball to the next player. The first line that finishes the race wins. Try this race by seeing which players can make the most layups in 30 seconds or in a minute.

Players are fresh and have a much better attention span at the outset of the practice session. This is especially true of the younger players, who naturally have a shorter attention span than their older counterparts. So while they are fresh and enthusiastic, get right to the phase of the game you want to teach and practice at the session. Then once you feel that the primary objective has been reached, move on to the secondary or optional items.

When the kids begin to wear down a bit and are becoming tired of running the same things over and over again, you can surprise them—come up with a drill or contest, or even a game, that is fun and that hopefully brings some of the excitement back to the practice. Obviously, whatever it is should also help improve an aspect of play, whether it revolves around an individual skill or a function of the entire team.

If a coach isn't well prepared for practice, players can become bored and disinterested.

Have a Schedule, but Don't Set It in Stone

If your practices are to run smoothly and efficiently, you always need a schedule. In other words, know what you are going to do beforehand. Don't get the players on the floor and then hem and haw and ask quizzically, "Now what should we do today?" Always be decisive and be ready to go. Your players must have confidence in you and must feel that you know exactly what you want from them. If you appear indecisive and players begin questioning your decisions, you lose their attention. Creating the right atmosphere begins at practice.

Quick Tips _____

No one can overlook the importance of practice. That's when you fine-tune your team and get ready for the season. Of course, the season will not be nearly as long as an NBA season, but depending on the league you are playing in and the age of the kids, you are still going to have a good number of games. Therefore, you have to be careful about overworking your team—too much practice can actually become a liability, especially as the season wears on. By then, your team should know your basic concepts, as well as the offenses and defenses you like to run. They should also be aware of any special plays, like the trap or full-court press on defense and the fast break on offense. By this time, the teaching phase will taper off a bit, and so should the length and intensity of your practice sessions. Therefore, as the season wears on, make adjustments to your practices, especially if your team is performing to your satisfaction. Don't work them as hard, and let them have more fun.

Practices should be run quickly and efficiently. Move from one activity to another, and be sure that your team responds to your whistle. Use it to get their attention, to either stop what they are doing, start again, or huddle up. Make your vocal commands sharp but not intimidating, and never stop praising the team and individual players for doing the right thing and doing it well. Positive reinforcement never stops.

With practice, as with everything else, be creative and flexible. Your team should take everything you say seriously, but you will get better results if you aren't always a no-fun taskmaster. Use practice as a tool but not as a punishment. Use it to win over your team and make all the players better, not as a place where the team will slowly sour on the game. It takes knowing your players well, and it sometimes takes a balancing act. If you do it well, practices can be among the best times you spend with your team, as well as the time you become the most accomplished as a coach.

Did You Know?

As a coach, you are responsible for everything your players do. The legendary college coach John Wooden, whose UCLA teams won a record 10 NCAA national championships, used to start each new season by actually showing his players the proper way to put on their socks and tie their shoes. That's how detail-oriented Wooden was. His players loved him and his teams won.

A Typical Practice Session

The length of your practice may depend on the age group you are coaching. With the younger kids, at eight and nine years old, it might be best to go for just an hour. A 90-minute session is probably better for the older groups. Following is a step-by-step breakdown of how you might conduct a practice for the older group, about a 90-minute session. Just shorten it by 15 minutes for the middle group and 30 minutes for the younger kids. The basic structure remains the same:

1. **10–15 minutes before practice.** Ask your players to arrive 10 or 15 minutes early so there is time to dress properly and then have a very brief team meeting. At the meeting, you can tell the team what they will be working on at the upcoming session.

2. **10–15 minutes.** Next, it's out on the floor for stretching and warm-up activities. This should take between 10 and 15 minutes. Besides stretching, players can warm up by jumping and running in place, doing some jumping jacks and squats.

3. **10 minutes.** To get the players moving more, you might want to spend the next 10 minutes or so running some dribbling, passing, and ball-handling drills (which will be detailed in an upcoming chapter) that also keep the players running up and down the court. By doing this, you are getting them loose, relaxed, and ready to tackle that first important item, the one they need the most work on.

4. **20 minutes.** Whistle them in and tell them what comes next. If it is an especially difficult concept, you may have to spend the next 20 or so minutes working on it. But don't overdo it. If the players are having a problem, they will become frustrated. Take them to a certain point and then move on. You can come back to the same concept at the next session. If it is a new concept that involves a walk-through first, it should be done in slow motion. Once you finish, be sure to get the players running again. For example, you may be teaching the motion offense, where the players have to know where to go on the court after each pass. A concept such as this will almost always have to be walked through a number of times before the speed increases.

5. **15 minutes.** To increase the pace of the practice, you can spend the next 15 minutes or so working on various drills in which the players have to move faster. Depending on where you are in the season, this can involve increasingly complex fundamentals drills to improve dribbling, passing, and shooting. As a coach, watch each player for flaws in his technique; if you see any, work with that player to try to correct them.

6. **15 minutes.** At this point, you can whistle them in again and now work on the secondary item that you had planned. By this time, your team has been out on the court for about an hour. A few players might be starting to tire, while others might be losing a bit of the edge on their attention span. If they don't show

quite the same zip as they did early in practice, don't be too hard on them. As conditioning improves, so should the players' stamina throughout the practice session.

Did You Know?

Young players who take to the sport and want to get better will probably want to practice whenever they can find a basket and the time. In fact, some of the great players in history almost practiced to excess. When he was in high school, Michael Jordan was playing and practicing basketball so often that his father had to remind him how important schoolwork was. The legendary Pistol Pete Maravich used to dribble a basketball out the car window as his father drove slowly down the street. Even when he was at a movie with his friends, Maravich always sat in an aisle seat so he could dribble the ball with one hand as he watched the film. Scottie Pippen said he practiced dribbling so often that the ball began to feel as if it was part of his hand. The great Jerry West took hundreds of jump shots every time he had the chance to use a basket. No wonder he was known as Mr. Clutch in big games. Carol Blazejowski, one of the first great women collegiate stars in the 1970s, always played pickup games with boys so she could challenge herself to keep up with them and improve her game.

It doesn't hurt to tell stories such as this to your players, but don't make it sound as if this is what all of them should do. Practice is extremely important, but only a special few will push themselves as these greats did. As long as your team gives you a solid effort at each practice, you know you're doing your job well.

At some point during each practice, make sure your players practice their free throws.

7. **15 minutes.** The last 15 minutes of your practice session should be devoted to something that is fun for the players but that also helps them improve a skill and gets them into better physical condition. You can run some special drills or have the aforementioned dribbling relay race. Or you can have the players alternate taking short jump shots and then layups to see who can make the most baskets in one or two minutes. Or you might have everyone take 25 or 50 free throws to see who makes the most. It's always a good idea to have your players practice free throws at some point because these are very important in games. Some coaches always end practice with all their players taking 25 or 50 free throws. Some might finish with a few wind sprints, especially if the practice consisted of a great deal of walk-through time.

> ### Coaching Corner
>
> As the season progresses, a coach can use the final 15 minutes of practice to both teach and review special situation plays, such as the full- and half-court press, last-second plays, out-of-bounds plays, and when to call timeouts. Do this only after the team has been exposed to these situations. It is ideal for older kids.

As you can see, a good coach can accomplish a great deal during a 60- or 90-minute practice session. Now that we are about to get into the real nuts and bolts of the game, you'll find myriad drills, offensive and defensive strategies, and every other facet of the sport that you can incorporate into your practices. Sticking to the format we have outlined here, your practices should go smoothly and have the desired effect of making your players better players and bringing your entire team together, giving the players the enthusiasm they need to play the game and the camaraderie they need to play together as a team.

The Least You Need to Know

♦ Always try to make your practice sessions convenient for all your players. They should always have transportation both to and from practice.

♦ Try to limit sessions to about 60 minutes for the 8- and 9-year-olds, 75 minutes for the 10- and 12-year-olds, and 90 minutes for the 13- and 14-year-olds.

♦ After warm-ups, always start your team with what you consider the most important thing that has to be done. That way they are fresh and ready to go.

♦ Run your practices smoothly and efficiently. Always know what you want to do, yet be flexible enough so that the routine changes and the kids don't become bored.

♦ Always have some kind of fun activity toward the end of practice when the players begin to get tired. This will perk them up and gives them a good feeling when practice ends.

Chapter 9

Teaching Individual Skills

In This Chapter

- ◆ The importance of presenting the fundamentals in a clear and concise manner
- ◆ Proper demonstration of techniques
- ◆ Accurate execution of fundamental skills
- ◆ When some kids don't get it

In coaching youth basketball, you will undoubtedly be handed a mixed bag of players. At the upper level, you may find some kids who have already been playing the game for six or seven years, others who have been dabbling in it for two or three years, and a few who are virtually just beginning. At the youngest level, the majority of players will be inexperienced and ready to absorb everything you teach them. From learning the basic fundamentals of the game to mastering the more advanced skills and techniques to blend together into a team, the team will continue to look to you.

This chapter delves more deeply into the qualities that are needed to teach some of the more complex techniques and skills of the game. Every coach knows he has to start at the beginning. Thus, the better equipped you are to teach your young players, the better the chance you can not only teach them about basketball, but also create a situation in which they will appreciate what a good teacher and leader can do for them.

Did You Know?

Even at the professional level, coaches often influence some players in ways that transcend their sport. When the New York Giants were one of the National Football League's best teams in the 1980s under Coach Bill Parcells, George Martin was a top defensive end. Once his career ended, Martin said that Coach Parcells talked to him about everything from developing a post-football career to ways of raising kids. Martin always credits his coach with being not only a fine football coach, but a major influence on his life as well.

Make Your Presentations Clear and Concise

Whether you are teaching a basic or a complex skill, you must always be sure to present the most salient points in a clear and concise manner. This is especially important at the younger age levels, where previously learned knowledge of the game is probably lacking. One of the first things you must remember is never to assume. Many coaches make this mistake at all levels. They assume that their players already have some degree of knowledge about what they are teaching and thus leave out some important elements, which can sabotage the entire point of the lesson. In a sense, it is almost safer to assume that while some or all of the players may know how to do a certain thing, they don't always know how to do it properly. Therefore, always start from the beginning.

There are other reasons why a presentation has to be done carefully. You always have a variety of players on your team. Their athletic skills vary. They have different motivational levels. Some have a strong desire to learn and improve, while others might simply go through the motions because they are out there just to have fun. A few might not really want to be there at all. In addition, the intelligence levels of your players can vary. Some will "get it" very quickly, while others might not. So never rush through a presentation and expect every member of the team to understand and remember what you said. Especially when dealing with physical athletic skills, much of the teaching involves repetition. Don't become frustrated with the team or any of the players if they ask to hear something a second or third time. Instead, just appreciate the fact that they want to learn it the right way.

Make Adjustments Based on Age

In many ways, the eight- and nine-year-olds represent the most difficult age level to coach. These are the kids who generally have the shortest attention spans, are going through many emotional changes, and, because so many of them are just starting to play, may be there for reasons other than simply wanting to play the game. It may be that their parents want to get them into sports, participate on a team, and expand their still-developing horizons. Many of these kids are in a competitive situation for the first time in their lives, and you may also be one of the first people to tell them no. For these reasons, it is even more important to be clear and concise in any oral presentation or instruction when dealing with the skills of the game.

Always entertain questions at some point in the practice. But make it at the same point each time. In other words, if you have just finished explaining the importance of a good passing game, then give the kids a chance to ask questions. Don't allow them to throw up a hand or call out right in the middle of your presentation. By taking questions, you will have a better sense of how many of the players understood what you were teaching. If you have to repeat some things, do it willingly. Just be consistent and always take the questions after the initial presentation has been completed.

When working with the youngest age level, always make sure that everyone understands exactly what you are teaching.

A clear and concise presentation is essential in coaching.

Always Provide the Proper Demonstrations

As with all sports, talk is never quite enough. Once you have explained a skill to your team, you have to demonstrate it. This is extremely important because many players need to see the movement, form, and action of a skill to really understand it. The majority of coaches have played the game, though to varying degrees. Some may have played only through high school; others have played through college. Some may have played only recreationally, but have a good knowledge of the sport and a strong desire to coach. And, in truth, some great coaches have been only average players, especially at the youth level; however, it is very important to demonstrate all the points you are making when teaching a skill.

Did You Know?

More often than not, when a former superstar professional athlete becomes a head coach or manager, he doesn't find the same kind of success he had on the playing field. It isn't that he doesn't know the game or strategies. It's something else. Players who were superstars are usually also hard-working perfectionists, and they find it difficult to accept less from players who don't have their talent. That often leads to a lack of patience. So don't worry if you weren't the greatest player in the world. If you know the game, enjoy working with kids, and have patience and the ability to teach, you can become a great youth coach.

As hard as it is for some coaches to admit, sometimes they need help. This might not seem like conventional advice, and it might hurt the pride of a few, but for the good of the team, they do have to provide the correct demonstration. This is not to demean a good coach. It's just that some coaches may not have all the consummate skills of a player. For example, if a coach is trying to teach the behind-the-back dribble yet cannot himself do it smoothly and easily, he really should bring someone into his practice who can show how it's done. It may be another coach or perhaps an outstanding local high school or college player. In other words, you have to be sure that your team can see how the skills are accomplished. By seeing the actual physical movements, players can better understand the concept more quickly than if you explain it verbally 10 times.

Quick Tips

Whenever you present a demonstration to your team, always be sure you do it slowly enough to be watched and studied. If you run through it too quickly, kids can't take in all of the movements and the forms needed to be successful. As the demonstration continues, you can pick up speed until you are running it at game tempo.

The other important thing is that they must see the skill done correctly.

Once again, you must be cognizant of the age level. With the younger kids, you always must be aware of commanding their attention. If you present a demonstration and have them walking through it very slowly several times, then they aren't moving around much. Too much slow motion definitely causes lapses in attention. So with this age level, try to do the demonstration slowly so that they can see it, but then get them moving again. Even if you feel that the skill you have been demonstrating is still not fully understood, break it up with a drill or a game that will get them moving and motivated; then whistle them in and demonstrate the skill you are teaching once again.

Ensure That Execution Is Accurate

We just finished discussing the need for accurate demonstration of individual skills, and the occasional need to have an older player or another coach come in and help you demonstrate. Once you have your team beginning to work on the skills you have been demonstrating, make sure that players' execution of the skills is accurate. If you demonstrate something slowly and carefully and then allow your players to execute it poorly, they will soon fall into sloppy habits so that even the perfect demonstration will have been for naught.

Quick Tips

Always watch carefully when your players are learning skills for the first time. If, for example, a young player can only execute the crossover dribble by turning his palm upward and carrying the ball across his body, he's committing a palming or carrying violation. If you don't correct him immediately, this habit can become the norm for his dribbling technique and the refs will whistle a violation constantly. The longer you allow bad habits to continue, the more difficult they are to break.

Again, you can have your players begin slowly, just as the demonstration began. Then they can pick up the pace; as they do, make sure the execution doesn't change. If some players are losing the technique when they speed up, slow them down again and make sure they do it properly. In fact, it is probably worth *overlearning* basic skills in these age groups. The tendency for many kids is to think that they know something as soon as they do it once or twice. But executing the various skills takes practice and repetition. It has to become automatic, not something the player has to think about. If you teach a particular skill at one practice, make sure you continue to review it at subsequent sessions, or the execution can slowly fall apart or be lost completely. Repetition, therefore, is one of the key ingredients in coaching basketball at the youth level. There is simply no substitute for it.

Simply having players repeat a skill can get boring. But since repetition is important, you can now use drills to put some variation into your practice and have the players execute the skills you want to see at the same time. For example, if you are teaching the crossover dribble, you might begin by having your team walk through it at a slow pace. That gives you a chance to check everyone's execution. Once you are satisfied, you might then go through a basic dribbling drill, such as having the players weave in and out of a series of cones so that they will have to use the crossover dribble to complete the drill. Again, you watch the execution of the technique with each of your players. Finally, you might want to run a full-court press drill, in which the player with the ball has to use the crossover dribble in what could be a game situation. By varying the practice and the drills, you are keeping your players' attention, but you have also geared everything to executing and improving one particular skill.

Execution Through Drills

Drills allow you to refine the techniques you are teaching. It's one thing to describe a skill, then demonstrate it, and finally watch as your players execute it. But even if everyone has mastered the skill, in some situations players have to improvise and perhaps use the particular skill in a different way. For example, a player who is trapped near the sideline or baseline and finds herself falling out of bounds, can use the basic two-hand chest pass to bounce the ball off a nearby opponent's leg so that it goes out of bounds and her team retains possession. That's why drills are such an important tool in the teaching process.

One drill may not be enough to get the job done when teaching a skill. When devising your drills, ask the following questions:

Quick Tips

As the season progresses, you may want to add more challenging or time-related competitive drills to evaluate your team's improvement in certain skill areas. This is yet another value of drills and is probably most applicable with the older age groups.

◆ Are the drills successful? Are they serving the purpose you intended?

◆ Are the players enjoying the drill? Obviously, you don't devise practices or drills solely for the players' enjoyment, but if the players are motivated and enjoying a drill, they may work even harder at it.

◆ How much time are the drills taking? You have only a certain amount of time at practice, and you must get the most value from the time. If a particular drill is going to take half of your practice time to be effective, perhaps it should be replaced.

◆ Are these the best drills you can find to help your players execute, understand, and begin using the skills smoothly and easily?

Execution Through Positive Reinforcement

You must remember one other thing throughout this process: Always use positive reinforcement to encourage your players. Nothing can turn kids off faster than a negative attitude. They will take criticism if it's in the form of correction. They can be told they didn't execute a skill the right way if you take the time to show them the right way. And they can probably accept the fact that they aren't improving as rapidly as a teammate if you keep encouraging them and convincing them that they ultimately can improve. Positive wins, negative loses. And we don't mean the outcome of the game.

In other words, if one of your players just can't figure out how to set a screen, he won't react well if you say,

> "What's the matter with you, Bob? This is not a difficult concept to grasp. Don't be stupid. Watch what I do and then you do it. And I don't want to hear any more of your excuses."

This kind of negative tone will help you lose the player for good. However, there is a positive approach that goes something like this:

> "Okay, Bob, you've almost got it. Just remember: You stop short, then turn and face the ball. Only stand still. Don't move toward the defender because then you'll be committing a foul. Just think of yourself as a statue on the court and allow the play to develop around you. Okay, let's try it again."

With a positive approach, the player is likely going to try harder. And when he finally gets it, be sure to praise him, or maybe "high-five" him, and tell him you always knew he could do it.

Kids Who Don't Get It

One of the most difficult aspects of youth coaching arises when the majority of a team understands a concept, technique, or skill, but a couple of players don't get it. This can be a dilemma for the coach. Eight kids are ready to move on, but maybe two, three, or four aren't. Do you stop and work with the slow kids again and hold the others back? Or do you go on, hoping the kids will find a way to catch up? It can really be a balancing act. However, you have to remember one thing: You are everyone's coach. You are there to teach your players the skills and techniques of basketball, and your obligation to the slowest kid on the team is the same as it is to the best player.

Every time you start a new season, you should be prepared for some kids to be slower than others. You can do a number of things so that the slower kids get the attention they need while the kids who are progressing more quickly aren't held back. One way or another, you always have to be nurturing, especially at the younger age level. At the same time, you've got to decide which steps to take with your slower kids. This may depend on your expectations for winning and losing. If you wait for the slow kids, your entire team may not learn as fast as it can. That can cost the team games. But you shouldn't be concerned only about winning. Then again, even without the won-lost equation, holding the rest of the team back can make the better players lose interest. It almost sounds like a Catch-22, but fortunately, there are other ways to go.

One thing you can do is pair the slower kids with each other in drills. That way they won't be overmatched against some of the better kids to the point that they become discouraged. If they are slow to grasp a concept or technique, you might ask if they can stay a while after practice so you can continue to work with them, or perhaps even come a few minutes early for the extra help. If you do that, be sure to inform the parents and make sure they have transportation available. Remember, repetition is the best tool for teaching skills, even with the slower players. But as mentioned early, try to vary the lessons and the drills. Too much of one thing can begin to sour a player on the game.

Did You Know?

George Mikan is widely considered basketball's first great big man. The 6-foot, 10-inch Mikan was a star for the old Minneapolis Lakers, won several scoring titles, and led his team to five NBA championships in the late 1940s and early 1950s. But when Mikan began playing at DePaul University, he was one of the "slow kids." He appeared clumsy and uncoordinated. That's when his coach, Ray Meyer, started from scratch. He had Mikan do simple things such as jumping rope, running figure eights around chairs, boxing, dancing, lifting weights—anything to improve his coordination. He also had him shoot hundreds of hook shots from both sides of the hoop. By his junior and senior years Mikan was a star, and he became even better in the pros. So there is always hope for the kid who can't keep up with the others at first. Don't let him quit.

Bring in Some Help

As a youth coach, chances are good that you will be working alone without an assistant coach. After all, this isn't the NBA or a Division I collegiate program. However, there is no harm in bringing in a volunteer to help you in certain situations. It might be a very good local high school player or even a college player who enjoys working with kids. You can use the helper to do a number of things. He can demonstrate techniques to the entire team, or he can take some time to work with the slower players while you continue your work with the others. If you do this, however, you should probably have your helper also spend a little time with the rest of the team. That way, the slower players won't feel as if they are being singled out. If the helper is a local star player who the other kids know, they will want to spend some time with him as well.

Bringing in help in no way diminishes you as a coach. In fact, it shows that you have a strong sense of responsibility to all your players. If you were stubborn in this situation and insisted on going it alone, your slower players might not get the attention they need, or your better players could be held back. By having someone assist you on a temporary basis, you will be better prepared and able to teach the individual skills of the game to all your players—and hopefully have them all ready to contribute to the team in the upcoming games.

Bringing in someone to assist you with demonstrations or with slower kids can only help your overall coaching effort.

An Ongoing Process

With players from all three age groups—the youngest, middle, and oldest—basketball will remain a teaching process right through the season. Game situations will give you an opportunity to assess your players' form and execution of the individual skills you have been teaching. It isn't unusual for a player to perform well in the controlled atmosphere of practice, where you can whistle the action to stop at any time and once again shift into the teaching mode. Obviously, you cannot do that during a game. The time to correct errors in form and execution is at the very next practice after the game. Once again, use positive reinforcement, especially with your weaker players who may begin to feel that they are not good enough. Always tell all your players, from the best to those who have to struggle a bit, that through hard work, everyone can contribute to the team effort and will continue to improve their individual games.

Did You Know?

Michael Jordan is widely considered the greatest basketball player ever to lace up a pair of sneakers. But it wasn't always that way. When he was playing for the Laney High School JV team in North Carolina, sophomore Jordan was upset because another player was picked to join the varsity late in the season. The reason was that the other player was taller and the team needed height. Yet when the varsity when to the regional playoffs that year, the only way Jordan could go to the game was to take the place of a team manager who got sick. So while others played, Michael Jordan handed out towels, something he would always remember. "I made up my mind right then and there that this would never happen to me again." The rest, as they say, is history—history and perseverance.

Teaching the skills of basketball is a skill in itself. As with most things, you will become better with experience. You may decide that the older age level is your strongest niche, or you may get the most satisfaction by working with the youngest kids. Either way, the more you know about the game and about teaching individual skills, the better prepared you'll be to do your job well. The next chapter focuses on the fundamental skills of dribbling, passing, shooting, and rebounding, where the teaching concepts provided in this chapter can be put into action.

The Least You Need to Know

♦ It's important to present what you teach players in a clear and understandable format that is flexible enough to allow for the differences among player skills, abilities to learn, and age.

♦ If there is a particular skill that you don't feel you have the ability to demonstrate properly, don't hesitate to bring in someone—a local high school or college player, perhaps—who can demonstrate the skill very well.

◆ Always be sure that all your players are executing a new skill with the proper technique. If you let bad habits form, they can be very difficult to break.

◆ Be patient with those players who take longer to understand a concept than other players. It might even be helpful to bring in an "assistant" to work with them. It can be an established high school or college player who the younger kids know and respect.

◆ Remember, teaching and coaching is an ongoing process. The more *you* know and continue to learn, the more you will be able to teach your players. Your basketball education should never stop.

Chapter 10

The Basic Fundamentals

In This Chapter

- ◆ Dribbling
- ◆ Passing
- ◆ Shooting
- ◆ Rebounding

Now it's time for the nuts and bolts of the game itself. The previous chapters outlined and discussed a necessary foundation for coaching success, allowing the coach to get his ducks in a row and prepare his team for what follows: learning the fundamentals of the game, teaching individual skills, and working together as a team through both the offensive and defensive strategies that enable players to really learn how the game is played.

This chapter begins by discussing the four basic fundamentals each and every player must know. Before a player can be expected to successfully compete in a full-court game, he must have a firm grasp of dribbling, passing, shooting, and rebounding. These basic fundamentals are used in nearly every facet of the sport and in every kind of situation. No matter what type of offense or defense you decide to have your team play, your players will not be able to execute it well without using these skills. In fact, these fundamentals must become second nature to the players so that they don't have to think about them, but just use them instinctively as they move up and down the court during a game.

Dribbling

Today it's called "putting the ball on the floor," but no matter what term is used, dribbling the basketball is a necessary and crucial fundamental for every player to master. Besides passing, it is the only way a player can advance the basketball up the floor, drive to the basket, and work his way into position for an open shot. A good *ball handler* can control the offensive pace of the game, help defeat a pressing or trapping defense, and set up teammates for making baskets. In today's game, the point guard is often the best dribbler or ball handler on the team. On offense, the ball is in his hands much of the time. But it isn't always that way in youth basketball.

As a coach, it is your job to convince every player on the team of the importance of this fundamental skill. Most players probably know this already. If they watch college and professional games, they can see how today's players dribble equally well with either hand, change hands quickly, and sometimes put the ball behind their backs and between their legs while continuing the dribble. They do it without looking at the ball; instead, they watch the rest of the court so that they can make a play. Dribbling has to become almost automatic or second nature to players. However, this doesn't happen overnight. There is a long road from taking the first bounce to being able to shake a defender with some slick ball handling. As with everything else, young players have to "walk before they can run." You can play a big part in developing a player's ability to dribble, control the ball with confidence, and use this skill to the best of his ability.

Quick Tips

Remind all young players who want to improve their dribbling skills to always keep in mind the following basic tips:

- ◆ Keep the ball low.
- ◆ Spread their fingers and control the ball with their fingertips.
- ◆ Use a pumping motion with their forearm from the elbow to the fingertips.
- ◆ Keep their knees bent, and bend slightly at the waist.
- ◆ Don't look at the ball, and keep their heads up.
- ◆ Practice using both hands.
- ◆ Refrain from trying to imitate the flashy dribblers in the pros. Always learn the basics first.

Working with different age levels, you'll also find yourself dealing with players who run the gamut from no dribbling skills to fairly good skills. Much, of course, depends on the age of the players. Chances are, the youngest kids will need the most hands-on instruction and basic practice schedule. But no matter what the beginning skill level of your players is, you should begin by explaining the principles of the dribble and why they must be adhered to in order for a player to master the skill correctly.

Here's How to Dribble

Begin by reminding your players to always keep the ball low, never allowing it to bounce higher than the waist. When dribbling in heavy traffic, players should get even lower. The low center of gravity will give the player better control of the ball and also make it more difficult for a defender to steal it. Even the youngest players with the smallest hands should spread their fingers and allow the fingertips to control the ball. As the ball comes up, the player should meet it with her hand, giving just slightly with the hand as the ball makes contract, and then within a split second use the fingers to push it back toward the floor.

The dribbling motion is made with a pumping motion using the forearm from the elbow to the wrist and fingertips. Have each member of your team begin bouncing a ball using this motion so you can see who is doing it correctly and who is not. Then make your corrections with those who need it. This is also the first basic dribbling exercise for beginners, to continue to bounce the ball while standing still. It should be done with both hands, one after another. Right-handed players might have trouble at first using the left hand, and vice versa. That's the value of practicing, to bring both hands into play.

There are two additional dribbling exercises that beginners, as well as those who need more practice in the basics, can do. Both are very simple. One is simply to practice bouncing the ball while blindfolded. Obviously, the dribbler must stand in one place, but the blindfold will force him to bounce the ball without looking at it. Again, tell the player to make sure he does this basic drill by practicing with both hands. The second exercise is for the player to get on her knees and bounce the ball. By bouncing it this way, the player will get a better feel for the ball on her fingertips because of the shorter distance the ball has to travel to the floor when dribbling.

Coaching Corner

It's okay for beginners to look at the ball when they begin dribbling, but let them know that they have to learn to keep their heads up. As soon as they feel comfortable bouncing the ball, tell them to stop looking at it. It's okay if they lose control initially. Assure them that they will soon learn, as thousands of players have before them.

A good way to keep young dribblers from looking at the ball is to have them bounce it blindfolded.

Also remind your players that dribbling is a skill that can be practiced almost any place at any time. All they need is a ball and a place to bounce it. There is no need to be in the gym or to be playing a game. The more a player practices, the quicker he will become comfortable with bouncing the ball.

A good way for a young player to get the feel of the ball is to dribble it while on her knees.

Players Should Walk Before They Run

Once a player becomes comfortable bouncing the ball with either hand, he's got to begin moving with it. The object, of course, is for the player to be able to run, turn, and change speeds and directions, all while continuing to dribble. But he can't do this without the proper control of the ball. Beginners have to start slowly, just walking slowly as they dribble. Make sure they bounce the ball slightly in front of them as they walk. They can do this while walking forward and then backward, and then sliding slowly to each side. At first, they may have to look at the ball, but tell them to look as little as possible. It's better for a player to dribble the ball off his foot once or twice while not looking than to continue to look, so that he can do it successfully.

The progression here is relatively simple, although not always easy. Have your players pick up the pace from a walk, to a jog, and finally to a run, all while dribbling and looking at the ball as little as possible. At this point, you can run some sprints and conditioning exercises while the players are dribbling, so you are essentially accomplishing two things at once. The next logical step is for the player to learn to change speeds, especially accelerating with the dribble to burst past a defender. To do this, the player must lean forward, or *lean into the dribble*. As he increases speed, he must use a slightly higher dribble, controlling the ball from his waist to his chest.

Coaching Corner

You should remind beginners of a couple of things as soon as they start handling the ball. One is that they cannot dribble with both hands at once. That's a violation, and the team loses possession of the ball. They also cannot dribble, stop, and then dribble again. That's called a *double dribble* and is also a violation that results in the loss of the ball. The dribbler also cannot *carry* or *palm* the ball. This occurs when the dribbler allows the ball to rest or cradle in the palm of his hand while taking a step. Players should be aware of these dribbling violations before they begin falling into bad habits. As soon as you see a player commit one of these violations, blow the whistle and let her know about it.

Advanced Dribbling Moves

Once a player has a good enough mastery of dribbling that he can handle the ball with either hand while running and changing speeds and without looking at the ball, you can demonstrate some of the advanced dribbling moves he needs to learn as he improves and as the pace of the game becomes faster. A number of dribbling drills outlined in the next chapter enables the player to work on these moves and improve his skills. The following are some of the more advanced moves with the basketball:

◆ **The crossover.** This is an important move often used when a player is dribbling toward a defender with his right hand and wants to go left. He has to bounce the ball across his body quickly and pick it up with the other hand as he begins his move. A player should be able to do this with either hand.

◆ **The reverse dribble.** This move involves changing hands on the dribble while the player turns his back on his opponent. If the player is dribbling with his right hand and a defender begins to make a move for the ball, the player can turn to the right, letting his body protect the ball. At the same time he makes his turn, he picks up the ball with his left, completes the turn, and emerges dribbling with his left hand.

By turning his back to the defender, a ball handler can change hands and dribble the other way.

◆ **The behind-the-back dribble.** This is a more difficult move, but it's yet another way to switch hands when trying to dribble past an opponent. Instruct your players to bend more at the knees when they learn this move, at first going almost into a sitting position. They should aim to bounce the ball behind their heels so it will come up behind the opposite hip. Then they can reach back with their opposite hand to get the ball and begin moving to the opposite direction.

◆ **Fake and dribble.** When a player has the ball and a defender comes up to guard her, she should always hold the ball with both hands even with her waist in the *triple threat position*, which gives the player the option to also pass or shoot. If she wants to dribble, this position gives her the option of going left or right. Demonstrate to the players how they can fake going one way by moving one foot and the ball in that direction, and then quickly swinging the ball back and dribbling in the other direction.

As mentioned, the next chapter details a number of good dribbling drills that you can use with your entire team. Remember to emphasize to your players that dribbling can be practiced anywhere and at any time. It is one skill that a player can improve on tremendously on his own, by just practicing as often as he can.

A good maneuver to practice is faking one way and then quickly dribbling the other way.

Passing

Being able to pass the basketball well is every bit as important for players as is acquiring the ability to dribble. In fact, a crisp passing game is the fastest way to move the basketball around. In the early days of the game, when the quality of the ball made dribbling difficult, passing was the way to go. You moved the ball and then you moved yourself, the old timers used to say. That strategy is still very applicable today. Young players must learn how to pass well and use the various types of passes as soon as they begin to play the game. This is a basic fundamental that simply cannot be ignored; you, as a coach, must stress good, crisp passing from the very outset. In fact, proper passing and receiving techniques are often the most overlooked—and assumed—skills by players at all levels.

Coaching Corner

Before we even begin talking about making passes, let's pause for a moment to discuss the other half of the pass, which is the catch. A player can throw a perfect pass, but it won't do much good if it bounces off the hands of the receiver. Here are a few tips to know about catching:

♦ A player should catch the ball with two hands whenever possible.

♦ If the pass is arriving above the waist, the player should place the palms of his hands toward the ball with his fingers up. The fingers should be spread with the thumbs behind, almost touching. This will keep the ball from slipping through the player's hands.

♦ A pass arriving below the waist should be caught with fingers down toward the floor with the palms facing the ball once more. This time it is the little fingers that are almost touching and that will prevent the ball from slipping through.

♦ A player should always keep his eye on the ball until he catches it, and allow his hands to give slightly as soon as the ball hits them. The "soft hands" approach allows a player to catch the ball and then draw it in close quickly so a defender cannot slap it away.

Passing drills allow players to practice both passing and catching at the same time. Remember to emphasize that players must always be ready to receive a pass.

There are four basic types of passes, plus a couple of variations. Let's start with the basics:

- ◆ The two-hand chest pass
- ◆ The bounce pass
- ◆ The overhead pass
- ◆ The baseball pass

The Two-Hand Chest Pass

The two-hand chest pass is perhaps the most basic pass in basketball and one that has been around a very long time. Ironically, in today's fast-paced college and professional games, with bigger and quicker players, this pass is not used as frequently as it once was. But it should still be very basic to all of your players and should be the first pass they practice. The pass is thrown by gripping the ball with both hands, one on each side, with fingers spread wide with the thumbs directly behind the ball, again almost touching. The pass is delivered from chest level. Make sure the player takes a step in the direction he is passing and then pushes the ball straight away from his body. As the arms straighten, he should give a final strong snap of the wrists to give the pass its power. Also make sure he keeps his elbows in close to his body; when he follows through, his arms should be extended with the palms outward, fingers pointing toward his target.

Every young player must practice the two-hand chest pass with the form shown here.

Snappy, quick two-hand chest passes are usually used in short- and medium-range passing situations. Bigger, stronger players can use this pass for longer distances. However, the kids at the lower age levels may still have problems with this pass. They have smaller hands and sometimes are not strong enough to get a good wrist snap. If you see some young players unable to execute with both hands, allow them to begin with the one-handed push pass. The difference is that one hand guides the ball and the other pushes it toward the target. This allows the younger players to become familiar with the passing game; as soon as they're big and strong enough, they can begin using the two-handed chest pass.

Some very young players still don't have the strength to throw the two-hand chest pass. They can use the same technique but push the ball out with one hand.

The Bounce Pass

The bounce pass can be used in heavy traffic, especially when the passer feels there is a chance that a chest pass might be intercepted. At the upper levels of the game, it is also used because it's more difficult for taller defensive players to bend down and pick it off. The ball can be thrown with one or two hands and is delivered from a lower position than the chest pass, closer to the waist. It generally isn't delivered with the speed of the chest pass, but the technique has to be precise.

When throwing a bounce pass, players may want to bend at the knees to better see the passing lane. They should aim to bounce the ball just over halfway between themselves and the receiver. That way the ball should be received at about waist level.

Bouncing it too soon will bring it up too high for the receiver to make an easy catch, while bouncing it too close to the receiver will force him to bend down too low for a good reception. So it takes practice to gauge the distance of the bounce. Once a player gets the knack of throwing this pass, he can put some backspin on it if he feels he has to bounce it closer to the receiver. The spin will cause it to bounce higher to the target.

A good bounce pass will reach the receiver at about waist level.

Did You Know?

Ever since basketball grew up as a professional sport in the 1940s, some players have done things with a special kind of flare. This so-called flashy play has usually shown up the most in the passing game. A guard by the name of Bob Davies is generally considered the first player to throw the behind-the-back pass regularly in games. Then in the 1950s, Boston Celtics great Bob Cousy perfected the same pass, often using it on the fast break, and it brought ooohs and aaahs from the crowd. Cousy always said he threw his special passes not to be flashy, but because that was the best way to deliver the ball. Then in the 1970s, along came Pistol Pete Maravich. He might have been the greatest passer of them all. Maravich threw passes from every conceivable angle and in a myriad of ways. He passed from behind his back, between his legs, and around his neck. Sometimes even his teammates were surprised that the ball was suddenly upon them. Young players will see many fancy passes when they watch their favorite players at the collegiate and professional levels. Their coaches, however, should always remind them that even the great passers had to start with the basics. As for the flash and dash, that's always reserved for a special few.

The Overhead Pass

The overhead pass is often used to *inbound* the ball after it goes out of bounds. The player throwing it back in play will use this pass because the ball is held high and more difficult to block or tip away. Players getting a rebound also tend to use the overhead pass, which they can release quickly without bringing the ball down where it can be grabbed or tipped.

The pass is thrown with two hands held over the head. As always, the ball is held with the fingers spread and the thumbs behind the ball. The motion is similar to that of the chest pass, except that the arm straightening and wrist snap comes from above the head. The passer again takes a step toward his target and snaps his wrist just before releasing the ball. The motion is completed with a smooth follow-through. Some players looking for more power make the mistake of bringing the ball farther behind their heads. If you see a player doing that, quickly point out that the power comes from the wrist snap. Bringing the ball farther back only makes the pass less accurate.

The overhead pass is a great way to throw the ball over the defenders.

The Baseball Pass

The fourth and final of the fundamental passes is the baseball pass. This is just what it sounds like: The basketball is thrown with one hand like a baseball. It is used to make long passes, usually by a player who gets a rebound and spots a teammate streaking down the court ahead of the defenders on a fast break. It is thrown by the passer cradling the ball in one hand and bringing it up and behind his ear. He should step into the throw, let his elbow come forward first, and then snap the ball with his wrist. To make sure the throw is a straight one, the passer should roll his wrist inward with the palm facing out.

The baseball pass isn't always easy for very young players. Their hands may not be large enough for them to balance the ball in one hand long enough to bring it back and release it. But if they also play baseball, they will already have knowledge of the motion and should pick up the pass quickly as they grow and continue to play.

The baseball pass is used when a player has to throw the ball a long way.

Quick Tips

Though all four basic passes are thrown differently, some principles remain constant. These are things players should never forget when working on their passing games:

- ◆ Always spread their fingers when passing or receiving a pass.
- ◆ Power comes from snapping the wrist.
- ◆ Always follow through on each pass.
- ◆ Step in the direction of the target before releasing the pass.
- ◆ Don't throw the ball to where the target is, but where the target will be when the pass arrives.

The final tip is something you should make clear to all your players. They will often pass to a player who is on the move. If they throw to where he is, he may not be there when the ball arrives, leading to an errant pass. The ball could go out of bounds or be picked off by a defender. In either case, your team will lose possession of the ball. The trick is to *lead* the receiver, much as a quarterback does in football. This takes practice, both in scrimmages and in games. You can also devise some passing drills that will allow players to get the knack of passing to the spot. Once a player learns about his teammates and how they move, he will begin to pass by instinct and without thinking. When he does that, he is a step closer to becoming a bona fide basketball player.

Other Ways to Pass

We have discussed the four basic passes that every young player must know and master. Game situations sometimes dictate some changes in the passing game. For example, if a player stops his dribble and the defensive man is close to him, he may not have room to make a chest or bounce pass. Sometimes he can simply shove a quick one-hand push pass to a teammate off to his side. There may also be times when a player has to jump in the air to get his pass off safely.

Quick Tips

Players cannot always look at the receiver and make a simple pass. The defense is always looking to pick it off. To make it more difficult for the defense, the passer should practice faking a pass one way, then pulling the ball back and passing in the other direction. That helps to keep the defense off balance.

When a player is guarded very closely, a quick push pass to the side is often the best way to go.

Older players and those with more skills may also find themselves passing directly off the dribble. In other words, when the ball comes up, they don't push it back to the floor. Instead, they cradle it on their hand and in one motion throw a bounce or straight pass to a teammate. Finally, there is the behind-the-back pass, which is often thrown off the dribble as well. As before, the player cradles the ball in his hand as it comes up, and then swings it behind his back and releases it to a teammate. This takes a great deal of practice, and young players will more likely throw the ball away instead of making an accurate pass. Don't encourage players to do this in scrimmages or games, but at the same time, don't discourage them from trying it on their own and occasionally in practice. Remember, the game always has to be fun.

Shooting

Now the fun starts—at least, that's what most of your players will think. At the beginning, most kids consider putting the ball through the hoop to be the most exciting part of the basketball experience. After all, that's the object of the game, to make baskets and score points. It will take a bit longer before they realize that the same satisfactions can come from completing a great pass, making a steal on defense, blocking a shot, or snaring a key rebound. But let's face it: All players have to know how to shoot. That's still the focal point of the game.

Four basic shots have always been necessary to learn, although the order of importance has changed over the years. They are the layup, the jump shot, the push or set shot, and the hook shot. A player may not use all four of these shots every game, but he still should know how to execute them correctly. Besides knowing *how* to take them, he should also know *when* to take his shots. A player who shoots almost every time he has the ball isn't going to help his team, even if he has a pretty good shot. Instead, he'll get a reputation as a *gunner*, a guy who wants all the shots for himself and refuses to pass to his teammates. In return, they won't pass him the ball and the whole team will suffer.

This illustration shows just how the hand should make contact with the basketball when shooting.

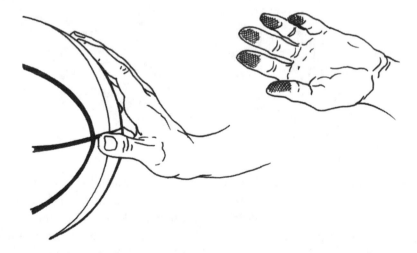

Therefore, you have to teach your team not only how to shoot, but also how to work the ball so that everyone on the floor has an opportunity to get some good shots. The younger kids especially should have a chance to shoot. A pecking order will slowly become established, with the older players and the better shooters taking more of the shots. Yet you should never let these few players take *all* of the shots, nor should you encourage a pecking order mentality. Otherwise, it won't be as much fun for the players being frozen out. Now let's look at those four basic shots.

Did You Know?

On March 2, 1962, Wilt Chamberlain of the Philadelphia Warriors set an NBA record by scoring 100 points in a game against the New York Knicks. In that game, the 7-foot, 1-inch center took an amazing 63 shots, but none of his teammates got mad. Wilt was always their leading scorer, and when they saw he had a chance to set an incredible record, they began feeding him the ball. That night, the big center made 36 of his 63 shots from the floor and 28 of 32 from the free-throw line. Later in his career, however, Wilt proved he could do more than shoot by leading the league one year in total assists, the only center ever to do so.

The Layup

The most basic shot in basketball is the layup. It is taken from directly under the basket and is a shot that a player, theoretically, should never miss. But it's one thing to shoot a layup with no one around you and another to shoot it while going to the basket at full speed with a defender breathing down your neck.

A player should always take the layup with one hand and should be able to make the shot from both the right and left sides of the basket. That means she should be able to shoot the layup with either her right or her left hand. When a player approaches the basket from the right or left side, she always puts the ball up against the backboard and banks it into the hoop. When a player approaches from directly in front of the hoop, she will generally push the ball softly over the front rim and in. But with young players, it's always a safer bet to come in from the side and use the backboard.

When shooting the layup from the right side, a player dribbles to the basket, takes a final step with the right foot, and then explodes off the left foot. As he goes in the air, he grabs the ball with both hands and brings it to a point just above his head. Then the left (or nonshooting) hand releases, and the shot is completed with the right (or shooting) hand. The shooter should aim for a point on the backboard above and to the right of the basket. When done correctly, the ball will hit the backboard on the way up, bank off it, and then fall back through the hoop. It is done exactly the same way from the left side, except that this time the shooter explodes off his right foot and completes the shot with his left hand. Coaches should tell players to look at the spot on the backboard where they want to put the ball and to always concentrate, even though this appears to be a simple shot. In a game, defensive players may try to jump with the shooter, bump him slightly, and sometimes even scream at him. By concentrating, a player can make the shot more often than not, even when he is fouled.

The basic layup is a shot that a player should never miss unless he loses his concentration.

Quick Tips

Younger and less experienced players may not be familiar with the layup. Here's how they should begin practicing it:

1. Stand to the right side of the basket, push the ball upward, and at the same time push off on the left leg and lift the right knee toward the waist. Then do it on the opposite side, using the right leg to push off, raising the left knee to the waist, and pushing up the shot with the left hand.

2. Once a player is comfortable shooting the layup from a standing position, he should begin jumping off the left and then the right foot as he takes the shot.

3. Next he should do it by taking two steps. From the right side, he should step with the right foot and then take off with the left and put the shot up. He should reverse these steps from the left side.

4. Once a player is comfortable shooting with two steps, he can start dribbling toward the basket slowly and taking a real layup, slowly increasing his speed and the explosiveness of his jump.

Instruct your players to practice developing power and explosiveness in their take-off foot. With the layup, a player wants to get as high in the air as she can. The higher a player can jump, the easier it is to make the shot and the less likely it will be blocked. Also remind your players that there is no need to push the ball at the backboard with any real power. If they do that, the ball will probably bounce back off the rim. Just let it gently roll off the fingers toward that spot on the backboard, and it should carom into the hoop perfectly.

Once a player has the layup down pat, he can slowly work on other shots from close in, such as the reverse layup, in which he goes under the basket and lays it in from the other side. But, as always, before you even demonstrate something like a reverse layup, make sure your players have the basic layup fully conquered.

The Jump Shot

The jump shot has become the most popular and universal shot in basketball today. Players take jump shots from everywhere on the court, including three-point land. All your players will want to shoot the jumper, and the older ones are probably shooting it already. It's your job to make sure all of them are using the correct shooting technique. That doesn't mean that every jump shooter is going to look like a clone of his teammates, but certain principles of form should definitely be followed for maximum effectiveness. Here are the basic points to emphasize to all jump shooters:

◆ A player should always use the same form and technique when shooting the jumper from any distance and any place on the floor.

◆ A player should always square his body to the basket before shooting, no matter where he is on the court.

◆ The nonshooting hand should act as a guide almost to the point at which the ball is released.

◆ The shot should be released above the head.

◆ When shooting, the player's eyes should be focused on the rim.

◆ At the release point, the ball should roll off the fingertips, with the arm straight and the hand smoothly following through.

Once again, there will be a difference between the younger players and the older ones. The kids in the youngest group are often not big or strong enough to shoot a conventional jump shot. The older kids probably already have developed one. So your approach will be different based on the varying ages and skill levels of the players.

Working with Younger Players

Most kids at eight and nine simply won't be able to shoot the jump shot. However, you can still provide them with the proper form so that they will grow into it. Trying to shoot a jumper and not reach the basket would be far more frustrating than having the simple ability to push the ball into the air with enough force to get it over the rim. Though the young player may struggle to get the shot up, the form and rhythm should be the same he'll use later when taking a conventional jump shot.

The youngest players aren't strong enough for a real jump shot. Let them bring the ball down low and push up hard.

As with all jump shots, the ball should be held with two hands. The shooting hand is behind the ball, fingers spread, while the nonshooting hand is placed on the side of the ball to serve as a guide. Allow the young player to bring the ball down lower than normal, as long as he keeps it tight to his body. In fact, he can start with the ball below his waist. Next he should bend at the knees and then try to pop them up quickly, to give him thrust and at least take him a short distance off the floor. At the same time, he should push his shooting arm upward, extending it toward the basket, with the ball still guided by the nonshooting hand. Just as the arm is reaching full extension, the shooter should snap his wrist forward, let the ball roll off his fingertips, and follow through so that the thumb is pointing downward and the fingers are off to the side.

By shooting from in close, the young player can put a high arc on his shot just to get it above the basket so there is a chance it will fall through. As he improves and becomes more confident, he can begin to move farther out, and as he grows can begin holding the ball higher and eventually take the conventional jump shot.

The Jump Shot as an Offensive Weapon

The jump shot has become a powerful offensive weapon, not only because it can be taken quickly off the dribble, but also because players can shoot it while high in the air, making it more difficult to block. Again, with older players who already have jump shots, the first thing you should do is check their form. If they are off-balance when shooting, are holding the ball too low, or are not releasing it properly, make corrections immediately. Bad habits are sometimes difficult to break, and the proper form will always ensure more accuracy.

Even when you begin working with your better players, have them start shooting from no farther than 10 feet out. That way, they won't worry so much about making the shot as taking it properly. The jump should always be made with the body squared to the basket, with the feet even and shoulder width apart. Players should jump straight up, coming down on the same spot or just slightly forward. The shot should always be taken at the top of the jump. Those who shoot while still on the way up or on the way down will lose some accuracy. The shooter should always aim at the same spot, either just over the front rim or in front of the back rim. He should aim for the same spot each time, never changing the target. Consistency is very important.

If you can shoot a jump shot with perfect form every time, chances are good that you will be successful.

The older player doesn't have to hold the ball nearly as low as the young kids. Otherwise, the technique is almost the same: grabbing the ball with two hands, with the shooting hand behind it, bending at the knees, and then jumping in the air. As he jumps, the shooter raises the ball above his head. With his eyes focused on the rim and the ball in shooting position, he removes the guide hand, and then releases the ball by straightening his arm and snapping his wrist forward and into the follow-through position. Again, the fingers are spread and the ball rolls off them, leaving the middle and index fingers last. Just before the release, the elbow should be under the ball, not sticking out at an angle. The wrist should be cocked backward, almost as if the shooter were carrying a flat tray.

Did You Know?

In basketball, a soft touch isn't someone who'll lend you money without asking questions. Instead, it's a shot that has a better chance of going in the hoop due to the way the shooter puts it up. If the ball does not come off the rim hard, the shooter has a soft touch. The ball is more likely to bounce around the rim with a chance to go through the hoop. If it clanks hard off the rim and flies 10 feet away before coming down, the shooter has a touch like a rock. Most players will develop a sense of touch on their own. Everything counts—the way the ball feels in the hands, the way it is released, and its flight to the basket. A shooter using the proper form will put a backward spin on the ball, which helps give it *touch*. He also should not shoot with an overly high arc, and he should hold his arm steady and the wrist in the follow-through position for a second after the ball is released. A player who breaks the motion too soon could affect the accuracy of the ball and alter its touch.

Once a player has mastered the technique of the jump shot, he can begin to increase his range, shooting from farther and farther out until he is comfortable from most sections of the court. Of course, if a player finds that he is much more accurate from 15 feet than 20 feet from the basket, he should try to work in closer for his shot. Don't let your players *force* shots from too far out. If they don't have the confidence that they can make it, they may alter their technique or release to compensate for the increased distance, and this can easily lead to bad habits.

Very rarely will players have an open jump shot without a defender guarding them. Often a player has to create his own shot. To prepare for this, the shooter must also practice taking a jump shot off the dribble and after receiving a pass. In both cases, he will probably have a defender trying to stop him. To shoot off the dribble, the player must practice coming to a quick stop and immediately going up in the air to take the jump shot. Once he is in the air, all the techniques of shooting apply. When catching a pass, the shooter must stop as soon as he has the ball, and then get up in the air before the defender can react. Quickness is the key in both situations, and practice is the best way to improve quickness.

This sequence shows the proper way to release the basketball on almost all shots.

Fact of the Game

No two players will shoot the jump shot exactly the same. Some may hold the ball a little higher or a little farther back than others. Some may use their guide hand a little differently and take it off the ball sooner. Players should always remember that the most important thing is to take the shot exactly the same way each time, no matter what the situation is or how far they are from the basket. If a shooter's technique varies or changes in any way, he will lose some or all of his accuracy.

One-Hand Push Shot

Long ago, the two-hand set shot was a formidable offensive weapon in basketball. Players could hit this shot from far out, standing squarely on the floor and flicking the ball with both wrists. This shot is obsolete today, but the one-hand push shot still has some purpose. Players use it occasionally when they are unguarded with little or no defensive pressure. Many others use the one-hand push from the free-throw line.

The shooting motion for the one-hand push is identical to the jump shot. The only difference is that the shooter doesn't leave the floor. Instead, he places his feet about shoulder width apart, with the knees bent just slightly. The right-handed shooter has the right foot slightly in front of the left, with his body square to the basket. As with the jump shot, he then brings the ball over his head, releases it, and completes the shooting motion and follow-through. The one difference with the one-hand push shot is that the shooter uses his legs, straightening them as he releases the shot and following through by going up on his toes. By using his entire body this way, the shooter creates a great deal of range for his shot.

The figure on the left is too low; on the right, the player is leaning forward. The proper one-hand push shot form is in the center.

Coaching Corner

Free throws are taken from the foul line, 15 feet from the basket. Therefore, it is not a long shot. The player is standing alone, isn't rushed, and isn't guarded. Why, then, do players miss so many free throws? Always remind your players that the key to success at the free-throw line is to relax. A tense shooter will not fare well. That's why you see players bounce the ball several times, spin it in their hands until it feels right, and then take a deep breath, exhaling slowly. Once a player is relaxed and shuts out all the distractions around him, he can take the free throw. Most players use the technique of the one-hand push shot. A foul-shooting percentage of 75 percent or better is considered very good. The absolute best will shoot just over 90 percent. Never diminish the value of the free throw. It's impossible to count the number of games that have been both won and lost at the free-throw line.

In today's fast-paced game, most players don't find themselves unguarded long enough to set themselves and take the push shot. But there is no harm in having the very young players practice the technique. By using their legs and entire body, they will have more range than with their jump shots. And because the shooting motion is the same, they are almost rehearsing for the time they can shoot the jumper from the same distance.

For young players just learning the free throw, let them practice the type of free throw that is the easiest and the most accurate for them. Always set aside some time for each player to shoot free throws, and encourage the players to practice on their own. They should not be satisfied until the mechanics of the free throw become automatic.

Quick Tips

There is one immediate benefit to knowing how to shoot the one-hand push shot. Very few players, even in the pros, will shoot a jump shot from the free-throw line. Foul shots today are almost always one-hand push shots. When a young player begins developing the one-hand push shot, he is also developing a foul shot, and making free throws are always the mark of a good player and a good team. That's why it is still important for coaches to teach and encourage this sometimes forgotten shot today. However, there is one major advantage of the push shot over the jump shot for young players learning the game. With the push shot, the player hasn't left the ground and therefore can decide not to shoot, but he can pass or dribble. Once the player leaves the floor for a jump shot, he has to shoot or pass the ball before his feet touch the floor.

The Hook Shot

A shot that is often taken close to the basket in heavy traffic—the hook shot—is usually used by a center, a big man. In some ways, the hook shot is a lost art today. Since most young teams aren't going to have a dominant big man, it won't hurt players to practice the hook shot. It can be used in certain situations, and by the nature of the shot itself, young players can get the ball up to and into the basket. But since it is a shot taken with a long sweep of the arm, it takes a great deal of practice to shoot accurately.

Did You Know?

The last great hook-shot artist was Kareem Abdul-Jabbar, the Hall of Fame center of the Los Angeles Lakers in the 1970s and 1980s. Abdul-Jabbar's famed *sky-hook* is often still considered the most unstoppable shot in basketball. It was a thing of beauty to watch. It didn't hurt that Kareem was 7 feet, 2 inches tall; however, he still worked to make the shot perfect.

The hook shot is difficult to stop because it is taken from high over the head, with the shooter standing sideways to the basket and to the defender as well. That puts the shooter's body between the ball and the defensive player. Young players should not depend on this shot in a game until they know they can make it, and that takes practice. A player with a large hand will have more success controlling the hook shot. That's another disadvantage to young players. But if one of your players asks about the shot, there is no harm in showing him how it's done.

Though the hook shot is not used often, it won't hurt to learn the proper form of this classic move.

A player ready to take a hook shot with his right hand begins by striding forward with his left foot. He positions his body sideways to the basket and begins an upward sweep with his right arm, cradling the ball with fingers spread. He then rises up on the toes of his left foot and at the same time brings his right knee up as he continues the upward arc of arm and ball. The ball is released at the highest point of the arc, with the shooter flicking his wrist and letting the ball roll off his fingertips with a backward rotation. The shot can be aimed directly at the basket or can be banked in off the backboard. Once again, this is not only a shot that is difficult to master, but also one that won't be used that often in a game. So it should be tried and developed only after all the other shots have been mastered.

Rebounding

Because no one can make every shot she takes and no player hits every shot, there will be many missed shots during a game. When a ball bounces off the rim or backboard, it is up for grabs. The player who gains control of the ball after a missed shot is credited with a *rebound*. Rebounding is a very important facet of the game for both the offensive and defensive teams. An offensive rebound gives the team another potential shot at the basket after a miss. A defensive rebound means that the offensive team did not score and that the defensive team now has the chance to go on offense.

A good rebounding team has a big advantage every time it goes out on the floor.

The problem is that rebounding is not as easy as it sounds. At the upper levels right into the pros, the stronger, taller players are usually the best rebounders. But a tough, smaller player can also get that loose ball. Every player on the team should know what it takes to be a good rebounder. However, rebounding not only requires players to get into position and exhibit excellent timing when they jump, but it also takes aggressiveness and a strong desire to go get that loose ball. That's why you often hear rebounding described as "the battle under the boards."

Go Get That Ball

Rebounding is probably the roughest and most physical aspect of the game. When two or three players leap for a rebound at the same time, bodies often bang together. Players are occasionally knocked to the floor, sometimes from a foul and sometimes just from aggressive play. That doesn't mean that rebounding is all brute strength. Sometimes the smaller player with less jumping ability will get the rebound because he has worked himself into the best position in front of his opponent, effectively *boxing* him out. When working with the youngest players, it isn't always the best idea to encourage too much aggressive behavior. When teaching rebounding to eight- and nine-year-olds, it's better to emphasize the technical aspect of the skill. As kids get older, they become more naturally aggressive and, as a coach, you have to gauge their natural toughness. It's difficult to teach or demand that a player be tough. With the older kids, you can point out that they need to be more aggressive and let them know that they must have a willingness to mix it up underneath if they expect to be effective rebounders.

A good rebounder knows how to get position, jumps as high as he can, and grabs the ball with authority.

Every player should learn how to box out when going for a rebound. It is an important skill to master.

Fact of the Game

Boxing out has nothing to do with prize fighting. It is what the rebounder does after he gets into position under the basket and is ready to go for the ball. He has to prevent his opponents from taking the inside position by getting low and spreading his feet and arms out wide. By doing this, he is blocking the path to the basket, effectively boxing out the opponent behind him. The boxed-out player cannot push or pull the player in front of him, or he will commit a foul. The only chance he has then for the rebound is to jump higher than the other player. For this reason, boxing out is an extremely valuable tool in the rebounding game.

The rebounding process begins as soon as a shot is taken. Tell your players to watch the flight of the ball carefully and try to anticipate where it will come off the rim, whether it will bounce to the left or right or come directly off the front. At that point, the rebounder moves for position, trying to quickly slide or cut in front of opposing rebounders. Once in position, he is ready to box out. All the players on a good rebounding team will try to box out an opponent. For example, the player guarding the shooter should try to block his path to the basket so he cannot follow his shot and get an offensive rebound.

Position and boxing out are only half the battle. Once the ball comes off the rim, a player has to go hard to get the ball. He has to jump as high as he can and, whenever possible, grab the ball with both hands. If he can't grab it, he can also try to tip it to a teammate. Once a player grabs a rebound, he has several options:

◆ He must first control the ball and bring it down with both hands, with his elbows extended out to protect it.

◆ He must never bring the ball down to waist level or lower. That makes it too easy for an opposing player to slap it away or tie him up for a held ball. He has to try to keep it high in the air.

◆ Once a player gets a rebound, he should pivot immediately and look at the entire floor. If he sees a teammate starting down court, he can throw a quick overhead *outlet* pass to him. If he sees a teammate already far down court, he can throw the baseball pass to him.

◆ If all his teammates seem covered, he can then dribble out of traffic before making a pass.

Offensive Versus Defensive Rebounding

In most situations, more defensive players are closer to the boards than their offensive counterparts. For that reason, there are always more defensive than offensive rebounds during a game. If the defensive team has two or three good rebounders, it will be very difficult for the offensive team to get the ball for a second shot. But it can be done. Once a teammate launches a shot, offensive players looking for a rebound must be quick and aggressive. Otherwise, they will be boxed out. They can try to slip and slide, or even fake their defensive man one way and then go another to try to get inside him. If they can, it's their turn to box out and hold their position.

Always let your players know that if they get an offensive rebound under the basket, they should go right back in the air and try to lay the ball in. Chances are good that they will be fouled. If

Quick Tips

There is one absolute no-no when a player grabs an offensive rebound. He should never bounce the ball before going back up for a shot. This just creates trouble. The ball can be tipped away, or by the time it comes up, the defender is prepared to make a grab for it or perhaps tie up the rebounder for a held ball.

they feel that they can't get a shot or that the shot will be blocked, they can look to pass outside to a teammate who has the option of taking a jump shot, driving to the hoop, or just settling the team down and starting the offense all over again.

> **Quick Tips**
>
> This is one tip that is actually about a tip. If an offensive rebounder goes in the air and feels that he can reach the ball first but cannot grab it, he can actually try to tip the ball back into the basket. A tip-in can be accomplished with one or two hands. The skill comes in getting enough of the hand on the ball to direct it back into the hoop. Obviously, this is something that takes practice. A player can flip the ball up against the backboard alongside the hoop, and then jump in the air and try to tip it in. After a while, he'll find that it isn't as difficult as it looks.

Rebounding is an integral part of the total team game. Every coach should know the value of teaching this basic fundamental. To do this, some coaches even have put a cover on top of the basket so that every shot essentially becomes a rebound. That's just one way to practice. Any way you decide to do it, there's no question that the team that gets the most rebounds in a game has greatly increased its chances of winning.

Dribbling, passing, shooting, rebounding. These are the four basic fundamentals of basketball. In the ensuing chapters, we'll find out how these four skills are integrated into every other aspect of the game.

The Least You Need to Know

- There is no substitute for sound fundamentals. Young players should practice dribbling, passing, shooting, and rebounding skills as much as possible.

- All your players should learn to dribble with both hands and reach a point where they are comfortable dribbling without looking at the ball.

- Be sure that all your players practice each kind of pass—the chest pass, bounce pass, push pass, overhead pass, and baseball pass. All will be useful in different game situations.

- Though the jump shot is the primary shot used in basketball today, never neglect the basic layup or the one-hand push shot, which players will use from the foul line. Older, taller players can also work with a hook shot that they can use close to the basket.

- Rebounding can win basketball games. Even smaller players can compete under the boards if they know how to get position, box out, and have a real desire to get the basketball.

Chapter 11

Running Drills

In This Chapter

◆ Dribbling and ball-handling drills

◆ Passing and catching drills

◆ Shooting drills

◆ Rebounding drills

They may sound boring and military-like, and repetitious and regimented, but drills are the linchpins that make a good basketball player and good basketball team. Through drills a coach can begin to put into practice the skills and strategies that he has taught his players and his team. By running drills, not only do players improve upon their skills, but they also begin to learn to work together with their teammates. Drills are the tools by which players can get the kind of repetition they need, but in a variety of different ways. The variety of drills that a coach decides to use will ultimately get his team ready for the real thing: the games.

In this chapter, we outline some basic drills that a coach can use to go with the basic fundamentals of dribbling, passing, shooting, and rebounding. There are countless others, of course, but you can build on these fundamental drills to get your team started.

Dribbling and Ball Handling

Dribbling and ball handling are not one in the same, but they certainly go together. While dribbling is an individual skill, ball handling is inclusive of dribbling because it takes into account everything a player does with the ball. If a player cannot handle the ball well, it's doubtful that he will be a solid dribbler. For young kids just starting out, getting a good feel for the ball and being able to control it in nondribbling situations is something that should be practiced as they are working on the dribble.

We begin with simple drills and progress to more complex ones. Some are individual player drills, while others are team drills. Remember, even the simplest drills can benefit older players if they are used as warm-ups or are done when players practice on their own. Any time a player spends with a basketball in her hands is beneficial to her overall game. Dribbling and ball handling must become natural for players in these age groups if they want to continue to improve and move to the next level of the game.

Coaching Corner

Because your practice time is limited, you can run only so many drills. Even if you alternate dribbling, passing, shooting, and rebounding drills, you can't spend a great deal of time on any single one. Impress upon your players that they shouldn't limit drills to team practice. Many drills can be practiced anywhere. Players usually just need a basketball and a hoop. Remind players that if they have access to a hoop, they shouldn't practice just one drill, such as shooting. Encourage them to become well-rounded players by practicing a variety of drills.

Slaps and Squeezes

The slapping and squeezing drill may seem like an innocuous drill for very young players, but it is important. This is a drill players can do at home in their own room because they won't be bouncing the basketball. The purpose is to allow a young player to get a better feel for the ball while strengthening the wrists and fingertips.

The drill is done by having the player simply balance the ball with his hand under it at waist-level. Then, in one quick motion, the player should bring his other hand across his body toward the ball while also swinging the ball toward the free hand. The free hand then slaps the ball hard right in front of his waist. Then the player should squeeze the ball hard with both hands for a few seconds. Have the player do this several times, and then switch hands and slap the ball with the other hand. The drill will get the player used to grabbing the ball hard, which he will have to do at times during games, while the squeeze strengthens the wrists and fingers.

Around the Legs

Moving the ball around the legs is another drill that is invaluable for young players who are just beginning to learn the game. Again, it stresses ball handling and allows the player to get a feel for moving the ball and controlling it with the hands. The player bends at the waist and slightly at the knees, with his feet together. He then begins by swinging the ball behind his legs at the knees with his right hand as he reaches back with his left. He transfers the ball to his left hand and swings it back in front of his knees, where he picks it up with his right hand again. He continues to move the ball in this circular motion, picking up speed as he gets better at it. Once a player has the knack for this, he can reverse the ball direction and do it again.

Swinging the ball around the legs at the knees is a great drill for young players to improve ball-handling skills.

A player can try several variations on this drill once he has the basics mastered. One variation is to spread the legs and pass the ball between them. The player begins with one leg at a time. In other words, he swings the ball around with the right hand behind the right knee and then brings it between the legs and transfers it to the left hand. Then, with the left hand, he swings the ball back in front of the right knee and takes it with the right hand again. Now the player goes around just one leg. He can then switch to go around the left leg. Once he masters this, he can alternate between one leg and two. In other words, he slides the legs apart, swings the ball around the right leg before taking the ball behind the leg, and then slides the legs together and takes the ball around both legs. The next time around, the player slides the legs apart and brings the ball around the left leg only. Next, the player slides the legs together and goes around both legs once more. In this variation, the player has to coordinate his ball-handling skills with some footwork.

A ball-handling variation is to swing the ball around one leg and then the other.

A second variation is to keep the legs spread, swing the ball around the right leg, and then bring it between the legs again. The player then picks up the ball with the left hand, bringing it around the left leg and between the legs again to the right hand. He continues the motion until he can do it smoothly. The player then can pick up speed and reverse the ball's direction. Now the player is making a figure eight around and between his legs.

Fact of the Game

Basic ball-handling drills are something players practice right into the pros. Often you'll see a collegiate, NBA, or WNBA player swinging the ball around his or her legs and waist at breakneck speed, bouncing the ball in between and making it look as if the ball's on a string. Professionals have been doing these drills for many years and have an amazing feel for the ball. A youngster of eight or nine years should know that these drills are performed by professionals as well.

Around the Waist and Head

Moving the ball around the waist and the head are two elementary ball-handling drills. One involves simply swinging the ball around the waist, transferring it from one hand to the other behind the back, and then transferring it again at the waist in front of the body. The player should do this in both directions until she can do it quickly. Another variation is to use a similar swing, but this time move the ball around the head, transferring hands at both the front and the back. Have players do this in both directions as well.

Swinging the ball quickly around the waist is another great ball-handling skill.

Swinging the ball around the head is a ball-handling skill your players should practice.

Coaching Corner

Ball-handling drills get monotonous quickly. Coaches sometimes refer to them as nuisance drills, but they serve a definite purpose and are invaluable to younger, inexperienced players. Encourage players to challenge themselves with the drills and attempt to do them more smoothly and quickly. Never spend too much time on one drill, and encourage players to do them on their own.

Let's Start Dribbling

Earlier, we suggested that kids begin slowly, bouncing the ball in one spot to get used to the motion. Another basic exercise is to bounce the ball while blindfolded to get used to dribbling without looking at the ball, and to dribble on the knees for a shorter bounce, to get the feel of the ball hitting and leaving the hand. After learning these drills, young players should move on to a couple of other basic drills.

One simple drill is the two-ball dribble. The player stands in one place and bounces two balls at the same time, one with each hand. A player who can do this is well on his way to making the dribble an automatic function of his arm, hand, and the ball. Players shouldn't look at both hands at once, but they should get the feel of each ball hitting each hand. This isn't as easy as it sounds. At first, one or both balls may bounce away. But gradually, players will find they can bounce both balls freely and easily. After players reach this stage, they can begin walking in a straight line, dribbling both basketballs simultaneously. The better a player gets, the more he can do with the two balls, moving backward and forward, jogging slowly, and maybe even running. Obviously, a player will never dribble two balls at once in a game, but this is an excellent drill for overall coordination and confidence, and it helps players practice using both hands to dribble.

Though it might seem difficult at first, dribbling two balls at once is a great way to improve a player's skills.

Standing Crossover

The crossover dribble is one of the most important basic moves a player can master. This is accomplished by simply bouncing the ball across the body with one hand and picking it up with the other. It is used to change directions quickly, avoid a defender, or shake a defender for a shot. For young players just learning the skill, a good beginning drill is the standing crossover. Just instruct your players to bounce the ball with one hand several times, and then cross it over and continue bouncing it with the other. Then, of course, players can cross back so that they get used to switching the ball from one hand to the other.

Players can next cross over on the move. At first, have the player take just enough steps to make the

Quick Tips

When learning any new basketball skill, players should start slowly. A young player shouldn't expect to look like Allen Iverson or Kobe Bryant in two weeks. This is the best method for new players to learn—this, and practice, practice, practice, of course.

crossover dribble and then stop. Have the player start again and cross over the other way. Once he feels comfortable, have him walk while dribbling and practice crossing over from one side to the other and back again. Have the player also cross over while jogging and finally while running.

Coaching Corner

When running basic dribbling and ball-handling drills with your young players, encourage them to practice on their own, but also urge them to create variations of drills that they can do outside the team setting. For example, once they get used to swinging the ball around and between their legs, they can bounce it once and then continue the swing. Or, they can try the crossover while moving backward and to the side. Being creative prevents boredom and encourages creativity on the court.

Advanced Dribbling Drills

You can begin group dribbling drills with the youngest players, and you certainly can start running more advanced drills with the older groups. The speed and difficulty of the drills should be determined by the players' skills. All of the following drills help players work together as a team. In addition, some drills help get players used to taking instruction from you and reacting to the sound of the whistle.

Stop and Go on the Whistle

With this drill, each player has a ball and lines up alongside the others at one end of the floor. Tell players that at the sound of the whistle, they are to begin dribbling up the court. When you blow the whistle again, tell them to stop quickly and protect the ball. In other words, they should grab the ball with both hands and set a pivot foot. Once the whistle blows again, they begin to dribble quickly and then stop at the next whistle blast. Repeat this at varying intervals as they dribble up and down the court.

Changing Directions on the Whistle

Once again, have your players line up at one end of the floor with enough room between them to maneuver. At the sound of the whistle, have them begin to dribble. This time, when you sound the whistle again, don't have them stop. In this drill, you point in a direction; they should immediately begin dribbling in that direction. You can point right, left, or backward. The players must change direction immediately and continue to dribble. You can also use a signal for a crossover. Continue this as they move up and down the court. If a player loses the ball, he should pick it up quickly and rejoin the line.

Speed-Dribble Relay

The speed-dribble relay can be a lot of fun at practice because it allows players to compete, condition themselves, and work on their dribbling at top speed. Place two cones at one end of the court and two lines of players at the other. At the whistle, the first two players in each line should dribble as fast as they can to the cone and back. When the players return to the line, they should hand off the ball to the next player. The first group to finish wins the relay. Scramble the players into two more lines and repeat the drill.

One variation of this drill is to have all the players in the two lines spread their legs. The first players roll the ball between everyone's legs to the last player, who picks it up and speed-dribbles around the cone and back. This time he goes to the front of the line, turns, and rolls the ball between everyone's legs again to the last player, who takes his turn at dribbling the court at full speed. Again, the variation breaks the boredom and allows the players to have fun.

> **Quick Tips**
>
> This may seem silly at first, but a coach should always make sure there are enough basketballs at practice for each player and one for himself. It helps if the players are shooting around as a warm-up, taking free throws, or doing drills that require everyone to have a ball. If you're short on basketballs, you may be short on practice.

Kids can have fun with a dribbling relay race while improving their ability to dribble at full speed.

Dribbling Around Cones or Chairs

This is a classic dribbling drill that has been done for years because of its effectiveness. Place a line of cones or chairs (whatever is handier) at set lengths down the middle of the court. Each player must dribble around the cones, weaving in and out and using the crossover dribble as she approaches each obstacle. Players should consider each obstacle as a defensive player they are going around and should make their crossover moves quick and decisive. You can send a group of players down the line one after the other. Have each go around the final obstacle and dribble back again. Then send the next group. Players who negotiate this drill quickly and efficiently will definitely gain confidence in their ability to handle the ball in game situations.

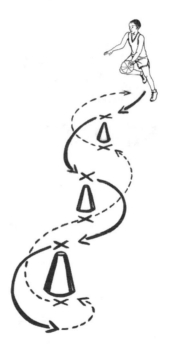

This classic drill is never outdated. It's challenging and fun, and it will make players better dribblers.

Follow the Leader

This is another fun drill in which one player can challenge the others. It can also be done several ways for variation. In this drill, each player has a basketball. One player is the leader. The others must follow him and do whatever he does. The players can follow the lines around the court or freelance down the middle. The leader can go right or left, use the crossover, and stop and go. The players behind him have to emulate his every move, all designed to improve the players' dribbling ability and get players to react to a change very quickly. Of course, everyone should have the chance to be the leader.

> ### Coaching Corner
>
> When running advanced dribbling drills, you may find that some players already have better dribbling skills than others. It won't do any good if the less-skilled players cause certain drills to break down. If you have this situation and want to run some advanced drills with your better players, you can run two drills simultaneously, with the more skillful players running the drill at a faster pace or the slower players running a secondary, less difficult drill. Either way, both groups of players will benefit from this approach.

Basic Passing Drills

A crisp, smart passing game drives an offense. In Chapter 10, we outlined the various types of passes each player must be able to make. And, of course, the players must be able to catch a sharp pass and to shoot, dribble, or pass again once they receive a pass. The following drills are designed to improve a player's ability to pass and catch, and to be able to move the ball quickly and efficiently after receiving a pass.

> ### Coaching Corner
>
> Young basketball players today often watch their favorite college and professional players on television, if not in person. They see some tremendous talents who seem to be magicians with the basketball. Unfortunately, many of these great players today like to showboat, to showcase their passing and ball-handling ability. As a coach, you cannot allow young players to emulate this. Often it simply isn't good sportsmanship, but more than likely your players won't have the skills to do it. Trying to showboat on the court can only diminish the developing skills of young players. Under these circumstances, it should be strictly forbidden.

The following passing drills vary from the basic to the more advanced. Young players can and should do the basic drills. Do not move them up to the more advanced drills until they are ready for them. Nothing discourages a young player more than not having the ability to do what his coach asks. So watch your players carefully; have them work just to the edge of their ability, but no further.

Two-Player Passing Drills

A basic passing drill is to have the players set up across from each other, beginning about 6 feet apart for the young groups. Each two players should use one ball to practice the various passes. Begin with the two-hand chest pass, and then incorporate the bounce pass and overhead pass. Work with each set of players, making sure they are using the correct form and snapping the passes crisply. Older players can begin 12 feet apart and also incorporate the baseball pass into the drill. Once the younger players are good enough to move back, they, too, can throw the baseball pass.

Having players standing opposite each other and snapping off passes is a basic way to begin to build a passing game.

This is a drill that will enable players to begin throwing the basic passes with more crispness and power. It will also enable them to get used to catching a crisp pass and then snapping it back quickly. Continue this throw-and-catch pattern until players are almost throwing the ball from sideline to sideline.

Two-Line Passing

This is a drill designed to get players moving at the same time that they pass the ball. Begin with two horizontal lines of players standing 6 to 10 feet apart a few feet behind the foul line. The player with the ball passes to the player opposite him, and then cuts hard to the baseline and eventually circles around to the end of the opposite line. The player receiving the pass fakes a pass to the cutter, passes to the player across from him, and then makes his cut to the baseline. Players keep faking, passing, and cutting. At either a prearranged signal, like the coach sounding the whistle, or a set number, such as the seventh pass, the passer actually makes a quick pass to the cutter for a layup.

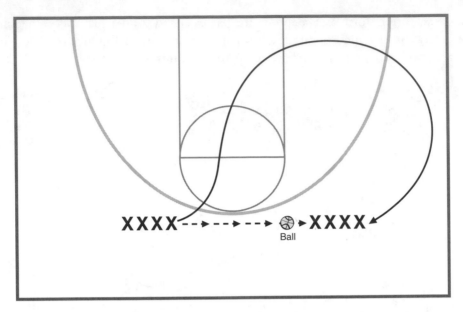

This basic two-line passing drill gets players passing and moving at the same time.

Once again, the passes can vary, with players using the chest pass, bounce pass, and overhead pass. The drill should be run as fast as the players' ability dictates. The drill not only will improve passing, but it also will get players used to cutting sharply to the hoop and getting a return pass. This is a drill that can be used with the young kids as well as the older ones.

Side by Side Down the Court

Another good passing and moving drill has two players moving down the court together about 8 to 10 feet apart. As they jog down the court, they pass the ball back and forth repeatedly, releasing it as quickly as they can after catching it. This gets players used to passing and catching on the run and leading the receiver. The better the players get at this basic drill, the faster they can run. When the pair gets close to the hoop, the player with the ball can take a layup; then the two can repeat the passing action coming back up the court.

More Advanced Passing Drills

With older players or even a good solid group of young players, you can work some more complex passing drills into practice. These usually have a dual purpose. Besides working on the passing game, they help the players' overall coordination, court

vision, and ability to react quickly. A creative coach can come up with his own variations, as long as the overall concept and purpose remain the same.

Passing Around the Square

Have four players set up in a square, two just inside the baseline and outside the foul
lane. The other two should be just beyond the foul line and also outside the foul lane
so that all four form a square. The drill is done with two basketballs. Players diagonal
from one another begin with the balls. They simply begin passing the ball to either
the left or the right and continue around the square. With two balls moving at once
a player has to receive it, make a quick half-turn and pass it away, and then get ready
to receive the second ball. When this drill begins moving at high speed, the players
really have to react quickly. By the time they pass the first ball, the second is on the
way to them. Of course, they should change direction and pass the other way as well.
They can also widen the square and try varying the types of passes.

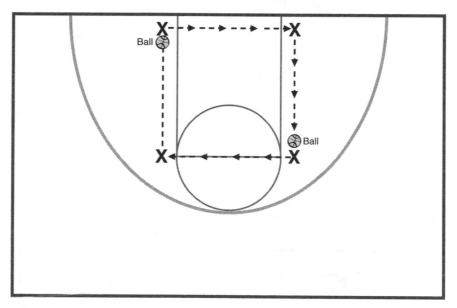

*Passing two balls quickly around a square is a great drill for reacting quickly, catching,
and passing.*

Star Drill with Two Balls

With this drill, four players form a square, with a fifth standing right in the middle.
Two balls are used. The player in the middle begins by throwing a quick pass to the
player in the upper-left corner of the square. He then turns and receives a pass from

the player in the lower-right corner. At the same time, the player in the upper-left corner passes the ball to the player in the upper-right corner, while the player in the middle passes to the player in the lower-left corner. The player in the middle then turns again and receives a pass from the upper-right corner, while the player in the lower-left corner passes to the player in the lower-right corner. Then they go around again.

Confusing? Check out the diagram, but you should get a sense of the crisp passing and timing needed for this drill. The player in the middle is the busiest, keeping two balls moving quickly. After a minute or two, another player should take the middle spot. You can also move the players farther back and have them throw different kinds of passes. Again, this is a drill for speed—passing and catching, quickness and coordination. When it's moving smoothly and quickly, it's a pleasure to watch.

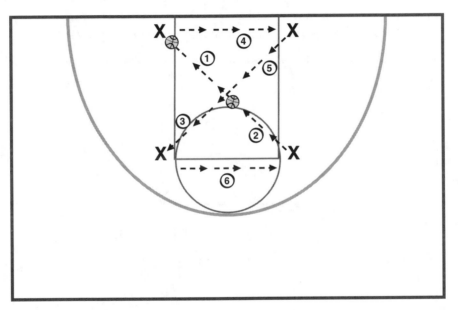

The star drill is designed for quickness in passing and catching.

Pass and Cut

This three-man drill will get players ready for moving the ball quickly up the court in three-on-one or three-on-two situations. The three players spread out on the half-court line, with the player in the middle holding the ball. At the whistle, all three begin moving. The player in the middle takes several dribbles, and then the player on the right cuts toward the middle in front of him. The player with the ball hits the cutter with a pass and then cuts behind him to the right before angling toward the hoop. At the same time the player on the left begins to angle toward the middle, takes a quick pass from the first receiver, and then whips a quick pass to the original player in the middle who is now coming in from the right side for a layup. Then start up the drill again with a different player in the middle. Passes should be made crisply, with the players picking up speed until they can do the drill at full speed.

Hoop Lingo

A three-on-one situation is when three offensive players break down the court with the basketball and there is just one defensive player back to stop them. By logic, a three-on-two situation is the same, but with two defensive players back to try to stop the offensive move.

Basic and Advanced Shooting Drills

The drill that players typically enjoy the most is shooting the basketball. In fact, one of your toughest jobs as a coach will be to convince your players that every phase of the game can be as rewarding and satisfying as shooting. But many kids will always enjoy hearing the roar of the crowd after they sink a long jump shot. That's okay, as long as they continue to play hard and learn the rest of the game. And let's face it: No coach can neglect shooting. A team still has to put the ball in the hoop to win the game.

Fortunately, shooting is a skill that players can always practice on their own. Some of the best players in the history of basketball would find a hoop and shoot hundreds of jump shots before they quit for the day. Free throws also require repetition. The more you shoot, the more automatic shooting them becomes. Nevertheless, some drills can be done at practice, and some have to be done as a team. The combination of team and individual practice will eventually make a great shooter. Let's get started.

Layups, Layups, Layups

The layup is probably the most basic drill in all of basketball. Nearly every team uses the basic layup drill as the first warm-up exercise on the court before a game. It's simply a matter of the team dividing itself into two lines on each side of the court before the foul circle. The first player from the right dribbles in for a layup and then runs to the rear of the opposite line. The player coming in from the left retrieves the ball and passes it back to the next player on the right, and then runs to end of that line while the second player goes in for a layup. This drill gets all the players loose. However, you should always emphasize that it is not strictly for loosening up. Each player should concentrate on making every single layup. This is a shot that no player should miss in a game if he goes in for it uncontested.

There are also variations for this drill. Obviously, after each player has taken a few layups from the right side, you should have everyone switch sides so that the shooter is coming in from the left and the player on the right is retrieving and passing it back. Finally, the shooters should come down the middle of the court and lay the ball over the front of the rim. You also can have players go under the basket from the right and then the left, to make reverse layups. Although these shots are considered easy, they are also important. No player wants to miss an easy layup in a game, and no team wants to blow the two points.

Layup Relay

Here's one that's fun and competitive and that also works on dribbling skills. Have your team form two lines under the basket just outside the foul lane. The first player on each line has a ball and, at the whistle, dribbles quickly out to the foul line, pivots, and dribbles back in for a layup. He then retrieves the ball and passes it to the next player in line, who does the same thing. The first group of players to finish the drill wins. You might have the team finishing second take a lap around the court to help conditioning and keep the players loose. Then switch the players around and do it again.

One variation of this is to have the players dribble out to the foul line, stop, and take a jump shot. This time the team that sinks the most shots wins. So this drill is a good way to practice two of the basic shots, the layup and the jumper.

Around the World

Players usually have fun with this one as well, and it's a great drill to prepare a team for shooting from different spots on the floor. A good starting point is to put two spots on the baseline on each side of the hoop, one outside the foul lane and the other near the corner of the baseline and the sideline. There should be a spot on each wing, one behind and to the left of the foul line, and the other in the same place on the right. The final two spots are just behind the foul line and just behind the key.

Players should dribble to each spot, stop, take a jump shot, retrieve the ball, and dribble to the next spot. The drill will keep them moving and shooting, as well as finding the spots where they need the most work. You can also make it a contest, seeing which players sink the most shots during their trip "around the world." You can have one or two players running the drill at both ends of the court as the rest of the players cheer them on.

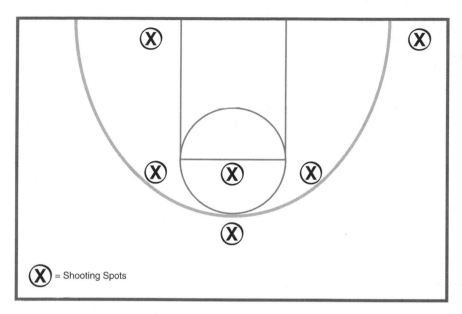

Shooting from different spots on the floor gives players confidence. The "around the world" drill can help greatly.

Shooting on the Move

It's great if a player gets the ball, doesn't have a defender nearby, and can take an open shot at the basket. Unfortunately, this doesn't happen too often in a game. Players have to learn to create shots and must know how to shoot off the dribble. Line up half your players about 6 to 10 feet to the left of the foul line. The other half are in a line on the opposite side near the basket. Each player should dribble to the foul line and then go up with a jumper. The first player in the other line retrieves the ball, passes to the next player in line to shoot, and then joins that line at the rear.

Younger players can shoot from inside the foul line and dribble slowly to the shooting spot. It's important that they control the ball and use the proper form. The older players should dribble as hard as they can and go up with the shot quickly. You can increase the range, moving the players back, and then have them do it from the other side. It is more difficult for a right-handed shooter to dribble to the left and get the shot, so don't neglect switching sides.

Coaching Corner

With jump-shot drills, be sure to emphasize proper form. Players might concentrate on the drill instead of the shot. Every jump shot should be taken the same way, with the shoulders squared to the basket, a jump straight up in the air, a shot release from above the head, and a smooth follow-through. Don't let drills turn into players' bad habits.

Catch and Shoot

Players will also have to be proficient in shooting quickly after receiving a pass. Remind them that when they get open, a defender will see them; if they don't get the shot away quickly, the defender will be on top of them, making it much more difficult to shoot. In this drill, have half your players line up halfway up the foul lane, about 4 feet from it. Have the other players on the opposite side. The first player on one side should cut back to the center of the foul line. As soon as he gets there, the first player in the other line whips a pass to him; he goes straight up for the shot without bouncing the ball. The passer and shooter then go to the ends of the opposite lines.

This drill should be run smoothly and quickly. The pass is just as important as the shot. If the pass is low and the receiver has to bend down for it, he won't be able to get a quick shot off. The same occurs if the pass is too high or wide. The shooter should receive the pass just above his waist. Then he can go right up with the shot. Variations have the players use a bounce pass instead of a chest pass and have the shooters come from the opposite side.

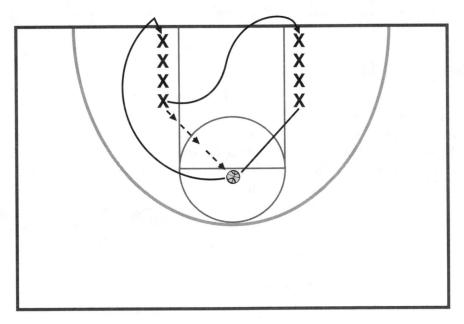

This is a great drill for catching a quick pass and going right up with a shot.

Another variation has the shooters fake left and then drive to the hoop for a layup if they hear a whistle during the drill. You can cover a lot of ground varying these drills.

Working off the Pivot

This is another drill that allows your players to work on several skills at once. Have one player stand at the foul line just outside the lane, with his back to the basket. A second player is stationed under the basket outside the foul lane on the opposite side from the pivot man. A third player stands with the ball behind the foul circle, about 10 feet from the pivot man.

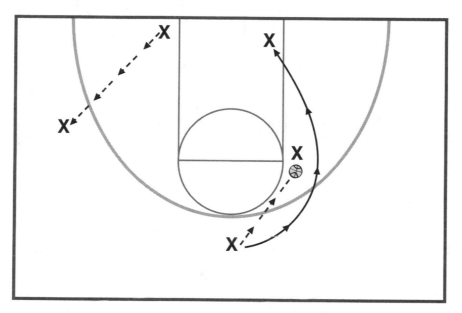

This drill allows players several options and works on several skills at the same time.

At the whistle, the man at the top of the key whips a pass to the pivot man and then cuts past him to the right on his way to the hoop. The player underneath breaks outside at an angle toward the wing, maybe 10 feet to the side of the foul line. As with the classic pivot play, the man standing in the pivot has the following options, all of which you can practice with the drill, telling the players which option to practice ahead of time, or letting the pivot man and wing man decide what they are going to do. Here are the options:

♦ The pivot man can simply turn and take a jump shot, or he can put the ball on the floor and drive to the hoop for a layup.

♦ The pivot man can pass back to the cutter coming around him, who then drives to the hoop for a layup.

- The pivot man can pass to the player coming from under the hoop to the wing. That player can take a jump shot or pass back to the original cutter for a layup.

- The pivot man can pass to the player coming from under the hoop to the wing. He can then whirl around and cut to the basket for a return pass and a layup.

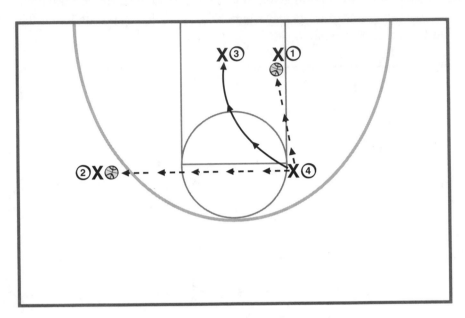

Once the pivot man has the ball, he can pass, shoot, or drive to the hoop.

As you can see, this is a drill that not only allows three different players to both pass and shoot, but it also gets players ready for the kind of plays they will run in an actual game. Thus, shooting drills are invaluable for more than just shooting. They add the other skills of dribbling and passing, as well as moving on the court, making sharp cuts, and incorporating options to pass or shoot.

Rebounding Drills

As emphasized in Chapter 10 on the basic fundamentals, rebounding is an extremely important skill. If a team cannot recover the ball after missed shots, it's in trouble. Once you have taught the fundamentals of rebounding—how to go after the ball and how to box out—you can practice a number of drills that will help sharpen the players' rebounding skills.

One-on-One Block-Out

This is a basic drill to allow each player on the team to learn how to block or box out an opponent in order to keep the best rebounding position. It is done with two players, one representing offense and the other defense. The defensive player is positioned inside the offensive player, a short distance from the basket. The coach shoots the ball and misses. The defensive player must turn for the rebound and at the same time box out the offensive player. One trick is for the defender to take a quick look at the eyes of the offensive player to see which way he is looking to go. Also, he should try to watch the other player's first step. Then he must try to seal off the lane that the other player will use to try to slide in front of him.

After a while, a good defender will almost do this by instinct. He must box out by using his body to feel the offensive player and with his arms spread wide apart. He has to be ready to jump for the rebound or move left or right if the ball comes off the rim or backboard in a way he didn't anticipate. Remember, not all rebounds are retrieved from the air. Some hit the court first and must be grabbed on a bounce.

Three-on-Three Block-Out

This is a similar drill, but now there are six players on the court: three offensive and three defensive. One defender is in the lane, and two others are outside the lane and close to the basket. The offensive players are stationed in front of them, away from the basket. When the coach takes the shot and misses, the three defenders must try to seal off the offensive players and get the rebound. The offensive players must try to get in position in front of them. Both offense and defense must watch out for fouls. Remember, this isn't football. Players cannot shove and push each other out of the way. The coach serves as the referee and calls any fouls. Players should take turns playing the box-out positions so that everyone gets a turn at practicing this skill.

Did You Know?
Rebounding takes a combination of strength, quickness, and tenacity. Yet the tallest, biggest guy isn't always the best rebounder. Hall-of-Famer Bill Russell, who, along with Wilt Chamberlain, was one of the two best rebounders in NBA history, stood just 6 feet, 9 inches tall. Charles Barkley was only 6 feet, 6 inches tall, yet he was one of the best rebounders of his time. Sometimes the player who wants the ball most gets it. That's why it's important to let all your players work hard at honing their rebounding skills. Sometimes the smaller players will surprise you. Getting the rebound becomes a personal challenge, and they work extra hard to excel under the boards.

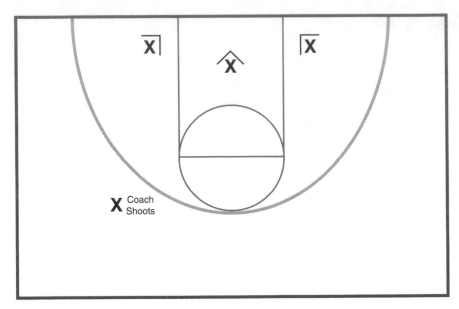

This is a drill that simulates game conditions as six players vie for the rebound.

Let the Younger Kids Just Move for the Ball

If you don't think your young players are ready for contact under the boards, you might run this simple drill to get them used to seeing the ball come off the rim and moving after it. Have two lines of players along the foul lane. You stand in the middle and put up a shot that will miss. Have the first kid in one line try to get it before it hits the floor, and then go to the first kid in the next line. If you can manage it, you can use two balls at once so that both kids can go after the ball. Keep the drill moving quickly so that all the kids are involved without too much time standing around.

Try a Tip-In Drill

This is an offensive rebounding drill that is probably best limited to the older kids. The youngest are too small and are not strong enough to try a tip-in, while some kids in the middle age group might be able to do it. Whether you want to run this drill with the middle age group is up to you. Evaluate your kids and then decide.

Form two lines of players on each side of the basket. The first player on each line has a ball, throws it softly up against the backboard on the side of the basket, and then takes a step, jumps in the air, and tries to tip it in. The players can try with one hand or two, spreading their fingers and trying to get their hand or hands under the ball so they can direct it to the basket. If they miss the first time, they can try again, but if the ball doesn't come off in a position to tap it, they can simply grab it as a rebound. Let each player do this several times. As with any drill, watch the players' techniques and make any corrections you deem necessary.

Rebound and Outlet Pass

One last drill concentrates on another important aspect of rebounding: the transition from defense to offense. This begins as soon as a defensive player grabs a rebound. You can set up this drill with two defensive and two offensive players. The defensive players should try to box out as before, so they are in a position to grab the rebound. This time, however, there are two more players on the wings, standing just beyond the foul line and about 10 feet toward each sideline.

You take the shot and look to miss it, creating the rebound. As soon as one of your defensive players grabs the ball, the two wingmen release and start downcourt. The rebounder should pivot, look for his teammate moving down the court, and throw either an overhead or a baseball pass to him. At the same time, the offensive player who has been boxed out should raise his arms to simulate game conditions and make the outlet pass a bit more difficult to throw. Don't always have the wingmen break straight down the court. They can crisscross with each other, just drift a bit to the outside, or sprint hard. That way, the rebounder will have to spot the man quickly and decide which kind of outlet pass to make.

As with all other drills, an experienced coach will undoubtedly come up with variations of the drills outlined here and may find others that also suit his purposes. Always evaluate your players' abilities and decide which drills will get the best results.

The Least You Need to Know

- ◆ Drills are the means of improving skills, refining techniques, and getting a team working together in practice.

- ◆ Players can put the basic fundamentals of dribbling, passing, shooting, and rebounding to use in ways they will begin to encounter in scrimmages and games.

- ◆ Drills should be fun, never boring, and never routine. Always vary your practices and keep your players moving.

- ◆ Don't create drills that are beyond the ability of your players.

- ◆ You can use drills to practice more than one skill at a time by combining dribbling and passing, or passing and shooting, for example.

Chapter 12

Who Plays Where

In This Chapter

- ◆ Guards, forwards, and a center
- ◆ Playing young kids in every position
- ◆ Fitting players to positions
- ◆ Older players often make choices easier

At one time, basketball didn't have clearly set positions. In the early days of the game, most of the players were small men who could play anywhere on the court. When the first big men began to appear, it was obvious they were more effective closer to the basket. Soon a basketball team had two guards, two forwards, and a center.

At the youth level, it is not always easy to assign positions. In fact, when teaching the game to young players, you should be certain that they acquire a thorough knowledge of all the positions and how to play them. This can sometimes involve difficult choices for a coach who has to decide exactly when it is most appropriate to put his best players at their best positions. Again, as with other facets of the game, part of the decision is dictated by the age level at which you are coaching. Now that we are approaching the team phase of the game, with various offenses, defenses, and strategies looming, the positions you assign your players become more important.

In this chapter, we look at the five positions on the basketball court, how they are defined, and the skills it generally takes to play each of them.

Let's Talk Positions

It's not difficult to generalize about the responsibilities of each position on the basketball court. Of course, when you generalize, it means that things don't always work just one way, and this is especially true at the youth level. For openers, however, this is how the five positions are viewed.

Hoop Lingo

The five positions on the basketball court would seem to be simple enough: two guards, two forwards, and a center. But as the years passed and positions became more specialized, so did the descriptions of the positions. The terminology evolved to point guard, shooting guard, small forward, power forward, and center. Today, numbers have often taken over when positions are discussed. The *1 spot* describes the point guard. Someone playing the *2* is the shooting guard. A player in the *3* hole is the small forward, while the guy manning the *4* is the power forward. The *5*, of course, is the center. That's rather dull terminology, to be honest, but it's well known to basketball fans everywhere.

The point guard is usually the best ball handler on the team and the player who runs the offense. Whenever possible, he brings the ball up the court and sets the team's offense in motion. His ball-handling ability will make him the surest bet to shake a defender and help break a defensive press. He also has to be an outstanding passer and have the instinct to get the ball to the open man. As with all backcourt players, the point guard should have a strong outside shot and be able to *penetrate* the defense when he goes inside to the basket. At the upper levels, the point guard is traditionally one of the smallest players on the team, though it isn't always that way.

The shooting guard is usually a little taller than the point guard and often has the best outside shot on the team. His job is generally to score more than handle the ball, but he should be adept enough to take the ball when necessary and maybe even play the point in an emergency. Shooting guards, like players at other positions, have become taller over the years and now go inside more and battle for rebounds.

The so-called "small forward" isn't necessarily small. In the NBA, a small forward may be 6 feet, 9 inches or 6 feet, 10 inches, or even taller. The position is more defined by the game the forward plays. The small forward is usually not as good of a rebounder or defender as the power forward, and also not as physical. He has to be a good scorer, however, who can shoot well from the outside and also go inside to the basket. The power forward, on the other hand, has to be physical and tough, as well as a good rebounder. But he can also be a top scorer. Players such as Karl Malone of the Utah Jazz and Chris Webber of the Sacramento Kings are two power forwards who can both score and rebound with the best of them.

The point guard is usually the team's best ball handler, with the ability to dribble past a defender.

Did You Know?

When Earvin "Magic" Johnson joined the Los Angeles Lakers as a rookie in the 1979–80, season he brought something unheard of into the National Basketball Association. He was a 6-foot, 9-inch point guard. Though he had the size of a so-called power forward, Magic could dribble, pass, and handle the ball as well as or better than any of the small men in the league. Not only did he truly bring a new dimension into the NBA, but he also showed that none of the positions on the floor could be set in stone. In fact, he proved it all over again in the sixth and final game of the championship series against Philadelphia that year, when he switched from point guard to starting center (Kareem Abdul-Jabbar was injured) and scored 42 points, grabbed 15 rebounds, and handed out 7 assists as the Lakers won the title.

The center, of course, is the big man, a player who must often have his back to the basket. Some centers, such as Wilt Chamberlain and Shaquille O'Neal, have been great scorers as well as outstanding rebounders. Some, like the legendary Bill Russell, were known more for defense and rebounding. A good center today must have both defensive and offensive skills, but he will help his team the most if he can dominate the game in close to the basket—scoring, rebounding, blocking, and causing offensive players going to the basket to alter their shots.

Quick Tips

In today's game, it's really difficult to define skill levels for the different positions. The well-rounded player really should be able to do it all. Sometimes size determines which position a player is best suited for, other times speed and quickness is the criteria. But players learning the game should try to acquire all the skills needed for each position.

Play Young Kids Everywhere

When you coach the youngest kids, you certainly can't look at them and decide who is a guard, which ones are forwards, and who is going to be the next Shaq. Even if one or two kids are much taller than the rest or a few are more mature physically and a bit heavier, you still don't want to give them a position and leave them there. These kids are with you to learn basketball, and that means learning the entire game, including how to play each of the positions on the court.

Fact of the Game

It's becoming almost cliché in all sports that the players are getting bigger and stronger as the years pass. Basketball is no exception. The young player today probably won't believe that there was a time when *all* of the players were too small to dunk the ball. One thing about the sport is true: A good big man was always able to dominate. In the 1920s, the early years of barnstorming professional teams, the original Celtics had a dominant big man. His name was Henry "Dutch" Dehnert, and he stood all of 6 feet, 1 inch tall and weighed 210 pounds. Today a player of that size would be a very small man. Yet Dehnert is the man credited with perfecting the pivot play, which the original Celtics used to win more than 1,900 basketball games. Dehnert could play with his back to the basket, was extremely tough, and yet handled the ball well. Those are the same qualities demanded of big men today, though most of them are at least a foot taller than Dehnert, an absolute big man for his day.

Because the game is becoming more specialized, it's increasingly important for players to have a thorough knowledge of all the positions. Obviously, the only way to really acquire that knowledge is to play all the positions. Therefore, your kids should become totally interchangeable on the court. Today's guard is tomorrow's center and

Thursday's forward. It isn't necessary to delineate between point guard, shooting guard, and small and power forwards with them. Just get them used to the basic positions. The youngsters who continue with the game and eventually settle into a position will have that knowledge of the other spots on the floor and will be better equipped to work within the context of the entire game. In other words, they will be better team players.

Long-Range Benefits for Young Players

Coaching the youngest players is a different kind of challenge. You may not have the responsibility of finding the best position for each player, but you have the added challenge of making sure that each and every player on your team learns *all* the positions. In Chapter 15, we describe a passing style of offense that allows the players on the floor to do this very thing by taking a turn at each of the positions. It's based solely on passing and movement. If that sounds familiar, it's the way the game was played in its earliest days, the only other time when there were no set positions.

This style of offense is a great way to teach the game and has definite long-term benefits. The smallest player on the team will have the opportunity to play the post and be the pivot man—in effect, the center. That way, all the players learn the responsibilities of all the positions, and it's a great way to start young kids learning the offensive game. Everybody plays, everybody handles the ball, everybody shoots, and everybody rebounds. When the players become old enough to settle into a position, they will know not only what playing that position means, but also how to relate it to the other positions on the court.

Hoop Lingo

For some sports terms, there appear to be no logical explanations. Words evolve to describe a play, a position, or a situation that seemingly has no relation to the sport or to what is happening during the game. The **post** in basketball is one of them. The word actually evolved from another word, **pivot**. The pivot man, as already mentioned, stationed himself just outside the foul lane near the foul line with his back to the basket. Once he received the ball on offense, he had several options. The **post** is actually used to describe where the pivot man stands. The high post is the aforementioned area near the foul line. The low post is closer to the basket, also outside the foul lane. Maybe the term came to be used because once the post player establishes position, the player standing on the spot doesn't move, like a post. An offensive player who is posting up stands in front of the defender, with his back to the basket. This can occur anywhere on the court.

Fitting Maturing Players into Positions

When you are working with older players, the top end of the middle group as well as the older group, things begin to change. At these levels, the games become more competitive, and you have to begin moving your better players into key positions. However, this doesn't mean that you must always follow the stereotypes. For example, your tallest player might be 6 feet, 2 inches—very tall for this age level. Your first instinct will likely be to make him your center. However, if that player also happens to be your best ball handler and shooter, it won't be the best situation for your team if he's always in the post. He can contribute more to the team effort if he is playing guard, handling the ball, passing to his teammates, and using his good shot to the best advantage.

By contrast, you may have another kid who is 5 feet, 8 inches or 5 feet, 9 inches, but who is husky and physically tough. He is a more logical choice for your post player. He'll make a good target in the post and can use his wide body to box out in rebounding situations. Many young players, as they mature and grow, begin to fall into their naturally best positions. You should always be aware of this at the upper levels and watch for the signs that show you where a kid should be playing. These decisions are based not always on size, but more on ability. Your point guard, for instance, doesn't have to be one of your smallest players. He should be the best ball handler, a player with the instinct to get all his teammates involved in the offense. In fact, you might well be coaching a team in which only the bigger and stronger kids have the range to shoot well from the outside. If you put them underneath because of their size, your team might not have an outside shooting game at all, and that would affect the overall way they play the game.

> **Quick Tips**
>
> Because players are more interchangeable at the youth level, coaches have certain options that college and even professional coaches don't have. Only in youth basketball can a player be the point guard on offense and the center on defense. For this reason, the youth coach must know the game very well and always evaluate the talents of his players so he can use them to the best advantage of the team.

Offense and Defense Doesn't Have to Be the Same

Yet another difference in youth basketball makes it stand out from the higher levels of the game. In most situations, professional, college, and even high school players are in the same position on both offense and defense. This isn't always the way to go with young players. First of all, if you have done your job, all your players will be familiar with all the positions. So there is absolutely nothing wrong with having a player at one position on offense and another on defense. For example, remember the 6-foot, 2-inch player who was not only the team's tallest, but also its best ball handler and shooter?

On offense, it was best to have the ball in his hands at guard. Defensively, however, you may want him underneath, where his height will enable him to block shots and rebound. Again, you have to make judgments and place players to maximize their abilities.

In addition, when you are working with the oldest group, the 13- and 14-year-olds, both the players and the games will be more competitive. While winning shouldn't be the end-all of your coaching efforts, there is certainly nothing wrong with winning a well-played game. To that end, you need your better players in the key decision-making positions, especially in the final minutes of close games. You may, for instance, have one player at point guard against teams that don't press defensively. But if a team goes into an effective full-court press, you may have to have another player—your best ball handler—take over at the point. This is another reason why all your players should work on their ball-handling skills.

Coaching Corner

Even with the older age groups, you are going to have stronger players and those who aren't as good. Yet in youth basketball, it is important that everybody plays. Once the competition level rises and the players want to win more, you will have to make different kinds of decisions regarding playing time. If you have slower players, always be sure that only one or two of them are on the court at the same time. The worst thing you can do is put all your weak players on the court at once. That can turn into a confidence breaker, a disaster for sensitive kids who are aware that they lack the ability of others. With one or two on the floor, they can be nursed through by the better players. You can also give your weaker players most of their playing time in the second and third quarters. That way, your better players can try to get a lead early and also play in the final quarter, when winning the game is on the line.

Coaching Cooperation Can Help with the Young Kids

When working with the eight- and nine-year-olds, you might try to do something unique. While at first this seems to go against the grain of competitive sports, it is something that can be very beneficial to young, developing players, kids to whom you are trying to impart not only skills, but also the love of the game. However, you will need the cooperation of the opposing coach.

Before the game, speak to the other coach. Point out your two or three least skilled players and ask if he is willing to play his equivalent players at the same time. That way, the kids won't feel overmatched when they are on the court. If the opposing coach agrees, your weaker players will be matched against players of nearly equal ability. That way they can learn, enjoy their time on the court, and hopefully come off with a good feeling about themselves. Some coaches may agree to this; others won't. Yet it won't hurt to try.

Don't embarrass a weak player by overmatching him in a game.

The less skilled kids will always understand that they aren't as good as some of the others. It's up to you not to embarrass them. You must consider that when assigning them positions. For example, you would never put a small, thin player with limited skills up against a tough, stocky, aggressive player. This is another reason why your players should learn all the positions. It allows you to set your match-ups and assign your players to a position that will fit a particular situation and allow the individual player to come away with the most positive experience possible.

The Least You Need to Know

♦ Make sure you know the responsibilities and requirements that go with each of the positions on the court.

♦ Teach your players how to play each of the positions early on.

♦ Be flexible about who plays in which position, and allow your players to grow into their natural positions.

♦ Don't overmatch your weaker players or play them all at one time.

♦ With the youngest group, don't hesitate to ask the opposing coach to play his weaker players when your weaker players are in the game.

Chapter 13

Basic Offensive Tips

In This Chapter

- ◆ Moving without the ball
- ◆ Setting and using screens
- ◆ Post and pivot play
- ◆ Pick and roll, back-door, and other plays

Now that we're getting closer to talking about full-court game action, it's time to begin working on plays that will become basic and valuable to both offense and defense. Players who have learned the basic fundamentals and have acquired the skills and knowledge that go with all the positions on the court should be ready to put all that to use within the team concept. All the individual skills in the world won't make a good player unless he can integrate his personal skills with those of the other players.

In this chapter, we concentrate on the offensive game, helping your players put the final pieces in place before they begin to work with various types of offenses and offensive strategics. By working on the skills and plays described in this chapter, your players will be a step closer and just about ready for the total team game. Everything described here—moving without the ball, setting and using screens, learning to use and take advantage of pivot play, as well as learning maneuvers such as the pick (screen) and roll and back-door plays—includes skills a player will use in games. These are also basic and important parts of a team's total offense.

You've Got to Move Without the Ball

Moving without the ball is almost a hidden skill on the basketball court. There's nothing mysterious about why it is a necessary part of the game, but many young players just don't think about it. If they don't have the ball in their hands, they tend to stand around and wait for it, maybe just moving a few steps here and there, but not really doing anything akin to perpetual motion. However, often what players do when they don't have the basketball is the key to a successful offense. In fact, if every player on the floor had the ball an equal amount of time, no one player would have it in his hands for more than 10 percent of the time he was in the game. Think about it: That means, theoretically, that 90 percent of the time a player is on the floor, he won't have the ball.

The offense that the coach decides to run determines to some degree the movement of the players on the court. But no matter what the offense is, chances are good that the players without the ball will be moving almost constantly. That is yet another reason why teams should be in tip-top physical condition. Add movement without the ball to running up and down the court, and a basketball player is constantly in motion. If a player gets tired and can't continue to move well, she can hurt the entire team's offense. If everyone on the team becomes tired late in a game, chances of playing well and winning are minimal.

Quick Tips

If the player with the ball stops his dribble and doesn't have a shot, he obviously has to pass. This is when it is important for a teammate to get open to receive the ball. You can teach your players a couple of quick keys. For example, if a defender is sticking very close to his opponent, that player can start hard toward the basket and then break back to get the ball. If the defender is on to this, the player can either outrun him to get open for the ball, or he can start back, pivot, and post up the defender, leaving him with his back to the basket but in a position to catch a pass. Teaching these keys to getting open is an important job for every coach.

Though movement will differ with different types of offense, here are some of the basic things every player must be aware of and must do when she doesn't have the basketball:

◆ Every player must be ready to both set and use screens. In addition, players must be ready to go to the offensive boards for a possible rebound and ready to box out when a shot is taken.

◆ Movement by an offensive player should keep his defensive man so busy that he will not be in position to help a teammate. This can be done by making the defensive man watch the offensive player's movement and turn his eyes away from the ball.

◆ Players must always work to set up their defenders so that they will be able to get open as a target for an outlet pass, a release pass, an inbounds pass, or a sequential pass in an offensive play.

◆ The offensive player must be working constantly to get himself open to receive a pass so that he can become a triple threat with the ball. That means getting the ball in a position to be a threat as a shooter, a driver, or a passer.

◆ Players should always be thinking of ways to set up a defensive man or to help a teammate get open.

Constant movement without the ball can confuse the defense, get a player open for a shot, and help teammates.

Movement on the court is characterized by quick, short steps, sharp cuts, fakes, and speed changes. Quickness is more important than pure speed, as is the ability to see the entire floor. If a player isn't aware of his immediate surroundings and runs into a stationary defender, he will commit a foul. As players grow and become bigger, the court may seem to become smaller. In fact, there has been talk from time to time about enlarging the court to accommodate the bigger, faster men who play in the NBA. Because young players are so much smaller, youth basketball is the perfect time for them to learn how to move without the ball. The lessons learned at this level can only help them as players grow older and continue to advance within the game.

Setting Screens

Setting screens, or picks, is an important offensive skill that every player should know. A screen is, in essence, a legal blocking maneuver in which an offensive player sets up in a spot where the defensive player will have to pass to cover his man. A screen can be set anywhere on the floor. The player setting the screen simply stops and stands still, with his hands at his side. In many cases, the player with the ball dribbles directly behind the screener, looking for a jump shot or trying to lose a defender so he can drive to the hoop. Here are some of the things that can happen when a screen is set:

♦ If the defender runs directly into the screener, he has committed a foul.

♦ If he goes in front of the screener, the ball handler can take a step back and shoot.

♦ If the ball handler leaves too much space between himself and the screener, the defender can fight through the screen and continue to guard his man closely.

♦ If the screener has not established his spot on the floor and is still moving into it when he and the defender collide, the screener has committed a foul.

Did You Know?

In the 1950s, when the National Basketball Association was in its infancy, teams had two or three set plays that involved screens. Teams often set double screens to get their top shooters open. They did it so often and became so adept at it that, although defenses knew it was coming, they could do little to stop the shooter from getting open.

Setting the initial screen, however, is only one part of the screening maneuver. The player setting the screen not only has options, but can immediately help the offense in other ways. For example, after the player sets and completes a screen, he should immediately turn and look at the ball handler, stepping back to prepare to receive a return pass. A player can also set a *slip screen*. In essence, this involves faking a screen, stopping for a count of one or two seconds, long enough for the defense to see it. At that point, however, the player releases from the screen and cuts to the basket. This is especially effective when the defense is rushing to double-team the ball handler every time a screen is set. In this case, the screener can release for a return pass that could lead to an easy hoop.

One of the bonuses of a successful screen is that it frees the ball handler to go up for a jump shot.

Once the ball handler passes by, the screener should open up and face the ball immediately. He should never turn his back and should always keep his eyes on the ball. Sealing off the defender gives him the inside lane in which to make a move. But he should always stay within the offense and not go off on his own unless he sees a big opening.

Quick Tips

A good screen can be set almost anywhere on the floor if the situation is right. Many screens are set around the top of the key as the ball handler moves right or left looking for a possible jump shot. But a player can also set a screen down low to the right or left of the basket so that the ball handler can cut to the baseline and drive underneath. He can then go in for the shot or even feed the ball back out to the screener for a quick jump shot. A screen set halfway down the foul lane can give the ball handler a clear line to the hoop. No wonder setting good screens at the right moment can be so helpful to an offensive team.

Working off the Post

In Chapter 11, we described a drill in which a player at the top of the key throws a quick pass to a player standing in the post, and then cuts off of him to the hoop. Several different things can happen on offense once the ball is passed in to a player on the high or low posts. Every player on your team should know how to execute these basic plays, since they are a fundamental part of the offensive game. With the younger kids especially, each player should have a chance to set up in the high post, take a pass, and exercise the various options of taking a shot, driving to the hoop, passing back to the cutter, or throwing the ball out to the wing and himself cutting to the hoop. These are all things that should be done quickly and smoothly.

Almost all teams have plays that work off the pivot. That's why it is very important for each player to know how to play the pivot and know what can happen if he's defending the pivot. If players don't know this basic offensive skill, someone will surely take advantage of them by posting up and running an offensive play. We will talk more about the defensive aspects of posting up in Chapter 14.

Quick Tips

When a player decides to post up, he should take a wide stance with his feet apart for good balance. He should always square his body to the passer. If the defensive player is using his weight to keep the post player from setting up, the post player should lean back into the defender and use his opponent's weight against him. If he does this and makes a quick move either with or without the ball from his posting spot, he might get the defender off balance just long enough to get free. Passes from the post should always be snapped off quickly and decisively.

In addition, a player with the ball in the post should practice his fakes. A quick fake in one direction before passing in another can freeze the defense just long enough to be effective. The post player should also learn to fake with his feet. He can freeze the defensive man, for example, by faking left by dropping his left foot back, and then suddenly turning and dribbling to the right.

You should also set up a series of drills, similar to the one described in Chapter 11, in which the pivot man can practice passing to cutters or kicking the ball back outside. You might also set your pivot man in the low post close to the basket, from where he can practice hook shots, short jumpers, and spinning layups, including an underhand scoop shot. Of course, it's easy doing this with no one playing defense. Have your drills include a defender guarding your post man so that he begins to get the knack of working off a defender. Then he'll have to depend more on fakes and quickness to get the job done.

Remember, a player can post up anywhere on the floor. While most plays are run off the high and low posts, you can also work with your players in other spots so they get the knack of posting up anywhere on the floor where it might help the offense.

Did You Know?

Professional basketball has had a host of top big men who helped their teams by posting up close to the basket. The first was 6-foot, 10-inch George Mikan, widely considered basketball's first great big man. Working with just a six-foot lane, Mikan would post up low, close to the basket, and became adept at hitting short hook shots underneath. Wilt Chamberlain came next. The 7-foot, 1-inch Wilt also loved to post up low, and he had more of a variety of weapons. He would spin inside for a finger roll over the rim or a slam dunk. He also had a turnaround jump shot from down low. Kareem Abdul-Jabbar, a 7-foot, 2-inch star, had one favorite shot, the sky hook. He had a much greater range on his hook shot than Mikan, so he could post up farther away from the hoop, opening the lane for his teammates. And he could hit the sky hook from almost anywhere. These were three great post-up players, all with different moves down low, but all outstanding for their time. That's more evidence of the effectiveness of playing well in the post.

More Tips for Offensive Players

Moving without the ball, setting and using screens, and posting up are all techniques that play a large role in most offensive game plans. All players should eventually learn other maneuvers as well, because they will also become integral parts of many teams' offenses. Many of these are part of the offensive game plan; others just happen in certain situations in which the players have to react by instinct. Let's take a look at some of them.

The Pick (Screen) and Roll

The pick and roll is a relatively simple play that, when executed well, can lead to many easy baskets for an offensive team. Guard John Stockton and forward Karl Malone of the Utah Jazz have run this play successfully countless times during their long NBA careers. The opposition knows it's coming, but the two players are so good at it that it's still difficult to stop.

By definition, the pick and roll is a maneuver in which a player sets a screen (pick) for a teammate with the ball and then cuts away from the defenders toward the basket for a quick pass and hopefully an easy layup. Once again, of course, there are options as with all screening plays. The roll often works best if the defense is caught switching men at the point of the screen or if the ball handler comes off the screen double-teamed by two defenders. That's when the screener can just roll right or left and move quickly to the hoop.

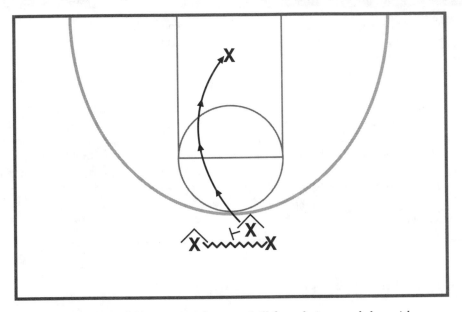

The pick and roll should be practiced first as a drill for technique, and then with defenders to give it a game feeling.

Most pick and rolls are run around the area at the top of the key. They should be practiced right to left, and vice versa. The player with the ball throws a pass to a player across from him, and then cuts inside and sets a screen. The player receiving the pass begins to move behind the screen. Depending on the defense, he can stop for a jump shot, cut off the screen and drive to the hoop, or at some point make a pass.

As soon as the player receiving the pass cuts past the screen, the screener can roll away from the defender and cut down the middle. If he's open, the receiver quickly returns the pass and hopes he can get an easy layup. If the player with the ball drives to the hoop, the screener can roll down behind him and be in position for a rebound or a back pass. But as John Stockton and Karl Malone have proved again and again for well over a decade, the pick and roll can be the road to many easy baskets.

The Back-Door Play

This is another basic offensive maneuver that requires a great deal of quickness, a sharp pass, and perfect timing. In essence, the back-door play occurs when an offensive player cuts away from the defender and moves behind the defense to receive a quick pass while breaking to the basket. The play is most successful when the ball is either outside or at the high post and no offensive player is under the basket, drawing the defense out. That gives the player going back-door the opportunity to sneak in behind the defense for the quick shot. The player going back-door can start from almost any spot on the floor and is usually away from the ball.

The basic play can be practiced with two lines of players at each sideline facing each other just outside the foul line. The player with the ball begins dribbling straight across at the player on the opposite side. That player takes several steps toward him as if he is going to receive a pass but then suddenly breaks to the hoop, in effect going back-door. The player with the ball hits him with a quick bounce pass, which is the most effective pass for this cut. As mentioned earlier, in actual game conditions, the back-door cut can come from almost anywhere if the situation warrants it.

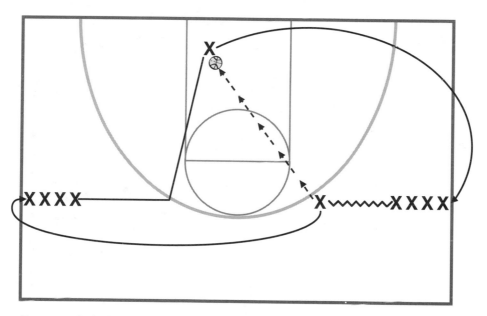

Practicing the back-door play is a solid drill. Its success depends on a quick cut and equally quick pass.

The Give and Go

The give and go is not all that different from the pick and roll or the back-door play. Each of these plays involves a player making a quick cut to the basket and getting a pass underneath. With the give and go, the player making the initial pass is the one who makes the quick cut and receives an immediate return pass from the player to whom she originally passed the ball. In this case, the player making the original pass can take one or two steps away from the ball, to give the defender the feeling she is moving away from the play. Then she makes a quick cut, positioning her body between the defender and the basket, and gets an immediate return pass.

A good drill for give and go practice is to have one line of players at the top of the key and a second line at the sideline even with the foul line on the right side. The player at the top of the key has the ball and passes to the player on the wing who has taken two steps toward him. After making the pass, the player up top takes two steps to the left, away from the play, and then cuts hard down the middle and takes the return pass from the wing player. That wing player then follows the cutter to the hoop for a possible rebound. During games, the give and go can occur from other spots on the floor as well.

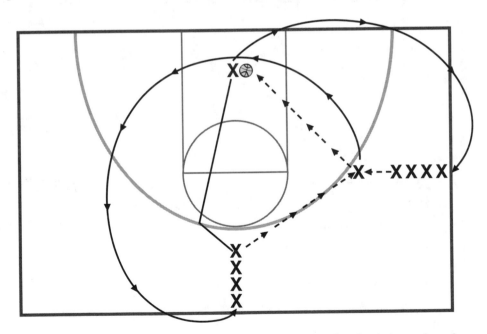

This is a good drill for the basic give and go. It gets players used to the timing and speed of the play.

Quick Tips _____

When a player makes a sharp cut on the basketball court, she is generally trying to take a defender by surprise and beat her to a spot, to either receive a pass or get in position for a rebound. Some players have enough speed to outrun a defender to that spot; however, a player also has to rely on changing speeds. A player ready to make a cut can take two or three steps at half speed, lulling the defender, and then can shift gears immediately to get a step or two ahead of the defender and get open.

Getting Good Shots

In previous chapters, we discussed the proper form of various shots, as well as drills to improve shooting in various game situations. However, once the action starts, it can sometimes be a different story. What seems easy in practice and in scrimmages isn't always easy in the heat of an action-packed game. The best shooter in the world won't be effective if he can't get the good looks and open shots in games.

Some players need help to get their shots, such as teammates setting screens or trying to isolate them on an open side of the floor. Other players have the ability to create shots or get good looks at the basket when there doesn't seem to be an opening. Both types of players can be effective in the right team situation. Of course, all players can do some things to get good shots in the game, apart from simply practicing shots and running drills. They include moving quickly, moving without the ball, faking, knowing how to use screens, displaying aggressiveness, playing a good passing game, and displaying a degree of coolness under fire, which is really a form of concentrating. Let's look at some of the key ingredients needed to get good shots.

Hoop Lingo _____

The simple word **drive** may be one of the most often used in sports, as well as one with the most diverse meanings. A baseball player hitting a ball hard is said to drive it. A long fly ball is a long drive. If a player at bat brings a runner home, he is driving in a run. A football team marching down the field is putting together a drive. A horse and jockey going all out to win a race are driving to the finish line. A driver is the golf club used to hit the ball off the tee. And, of course, in basketball a player taking the ball hard to the basket is driving to the hoop. So it's pretty apparent that in the lingo of sports, most driving has nothing to do with moving motorized vehicles.

Driving to the Basket

Some players have more propensities to drive to the basket than others. It's that way at every level of the game, including the pros. A player driving to the hoop, or "taking the ball into the hole," is looking to get a layup or another high-percentage shot very close to the basket—or at least to get fouled in the attempt. Driving entails moving very quickly past defensive players and often through a small opening while controlling the dribble. Players can drive from anywhere—at the top of the key, at the wing, or along the baseline. Here are some tips for being able to drive effectively:

♦ A player must be able to control the dribble at full speed and also must be adept at the crossover.

♦ A player must be able to *see* the opening in the defense and judge how quickly it will close up.

♦ A player driving to the hoop must be aware that he will sometimes take a hard foul from the defense and may be knocked to the floor.

♦ The driver must have the concentration to complete his move and hopefully make his shot despite the attempts to stop him.

♦ A player driving to the hoop should be able to shoot with either hand.

♦ When driving to the hoop, a player should still be aware of his teammates, in case he has to stop his drive and pass the ball.

♦ A successful drive begins with the offensive player getting his right or left foot and leg past the defender's body as quickly as possible.

A player can start a drive by faking and going around her primary defender, or by outmaneuvering her with a crossover dribble. Or, she can take a pass on the run and immediately begin going to the hole. Sometimes a player is open when she gets a pass. She can take a jumper, but if she sees an open route to the hoop, she can drive since the layup is a much higher-percentage shot than the medium-range or long jumper.

What can go wrong? When a player is driving in heavy traffic, the ball can be slapped away by a defender. If a player is going full speed down the lane and a defender suddenly fills the hole and isn't moving, the driver will be called for a charging foul if he continues into the defender. If a player sees that lane fill, he can always pull up for a short jumper or quick push shot instead of continuing the drive. When a player is driving to the hoop, he should always make an effort to shoot if he feels that he will be fouled by a defender. If he is in the act of shooting when he is fouled, he will be awarded two free throws instead of one.

When a player drives to the hoop, he's got to concentrate and finish his shot despite being surrounded by defenders.

Driving to the hoop can be rough. It's a very physical maneuver because there is usually some contact, with the possibility of a hard foul. In this sense, the player going to the hoop cannot worry about being fouled or even knocked down. Once committed to the drive, a player has to go hard and all out.

The Quick Release

It's one thing to be able to shoot the ball. It's another to be able to shoot quickly. In practice and in drills, a player can take his time to perfect his shooting style and technique. But once the action begins, it's often necessary to get the shot off quickly or risk not getting it off at all. A quick release, with the jump shot and also when the ball is inside in traffic, can often mean the difference between a hoop and a miss. Once again, the passing game becomes part of the shooting game. If a pass comes to an open player below the waist, there is no way he can get a quick release on the jumper. He'll have to move the ball too far. By contrast, if the pass is chest high, the player can almost go up and shoot in one quick motion.

Once players get to know each other as a team, they will also know the best way to deliver the ball to each of their teammates. That always helps. The sooner a player can make a move off a pass, whether it's to dribble, shoot, or pass again, the sooner another player will be open for a shot. A crisp passing game combined with quick shooting is one of the surest ways to make an offense work. Players can work on a quick release in drills that emphasize catching and shooting, and on their own by shooting off the dribble and releasing the ball on drives.

Getting the Jump Shot Off

The jump shot has become the primary offensive weapon in today's game. Some players become so enamored of the shot that they don't even try other offensive moves. There is nothing wrong with having a good jump shot. It can only make a player better. Still, every player should strive to have a well-rounded offensive game. The jump shot remains very important, so here are some do's and don'ts to impress upon your players:

- Players should shoot every jump shot with the same form.

- No player should shoot jump shots from beyond his normal range. This is the distance from the basket in which a player can comfortably reach the basket using his normal form. The normal range increases as players become older and stronger.

- If a player has a clear shot at the hoop from behind a screen, he should take it.

- Players should not force jump shots in heavy traffic. They should look to pass instead.

- Every player should practice different ways to get jump shots, including taking the shot off the dribble and executing the quick catch-and-shoot.

- Players should not take a lower-percentage jump shot if they have a clear path to the basket for a layup.

 Quick Tips

Some younger players don't have the strength to shoot a pure jump shot. Though taking a quick shot still applies, they should shoot the push and release shot described earlier. This shot doesn't encourage the quick shooting techniques of older kids, but it does encourage using the principles involved so it will come more naturally as they develop the pure jump shot.

Players can take their shots in still other ways. If a player catches a pass within range of his jump shot but the defender is upon him, he can fake the dribble or a pass and then step back for the jumper. This is done by taking a quick first step without moving the back foot, or the pivot foot. If the defender takes the fake and also takes a step back or to the side, the shooter can quickly bring his foot back and go up with the jumper. He can also try to freeze the defender by faking a pass, and then quickly step back and go up for the jump shot. Sometimes all it takes is a half step or a defender who freezes for a split second, and a quick player can get the shot.

A quick fake and a quick release can help a player get off a jump shot even when closely guarded on the high post.

A good shooter will also be sure to have total concentration on every shot. Remember, a defender often jumps with the shooter, thrusting his hand in the air—if not to block the shot, at least to distract the shooter. If the shooter hesitates, flinches, or tries to alter his shot, his technique will fall apart and the shot will more than likely miss its mark. The shooter must be able to shut out everything around him, hold his form together, and take the shot the same way he would take it in an empty gym.

Coaching Corner

It is practice that makes shooting natural and instinctive. Once a player has a feel for taking a quick jump shot, he has to be able to take that same shot in scrimmages and games without allowing the defense or the crowd to distract him. This takes confidence and intense concentration, an ability to play within oneself, and shutting out everything else except putting the ball in the basket.

Be Sure to Follow Every Shot

Some players like to admire their handiwork. They take a jump shot, hold the follow-through, as if posing, and then jump up and down in one place as they follow the ball to the hoop. If it goes in, they might raise their fist in the air and then turn and jog up court. What's wrong with this picture? Simple. What if the shot doesn't go in? Then the shooter is standing there posing while the defensive team has the advantage under the boards.

Always impress upon your players that once they take the shot and the ball leaves their hand, they must move on to the next phase of the game. In many cases, this means following their shot toward the basket. By following the shot, the shooter can make several positive things happen for the offensive game. First, if a jump shot hits the back of the rim, it can bounce straight out and over the first line of rebounders. By following the shot, there is always the possibility that the player can get an offensive rebound on a miss. Also, by following the shot, one of the defenders will have to move to box out the shooter, and that could free up one of his teammates for an offensive rebound.

All five players cannot *crash* the boards as soon as a shot goes up. That would leave the offensive team vulnerable to the fast break if a defensive player gets the rebound. Someone should always stay back, but it should be a player away from the ball. The shooter should always follow up for a possible rebound or to get a quick pass from a teammate who gets the ball. There is yet another good reason for the shooter to follow his shot. It is the shooter who often has the best feel or sense of where the shot is going. Once he releases, he often knows almost immediately if the shot has a good chance of going in or whether it might be long or short—and subsequently, where the ball's trajectory will cause it to wind up.

Quick Tips

One way to remind players of the best release point on layups is to tape the floor at practice to show players just where they should release the ball when they drive to the hoop. Soon, they release by instinct just where the tape had been.

Even on layups, players should leave themselves in position for a possible rebound. When driving to the hoop, they should always release the ball before they are past the rim. That way, if the shot comes up short, the driver will have a good chance to get the rebound. If they get too far under the hoop, their shot can hit the rim on the way up. Releasing early enough when they begin will develop good habits that will last much longer and always allow them the first opportunity to follow their own shots.

A Word About the Inbound Pass

When the ball goes out of bounds and is awarded to the offensive team, one of the players has to make an inbound pass. The pass is made from the sideline or end line and is designed to set the offense in motion once more. Most teams have some set formations on an inbound pass, which are discussed in Chapter 17. However, the pass itself is an important part of a team's offense.

Most players use the overhead pass when throwing the ball in. That way, the pass is more likely to clear the hands of the players trying to block or intercept it. Passes should be crisp and accurate. Sometimes an inbound pass will have to be thrown cross-court and at a considerable distance. Players should practice this to make sure they develop the strength and accuracy needed. They will also have to lead receivers who are moving to a spot to get the ball. A poor inbound pass that is intercepted will cause your team to lose the ball. So this, too, is an important part of a player's offensive tools.

The Least You Need to Know

- All of your players should know the importance of moving without the ball if they want the offense to work.

- Basic maneuvers such as setting screens, posting up, and running the pick and roll are important ingredients in every team offense.

- Players should have well-rounded offensive games. It's one thing to have an accurate jump shot, but this talent should be balanced by the ability to drive to the basket.

- Learning to shoot quickly and getting a good shot in tight situations can help both the individual player and his team.

- Don't let players forget the important little things, like following their shots for a possible offensive rebound.

Chapter 14

Basic Defensive Tips

In This Chapter

- ◆ Basic defensive stance and movement
- ◆ Defending on and away from the ball
- ◆ Picks, switches, and double-teams
- ◆ Helpful defensive drills

There's an old saying in basketball that goes something like this: *Offense wins games; defense wins championships!* Of course, nothing is set in stone. Offense doesn't win every game, and defense doesn't win every championship. The point of the saying, however, has a great deal of truth to it. An outstanding basketball team has to play tight, tough, denying defense. If a team cannot stop its opponent on the defensive end, it will have a difficult task trying to win the game.

In this chapter, we discuss the basic defensive techniques that every player should develop. These include knowing how to move, guard an opponent, deal with screens, switch players, and double-team. This chapter also outlines some basic drills that will develop players' defensive skills as well as prepare them for a more complete discussion of the types of defenses and defensive strategies that will follow.

Start with the Stance

There are no secrets when it comes to playing defense on the basketball court. No tricks, no shortcuts, no quick fix. Defense is simply hard work. A player who loafs on defense is a player who is beaten regularly by his offensive counterpart. Yet a player who may not be the best offensive player on his team can become one of the best defensive players—or *the* best defensive player—by virtue of hustle, hard work, aggressiveness, and desire. There is no substitute for these qualities when it comes to defending an opponent or a player's end of the floor.

Did You Know?

Although basketball players have been playing defense since the game's beginnings, one spectacular player really put defense on center stage and showed how it could influence the game. Center Bill Russell joined the Boston Celtics in 1956 after leading the University of San Francisco to a pair of national championships and then playing for the U.S. Olympic Team. Russell's presence in the middle of the Celtics' defense changed the face of the game almost from day one. Russell rebounded, blocked shots, altered other shots just by his very presence, stole passes, started the fast break, and won. He led the Celtics to 11 championships in 13 seasons, a run of titles never duplicated. During that time, Russell solidified his reputation as the greatest defensive player ever, and he and his Boston teammates helped create the axiom that defense wins champion-ships.

All players, even those in the youngest group, have to know and use the basic defensive stance. This hasn't changed over the years. A defensive player should stand with his feet comfortably apart, at least shoulder width, with one foot a short distance in front of the other. The defender should bend at the knees with the weight on the balls of his feet so he can move quickly in any direction. Hands should be kept out to the side, one hand up and one down. The down hand should be the one on the same side that the opponent has the ball, in case he tries to throw a bounce pass. If the opponent swings the ball to the other side, the defender should reverse his hands. A busy defender guarding an aggressive, creative opponent will sometimes seem to be making a windmill motion with his hands.

A young player using the defensive stance for the first time may be tempted to lean forward because he feels that gives him the best chance to steal or slap the ball away from his opponent. This is wrong and could be the most common trap in which young players find themselves caught. If a defender is leaning forward, he simply can't react quickly enough if an offensive player makes a move to dribble to the side or go around him. Because the defender is moving either laterally or backward, he should keep his weight centered and even slightly to the back. Even if the position seems a bit awkward at first, make sure your players stay with it because they will be using it for a long time.

The basic defensive stance never changes. All players should use it, from the youngest age on up.

Guarding a Player One on One

Two basic types of defenses are discussed in Chapter 18: the zone and the man-to-man (or just man) defense. With the zone defense, each defensive player is responsible for an area on the court, guarding whichever offensive player comes into that area. In the man-to-man defense, the defender is responsible for a particular offensive player and follows that player no matter where he goes on the court. In both cases, however, the defender will find himself in situations when he is guarding the player opposite him in a one-on-one situation. Here are five basic rules for a one-on-one defense:

♦ Always stay ahead of the dribbler.

♦ Never lunge at the ball.

♦ Point the ball with the front hand at all times. In other words, keep that hand down low to follow the dribble in case there is an opportunity to poke the ball away.

- When the man you're guarding passes the ball, slide in the direction of the pass at all times.

- Never leave your feet, except when trying to block a shot or a pass, and then only after your opponent has left his feet.

These are rules to live by when guarding a player one on one. Staying ahead of the dribbler means, basically, remaining between the dribbler and the basket. Once the dribbler gets ahead of the defender, he has beaten the defender. Of course, this isn't always an easy task. Some coaches always suggest that defenders play their man very tightly. "Stick to him like glue" is often the instruction given. But a good coach will tell his defensive player to take some other things into consideration when deciding how tight to play an opponent. Much depends on the speed and quickness of both players. If the offensive player is quicker and faster, the defender has to back off a bit so that the dribbler doesn't simply burst past him with his speed. The defender may learn this lesson only after a game has started, but he should learn it fast.

The defender should always have his lead hand down low. That's the hand on the same side the offensive player has the ball. In other words, if the offensive player is dribbling with his right hand, the defender has his left hand down low. The hand should be turned out so it can move quickly to deflect the ball. The opposite, or trailing, hand is up higher and ready to move up or down as the situation dictates. If the dribbler tries to cross over, the defender should quickly move the trailing hand down, to try to disrupt the move.

Quick Tips

Just because a player is defending someone away from the ball doesn't mean she can relax. She has to be ready to move just as quickly as the player defending the ball. The general rule when defending away from the ball is to take a position between the player being guarded and the ball. This is the position that the defender should try to maintain as the offensive player moves without the ball. That player is trying to get free to receive a pass or to break to the basket for a quick pass and shot. If the defender can keep herself between the offensive player and the ball, she'll have a much better chance of denying the ball or stealing a pass.

Remember to tell your players never to lunge at the ball. A good ball handler can avoid a lunge and then quickly beat the defender away from the direction of the lunge. A defender should also never be suckered into leaving his feet. The exceptions are when a defender tries to block a shot or pass. But again, a defender must be careful. He shouldn't leave his feet until the opponent has left his. How many times have you seen a defender leave his feet after the offensive player has faked a jump shot? By the time the defender comes down, the offensive player has taken off past him and is giving the offense a big advantage.

Defenders who jump in the air after a fake will find that the player they're guarding has burst past them.

Defensive Movement

Sometimes defensive players have to sprint up and down the court, to catch up to an offensive player who has gotten away. But most times, defensive players have to move side to side with a shuffling motion, sometimes called a *slide*. It's important that every player be able to execute this defensive slide with a great deal of quickness. If the player is sliding right, he should start with the right foot, sliding it to the side, and then slide his left foot; just as the left foot stops, he should slide the right again. It's almost as if the feet are chasing each other. From the defensive stance, the player should be able to move in any direction quickly using the slide step. The one thing the defensive player should never do is cross one foot in front of the other. This takes away the ability to change direction quickly and can leave the defender tangled up in his own feet.

Players have to be able to move quickly in all directions. If they have to move backward and sideways at the same time, they must use a *drop step*, which is achieved by stepping back with the foot closest to the direction the player is turning, and then sliding the other foot over and continuing the shuffle motion. With practice and with drills, players can learn to make these movements naturally and won't have to think about their feet. They'll be free to concentrate on the offensive player, the ball, and what is happening around them.

A defensive player who crosses his feet one over the other will soon stumble and be beaten by his opponent.

Individual Defensive Situations

Once a player learns the basic defensive stance and movement, as well as how to stick with his offensive counterpart, he will soon have to deal with specific situations on the court. Knowing some little things will make him a better all-around defensive player. You can show your players these different defensive situations gradually, moving from one to another as they improve and begin to understand the entire concept of defense. Let's take a quick look at some of the things a defensive player should know how to do.

Quick Tips

No matter what defensive skill you are teaching your players, never let them lose sight of the key ingredients of a successful defense—hard work, determination, doggedness, hustle, desire, aggressiveness, and more hard work! Defensive players can never loaf. They have to be on top of their games at all times. No matter what the skill level of the individual is, a player is a better defensive player if he gives 100 percent every minute he's on the court. Players who decide to take a break on defense are players who get beaten.

Overplaying Your Man

If a defender is playing his man straight up, he is directly in front of him and waits to react to the moves of his offensive counterpart. But in certain situations, he can look for an advantage by *overplaying* his man. This means the defensive player slides to either the right or the left of the offensive player in an attempt to force him to move in the other direction. There are several reasons for doing this. The defensive man may see one of his teammates just to his right, sliding over a bit and eying the man he is guarding. By overplaying to the left, he is forcing his man to go to the right. The offensive player may think he can beat his defender and may not see the other defender coming over for a *double-team*. If the offensive player falls into the trap, the player who is double-teaming might steal the ball, tie up the ball handler, or force an errant pass.

Stealing the Ball or the Pass

Grand theft basketball isn't a bad thing. In fact, there is no penalty for this kind of thievery—only the reward of a possible basket or game won. Good individual and team defense can often result in the pilfering of a pass at a critical time in the game. Stealing the ball can sometimes discourage and demoralize an offensive team. But it isn't a maneuver that should be taken lightly. If not done correctly, it can result in a foul being called or the defensive player being beaten badly.

Stealing the ball takes good timing and the confidence that the player can recover if he misses the steal attempt. Part of that ability to recover is in the way a player tries to make the steal. As stated earlier, a defensive player should never lunge at his offensive counterpart. This is especially true when trying to steal the ball. A player also should not try to steal the ball by stepping across. In other words, he shouldn't try to reach across his body with his right hand to slap at the ball as the opponent dribbles with his right hand.

The best way to try for a steal is for the defensive player to reach down with his outside hand and try to flick the ball away from the dribbler. If he misses, he should still be balanced in the defensive stance, with his hands in the proper position to continue guarding his man. If he is

Hoop Lingo

When you watch a basketball game on television, you are likely to hear the commentators mention the passing lanes. They might say the defense is shutting down the passing lanes or clogging the passing lanes. Or, they might mention that the offense can't find the passing lane. The **passing lane** is the imaginary line the ball creates when traveling from the passer to the receiver. Obviously, if there is a defensive player in the passing lane, the ball is not going to reach its destination.

successful in flicking it away, then it becomes a race to the ball. If the primary defender doesn't get it, a teammate might. Or two players can get it at the same time for a held ball. Even if the dribbler recovers it, the offense has been disrupted. So a good defender can continually flick at that ball without causing his overall defensive objective to be lost.

Players away from the ball can also make steals. If the dribbler is watching his primary defender, he may not see another defender coming over for a double-team. A defender coming from behind can reach in and flick the ball straight ahead away from the dribbler. This kind of double-teaming defense takes quickness and timing. A player should be pretty sure he can make the steal before he commits, because by trying to make this kind of steal he is leaving another offensive player open.

The correct way to go for the steal is to flick the ball away with the outside hand, without lunging at it.

Swiping the Pass

It takes a good deal of instinct to steal a pass. Sure, there are moments when a defensive player finds herself in the right place at the right time to pick off a pass that probably shouldn't have been thrown. But it's a real skill to be able to anticipate the pass, get into the passing lane quickly, and pick it off. A player guarding a ball handler who stops dribbling now knows a pass is coming. She can rush up very close to her opponent and try to disrupt the pass by waving her arms and staying close to the ball. Or, she can step away and create space in an attempt to anticipate the passing lane and go for the ball.

The space gives her not only time to make a move, but room to step in the direction the ball will also be released. As with stealing off the dribble, the defender should go for the ball with her outside hand leading so there is no contact and no foul. In other words, if the ball handler looks as if she will pass to her right, the defender should step back and then move to the left, with her left hand and left foot in the passing lane. Sometimes just flicking the ball away is as good as grabbing the pass because it disrupts the offensive flow and gives the defense a chance at the loose ball.

Denying the Ball

There is yet another way to disrupt the passing game. Instead of going for the steal, a defender can deny the ball to a potential receiver so the pass is never made. A defender guarding a player without the ball once again has to see the court and the passing lanes. If she thinks her opponent is trying to get in a position to receive a pass, she must position herself toward the ball and very close to the passing lane. The defender should maintain the basic defensive stance, but if the ball is to her right, she should also play her opponent to the right, with at least a hand and a foot in the passing lane. This will put her in a position to step in front of her opponent and grab the pass.

The trick, however, is having total-court vision. If the defender spends just a few extra seconds watching the passer, her opponent can quickly take a couple of steps back, creating a new passing lane and receiving the ball. If that happens, the defender must quickly step up as well and continue guarding her opponent who now has the ball. But by stepping back for the pass, the receiver sometimes takes herself out of shooting range. So once again, the defender has done her job. But it takes practice and instinct to be able to watch everything and to be in the right place at the right time.

The proper body position can sometimes prevent a pass or force the receiver to back up beyond shooting range.

Defending the Post

Denying the ball is another way to defend against an opponent who has posted up. Once an opponent has turned his back and posted up, the defender has two choices. If he wants to deny the ball, he has to play *ball side high*. That means seeing the ball and playing on the side of the post-up man closest to it. If the ball is to the right of the post-up man, the defender should play on his right shoulder and try to get his right arm in front of him. It may take some quick movement to stay ball side high, but if the defender can do that and keep an arm in front of his opponents, offensive players will be a little more reluctant to throw the ball into the post.

A player can also *front* the post, which means he plays between the post man and the ball. This way, if the offense wants to get the ball into the post, the players will have to lob it over the defender's head. This is a more difficult pass; more important, it enables the defender's weakside teammates to help defend the post by possibly intercepting or deflecting the lob pass.

A third way to defend the post is to simply play behind the post-up man and try to force him farther from the basket. Officials will generally allow the post-up player and his defender to lean on one another, as long as neither of them overtly shoves or pushes the other. So strength comes into play because the post-up will frequently try to back closer and closer to the hoop.

Dealing with Screens

A screen is designed to stop a defender in his tracks—or at least free up the player he is guarding for a jump shot or a drive to the hoop. Again, the defender has to make quick decisions, see the court, and then use his quick feet to try to defeat the maneuver. The best way to eliminate any effectiveness of a screen is to fight through it, which means going behind the screen and staying with the dribbler. To do this, the defender has to see the screen early enough and then try to beat the ball handler to the screen. If the ball handler gets there first, he'll try to go by the screener's shoulder, leaving no room for the defender to squeeze through.

If the defender is picked off and has to go behind the screen, the ball handler can step back and shoot a jumper. If this happens, the defender should turn and head for the boards, trying to box out either the screener or the shooter—or both. However, if he doesn't take a shot and the defender is caught behind the screen, he should watch for the ball handler coming out. The defender doesn't want to get caught in a switch where the offense has created a mismatch. In other words, if the ball handler comes out too quickly and the defender can't stay with him, he'll have to shout "Switch!"

Another teammate will have to take the ball handler, and the defender who is screened will have to guard the screener, who may be a lot taller and can then take the defender down low to the hoop.

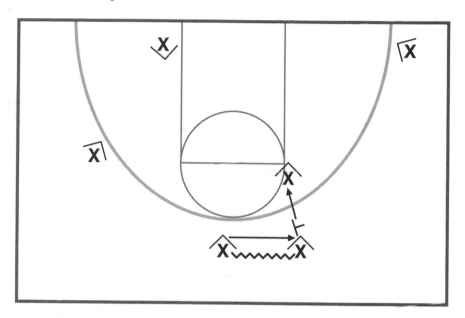

If the defender can get to the screener first, he will have an excellent chance of sticking with his man.

If the defender doesn't see the screen until the last second, he may commit a foul by running into the screener. If not, he again has to call for a switch because he won't be able to catch up to his man. If this happens, the screen has done its job and the defender has effectively been picked off.

Quick Tips

Tell your players to think of the letter *L* when they are guarding an opponent—one hand is kept down, and the other is up higher. In other words, if a right-handed opponent has the ball at his chest and seems to be ready to pass, the defender's left hand goes up and the right hand goes down. Instead of passing, if the opponent brings the ball down to dribble, the defender's left hand goes down and the right hand comes up.

In situations when the defender is picked off and has to switch, he is forced to defend the screener. Mismatch or not, the defender has to stay with the screener, using the same principles of defense already discussed. However, he also has to be cognizant that the screener may roll to the basket to complete a pick-and-roll play. If the screener begins rolling to the hoop, the defender can try to stay in front of him to prevent a pass down low. If he can't do that, he has to get behind him and use the post-up type of defense.

Blocking Shots

Many young players don't think they can block shots. After all, when they watch basketball on television, it always seems as if the shot blockers are 7-foot-tall centers. A smaller man goes in close to the hoop and, when he tries to shoot, a player 5 or 6 inches taller sweeps into the air and swats the shot away. Sure, that happens. But among young players, with most boys and girls close to the same size, it is certainly possible for a player to block another's shot at almost any point on the court.

Young players can block shots in several ways. As with older players, blocking a shot takes instinct and timing. Done improperly, the player can easily commit a foul or, if he goes in the air after an opponent who fakes a shot, can be beaten on the dribble. One way for young players to block a shot is to get the ball as the offensive man is swinging it up to shoot. To do this, the player has to watch the ball carefully. If he sees the offensive man begin to raise it as if he's going up with a shot, the player can step forward and try to slap the ball on the way up with his raised hand. Just remind your players that if they try this and slap the offensive player on the hand or arm, they will be called for a foul.

Did You Know?

The NBA has had many great shot blockers. At the collegiate and professional levels, the best are usually the big guys. Many players today feel that the harder they swat away a shot, the better and more intimidating it looks. A player who blocks a shot and sends the ball into the fifth row of the stands usually gets the oooohs and aaaahs from the crowd. But some of these power blockers should take a lesson from Bill Russell. The great Boston Celtics center was not only a superb shot blocker, but more often than not he tipped the blocked shot to a teammate, enabling Boston to run its devastating fast break. Sometimes Russell's blocks were 3-foot taps instead of 25-foot slams. But they always had a purpose, with the end result being another Celtics victory.

It takes even better timing to leap in the air and get the ball as the offensive player releases it toward the basket. To do this, the defender has to establish a jumping plane about 2 feet away from his opponent. That way, he won't jump into him and commit a foul. He also cannot fall for a fake and leave his feet. So he has to be certain that his opponent is going up for a jump shot. Then he can go up to try to block it. Even if a player doesn't block the shot, his effort might not be in vain. By just getting his hand close to the ball, he may distract his opponent enough to alter the shot. If he doesn't make the block, he should first box out the shooter and then turn and follow the shot.

It takes good timing to step in and block an opponent's shot before he releases the ball.

The Run-By

The final way a young player can try to block a shot is with the run-by. This entails running at the offensive player from the side and trying to slap the ball. This technique can be used if an open man gets the ball and starts to shoot. If the defender is close enough, he can try to run past and get the shot on the way up. Because he is running quickly to get to the shooter, the defender cannot jump in the air because his momentum will take him right into the shooter. By running past the shooter, the defender has a chance to leave his feet and reach for the ball from the side and block the shot without fouling. When it comes to shot blocking, always remind your players that if they foul a player in the act of shooting, that player receives two free throws (or three if he happens to be behind the three-point arc). Players should be confident when they make a move and should practice their blocking techniques to minimize the chances of a foul.

Time to Run Some Drills

Once again, drills become an important part of learning individual skills. A number of good, solid drills can make your players better defensively.

Stance and Stand

This is a very basic drill designed for the youngest kids. Its purpose is simply to get them used to the basic defensive stance. This can be done with your entire team at once. Have everyone standing on the court, with space in between player. At the command "Stance!" each player drops into the defensive stance, with the legs spread, arms out, and knees bent, as described earlier in the chapter. Let the players hold the stance for a few seconds, and then give them the command "Stand!" They can stand up straight and relax. Then repeat the two commands. This will get them used to assuming the defensive stance quickly at any time.

The Basic Slide Step

In its simplest form, the slide step is a good drill for young players, getting them used to the shuffle, or slide step, needed to play effective defense. Line up your players with plenty of space between them. Again, have them assume the defensive stance on command; then give the command "Slide!" They should take just two steps left, stop in the defensive stance, and then slide two steps right, stopping again. Once they all get it, you can begin to add variations that will allow them to move in all directions as well as at an angle, up and down. This gets them ready to move around the court in the defensive stance using the slide step.

One variation that can be used for all age levels is to have the players slide from side to side, from one foul lane to the next. Ask them to go as fast as possible, for a drill that will get them used to moving very quickly and changing directions in a flash. Eventually, especially with the older players, you can have them slide from one side of the foul lane to the sideline and back, eventually from sideline to sideline and up and down the court. When it becomes full court, it is known as the "zig zag" drill. Now you are not only working your team with the slide step and defensive stance, but you are getting them in game condition as well.

One-on-One Movement

This drill involves both an offensive and a defensive player. The main objective is to work on defensive movement. It can be done with three lines across the court, with three defensive players and three offensive players. The first time you run it, have the defensive players hold their hands behind their backs. The offensive players dribble toward the defenders and then move in one direction and back again at a slow pace. The defenders must stay in front of them just using their footwork, quickness, and speed. They should assume the defensive stance, with the exception of holding their hands behind their backs. Give your players a chance to play both the defensive and offensive roles.

This is a drill that can be embellished and made more inclusive as the players improve or with older age groups. For example, the next level frees the hands of the defensive players. Using the same three lines, players can now work both their hands and feet as the offensive players dribble at them. Now the defenders can get the knack of moving their hands as the dribblers cross over and go side to side. At the same time, because the defenders can now use their hands to swipe at the ball, the offensive players get practice with their crossover moves and dribbling skills, since they now have to protect the basketball. This is a drill that can be walked through at first, then jogged at half speed, and finally run at full speed, depending on the age and skill of the players involved.

Coaching Corner

Offensive players can cross over when coming up the court and when making quick cuts. In other words, one foot can go in front of the other as they break to one side. But crossing the feet is an absolute no-no for defensive players. If a defender crosses his feet, a good offensive player will leave him in the dust. When a defender has to change direction moving laterally or backward at an angle, he has to use what is known as the drop step. By using the drop step, the defender can turn his body while continuing to slide. This is done by dropping the back foot on the side to which the player wants to turn. In other words, if the dribbler is going hard right and starts to get the angle, the defender can turn his body by dropping his left foot back and then sliding the right foot over so he can either drop again or start to slide at a different angle. Like other defensive maneuvers, the drop step has to be done quickly and smoothly so that the defender doesn't lose any speed. In a nutshell, the drop step is to defense what the crossover step is to offense. Demonstrate the difference to your players.

Help and Recover

This basic drill begins as a one-on-one drill but can be expanded to include more players in various sets. It is a drill to see how quickly a defender can recover from being out of position and beat the offensive man to a spot. Start the defender just inside the middle point of the foul line. The offensive player is outside the foul line, a couple of feet behind the defender. At the whistle, the defensive player passes the ball to the offensive player on the wing. The offensive player immediately angles for the hoop. The defender has to slide over and try to cut him off before he can get a layup. Again, quickness is the key. The defender has to be under control: If he angles over too quickly, the offensive player can cross over and go inside him to the hoop. The object is for the defender to move the offensive player out of the lane. He shouldn't just try to cut him off and take a charge; instead, the defender should try to play him and force him off his angle and back outside.

One variation that makes it even more difficult for the defender is to put a pair of offensive players on each wing, with the defender in the middle. Now the offensive players have the option of passing to each other as they go for the hoop. The defender must try to fill the passing lane at the right time, force one of the offensive players off his dribble so he doesn't make an easy pass, or go for the player who finally tries to take the layup. This is a much more difficult drill for a defender, since a two-on-one, executed correctly, should win the battle most of the time. But it's still a great drill for players to practice quickness and anticipation.

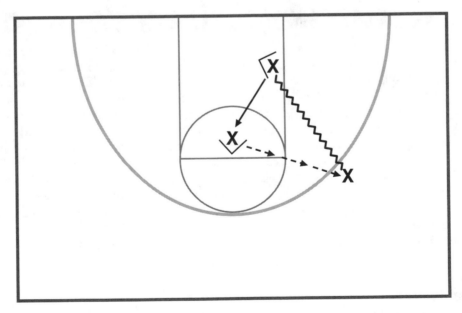

This drill allows the defender to beat the opponent to a spot on the court and force her away from the hoop.

Fighting the Screen

To get your players used to dealing with screens, just set up a ball handler, defender, and screener. But don't have the screener set up at the same spot every time. It's up to the defensive man to spot the screen and act accordingly. If he can get there first, he can go behind or over the screen and stay with his man. If the ball handler is able to dribble right off the screener's shoulder, the defender will have to go around the screen, which is what he doesn't want to do in games. The skill comes in spotting the screen early enough or being aware of it by a teammate calling it out—and then having the speed to get there first.

Dealing with screens takes practice. The defender won't win all the time. Offenses should practice setting them quickly and efficiently, and ball handlers should practice getting there first. But the defense always has to be ready since this is another integral part of the game.

These are but a few of the drills a coach can learn and devise for his team. We have talked about defending plays such as the pick and roll and the give and go. By running drills, you will sharpen your players' reactions and timing and better prepare them for the actual games. By way of review, here again are some of the important principles of defense, when defending players without the ball and then defending on the ball.

Defending Away from the Ball

Defending a player who doesn't have possession of the ball is just as important as defending the player with the ball. When teaching your players how to play defense when their offensive counterpart doesn't have the ball (in a zone or man-to-man defense), use these guidelines:

- The defender should maintain his position between the offensive player and the ball and should try to close the passing lane as long as he has help to cover the back door.

- The defender should keep the ball and man in sight at all times.

- Defensive players should always challenge their man's ability to receive a pass, in order to force him into a deeper area of the floor, diminishing the chance of a good, quick shot.

Quick Tips

Communication on the court is extremely important, especially for the defense. Defenders should call out when a screen is set, alert teammates who may have lost track of the basketball, and call out for help if they lose their man. Any help a player can give a teammate verbally will help the overall defensive effort.

♦ Defenders should always be ready to intercept a weak or *soft* pass, or at least get a hand on the ball.

♦ A defensive player must always be ready to pick up any open man if there is a chance that the offensive player will score.

♦ If a defender is away from the ball, on the *weakside*, he should drop into the middle and look to help teammates who are overplaying their men.

♦ When a defender is on the weakside, away from the ball, and sees his teammates double-teaming, he should look to zone an area of the floor and be ready to intercept the weak pass.

♦ Defenders should always be talking on the court, alerting teammates where the screens are and where the ball is if they need help.

♦ All defenders should be ready to step in and draw the offensive foul on a driver or cutter by getting good position early and not moving their feet.

Defending on the Ball

When teaching your players how to defend the player with ball, use these guidelines:

♦ A defender should never give up the baseline to a player she is guarding. Always force the drive to the middle, where there is likely to be help.

♦ Defenders should maintain pressure and position on their offensive counterpart until the player gives up the dribble.

♦ A defensive player should try to force the opponent into a difficult passing position, or try to force her to pass in a direction opposite to what she prefers.

♦ Defenders should always try to slide over the top of a screen and beat the dribbler to the screen.

♦ If a defender is screened, she should spin or reverse herself and try to get between the player who screened her and the ball, to prevent a return pass to the screener on a pick and roll.

♦ Defenders should always try to force their opponent into dribbling the ball to their weaker side, especially in the midcourt area or in the corners, since these are good areas for a double-team and a possible steal.

♦ Defenders should switch (change the players they are guarding) only as a last resort. But if it is necessary, they should switch quickly and decisively.

Playing defense is both simple and complex. It's simple in that once a player has learned the basic skills and techniques, hard work and desire can make her a good defensive player. Yet defense can be complex in the team sense. Whether a team is playing zone or man-to-man, a good team defense hinges on the players working together, melding their skills, and communicating on the court. If they can coordinate all of that and if everyone has the same work ethic, then the team will be praised by all for playing a tough "D."

The Least You Need to Know

- ◆ Good defensive play means learning the fundamentals, including the correct stance as well as both feet and hand movement.

- ◆ Defensive players must guard not only players with the ball, but also players who do not have the ball.

- ◆ A defensive player must know how to react to each offensive technique, such as screens, pick and rolls, and post-up plays.

- ◆ Quickness, combined with timing and instinct, is the key to stealing the ball or the pass and blocking shots.

- ◆ All the skill and defensive techniques are nothing if defensive players don't hustle and work hard every minute they are on the floor.

15

Types of Offenses

In This Chapter

◆ Let's talk offenses

◆ The passing game style of offense

◆ Running the offense

◆ Variations with different sets

There has to be structure to the game of basketball. Even with the youngest kids, a coach cannot let them go out on the court and just run around helter-skelter. After your players learn the basic fundamentals, you must still teach them how to apply their knowledge in a team situation. This means that you have to design an offense for them. It shouldn't be something too complex for their ability or an offense that requires too much specialization in the positions and roles of the individual players.

In this chapter, we present several variations of a basic offense that can work well for young kids learning the game. These offenses are designed to allow all the players to become involved and for everyone to experience playing the different positions on the basketball court. Yet at the same time, there are opportunities for the more talented players to get creative and improve their games, and for all the players to use the various fundamentals they have learned and practiced. As a coach, you will be able to tailor this offense to the talents on your team. Hopefully, the information provided here will create a framework upon which each coach can build an offense in which his team will flourish.

A Quick Look at Offenses

Various kinds of offenses are run by most basketball teams today. Some can be described as *set play offenses*, in which there is an exact position for every player on the floor. Because these offenses run a series of set plays, everyone has to know their roles for each of the plays and, for it to work, must carry out those roles to perfection. The second type of offenses are *pattern offenses*, which are based on repetition. Players run a repeating pattern over and over again, such as a three- or five-man weave, trying to get someone open for a shot. The third basic offense is the *motion*, or *passing-type offense*. This is a read-and-react offense that depends more on the initiative of the offensive players, and it will accommodate different levels of defense.

Four forms of the motion offense are presented in this chapter. We feel that the motion offense is the best type of offense to run in youth basketball. All age groups can run a form of motion offense, which also allows players to pick up the principles of offense while applying the fundamentals they have already learned or are in the process of learning. In these offenses, everyone on the floor has a sense of structure. At the same time, the motion offense strategies provide initiatives for the more talented players. This also allows players to have a chance to try each position.

Fact of the Game

In the very early days of the game, players had a difficult time dribbling a ball that was always out of shape and had raised laces. So they developed an offense based on both player and ball movement. They created a sharp passing game in which all the players (about the same size back then) played all the positions on the court. Soon, when a couple of early big men arrived, the pivot or post play developed, becoming just another addition to the crisp passing and movement game they continued to play. If the style of that game sounds familiar, it should be: It was very similar to the type of game being suggested for young players today.

There are certainly positive values in the other types of offenses. But the overall purpose of presenting these motion and passing offenses is to help younger players get a feel for the offensive game, or a "sixth sense" for reading the defense and knowing where they should be on the court. This is the best overall way to go at these age levels. The basic rules and principles are the same for all four offenses. First we look at the overall techniques used in the offenses; then we look at the offenses themselves.

The Principles of the Motion Offense

The four variations of the motion offense that are presented in this chapter differ slightly in the way they are set up and run. As you'll see, you have to choose which is best for your team—and you will base that choice on the abilities of your individual players. However, no matter which offense you choose to run, you'll find that the basic premise is the same. The offenses feature crisp passing, continual movement, and a chance for your players to utilize the individual skills you have been teaching them in practice and through drills. Let's begin with some of the basic tenets of the offense.

A crisp passing game is a must in the motion offense. Good players can sometimes pass the ball without looking at the receiver.

The following are common to the offenses presented here. As you go through this outline, you'll begin to see why these offenses are so good for young players:

- A player must move every time he makes a pass.

- The player must move with a purpose: to get open for a shot or to receive a pass, or to set a screen to get a teammate open.

- Players should be patient and should make simple passes.

- The player receiving the pass should be in the triple-threat position: knees bent, with one hand near the top of the ball and the other beneath it; and with the weight forward on the balls of the feet so the player can quickly dribble, pass, or shoot.

- Players should always try to receive the ball in an area on the court where they will be a threat to shoot or drive to the basket.

- The dribble should be used to advance the ball quickly out of the backcourt, to make a drive to the basket, or to open a passing lane.

- The team should quickly swing the ball around to make the defense shift.

- The team should make at least four passes before a shot is taken unless the ball enters the post area.

- One in every three passes should go to the post.

- A player shouldn't fight defensive pressure. Instead, the player should go "back door" or screen for a teammate.

- The players should keep the proper spacing and floor balance.

- All players are responsible for rebounding and defense.

Quick Tips

You can put up one overriding rule in capital letters when it comes to the motion offenses. The rule is simple: DO NOT STAND STILL! Because these are motion offenses, all players must also be in shape. So if you are going to use the offenses described here, make sure your team is in tip-top physical condition. Players who are out of shape will not be able to keep up with others when running the motion offense and will have no choice but to violate the cardinal rule—the one that says, DO NOT STAND STILL!

You should be able to see the virtues of these offenses immediately. The basic rules show the emphasis on a strong, quick passing game, with both ball and player movement. It's far from a run-and-gun, freelance offense that kids would probably enjoy more but that wouldn't give them a real taste of the game. This type of offense does, yet at the same time it provides opportunities for the more talented players. The offense also requires players to think on the court. They simply cannot go through a repetitive motion as if they were robots.

Think about these principles. Each one makes your players better because they are now involved in a true team concept. They're not running down the court and watching the star player take a long jump shot. The two or three weaker players aren't standing around while the better players work together looking for a score. Not only does everyone have a role, but they also must understand those roles and follow the basic offensive rules.

Players in the motion offense should take a shot when the opportunity is there.

Let's Check Out Some Specifics

Now that we have looked at the general rules for the motion offense, let's check out some of the specifics—notably post and perimeter play—and the general rules for screening, which plays a large role in all these offenses.

Once again, note that these general rules apply to all the specific offenses we suggest for young players.

Perimeter Play

Players on the perimeter, outside and away from the hoop, are just as important to the motion offense as those playing close to the basket on the inside. Since players often change positions in the offense, it's important for everyone to know what to do, no matter where they are on the court.

Cutting is a big part of the motion offense. A player, however, should not make two consecutive cuts in the same direction. If he changes direction, he will be much more difficult to defend and have a better chance to get open to receive a pass or take a shot.

The following basic rules will give your players a good offensive background for perimeter play:

- As soon as a player passes the ball, he should immediately do one of the following:

  1. Cut to the basket.

  2. Screen away, which means screening for another player away from the ball.

  3. Set a vertical screen going down low, or a rear screen coming up to the foul line.

  4. Replace an open designated spot on the court.

  5. Make a cut off the post.

- Players should maintain spacing of about 15 to 18 feet. The youngest kids can use spacing of about 10 to 12 feet, and the middle group can use spacing of 12 to 15 feet.

- Players should cut to the post areas when they are vacant.

- When the ball is passed to a post player, the passer should either screen the closest defender or slide to an open area, in the event of a double-team.

- When a player is without the ball, he should do one of the following:

  1. Look to move to the ball to receive a pass.

  2. Keep moving. Never stand in one position for more than two seconds.

  3. If possible, set a screen away from the ball.

  4. When overplayed as a receiver, go back door or screen away.

  5. When a teammate dribbling the ball approaches, slide on the perimeter or go to the basket.

  6. Look to use the low post as a screen to lose the defender and then move quickly away from the post for a quick shot.

Once again, you can see the passing, cutting, and screening that is at the heart of the motion offense. No one stands still. Players must move, set screens, cut to the hoop, look to go back door, and maintain their spacing so that two or three players don't get jammed up. No one player should be on the perimeter for too long, but all players have to know what to do when they are on the outside perimeter.

The Inside Game or Playing the Post

Because all players should move in and out of the high and low posts, the entire team should learn the principles of post play in the motion offenses. Once again, a number of general rules apply to each form of the offense:

- ◆ A player may be designated to always stay in the post area. This applies if you have a dominant post player or an excellent rebounder.

- ◆ As noted previously, everyone on the team is expected to play the post.

- ◆ The high post sets up on the side with the ball, while the low post always stays weakside, or away from the ball.

- ◆ When a player on the high post receives the ball, he should always look low toward the basket and then to the weakside of the court.

- ◆ When a player receives the ball in the low post, he should ...

    1. Look to score.

    2. Look for the high post breaking down the lane.

    3. Look to quickly pass the ball back out to the perimeter.

- ◆ On a pass to the high post, the low post should flash across the pivot.

- ◆ On the swing pass to the high post, the passer should break to the ball side of the low post.

- ◆ When the high post is vacant, the nearest player should move into it.

- ◆ The player moving into the high post should hold for a slow count of two and then ...

    1. Slide down low on the ball side and allow another player to replace him.

    2. Screen for the player in the low post.

    3. Step out and screen for a perimeter player.

- ◆ A player in the low post can do the following:

    1. Fill the vacant high post.

    2. Step out to the perimeter for a pass.

    3. Set a horizontal screen.

Obviously, you cannot state these rules or give your kids a copy of them and expect them to learn them without practice and demonstration. These rules should unfold as you begin to run the offense. You'll have to start by walking through the movement of the ball and the rules of the offense, and then pick up the pace. By showing your players where they have to be and where they have to go, and by reminding them as they begin to run the offense, they'll begin to learn most of the rules without realizing it. Passing and movement should become second nature so that the team can run the offense automatically.

However, these aren't the set play offenses that we mentioned earlier. Your players will have to think when they are on the court, watch their teammates carefully, and continually make decisions about where they will go next and what role they will play. In addition, they will have to be ready to go to the boards and rebound, and to make the transition to defense in a split second. So an effective offense won't happen overnight. Learning an offense takes time and practice. But with these offenses, none of the players get left out.

Coaching Corner

The constant movement and cutting needed to run the motion offense is going to sound confusing to many young players at first. As mentioned, you will have to walk them through it slowly, at first, until everyone knows his role. However, it also might help if you can show your team this offense in action. Perhaps you can obtain a tape of a team that uses it. Or you can go to a local high school or college game if the team uses a form of the offense. And if you're really lucky, you might find some older players who can come to a practice and demonstrate it for your team. None of this is an absolute necessity, but if your players can see the offense in action, they may get a sense of it that will make them learn it a little more quickly and easily.

Running the Basic Offense

The motion offense, including the different variations, is based on players rotating and always filling empty areas on the court. There are no set plays. The offense is based on teamwork and following the basic rules that were outlined earlier. Executed correctly, the motion offense is effective and difficult to defend. One of the most important aspects of this offense, however basic, is making sure all your players can both set and use screens effectively. In addition, players will eventually find themselves stationed at all positions on the court.

The basic motion offense, also called the high/low motion, has the team set up with a player on the high post by the foul line and another on the low post on the opposite side of the lane. The ball handler is on the perimeter in the middle and has two wings, one on the left and the other on the right. Once set up, players immediately begin moving, and the movement is dictated by the direction of the first pass. The principles described next apply to all variations—the high/low motion, triangle, box high, and box low (shell)—with the only changes being in the way the players are positioned. Positioning is determined by the talents and the size of the group of players you are coaching. Okay, let's begin running the offense.

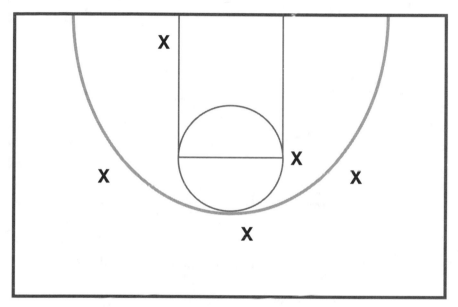

The motion or high/low motion offense begins with two players in the post and three on the perimeter.

If the first pass goes from the point guard to the high post, the low-post player breaks into the lane and tries to seal off his defender. If he can't get open, the low-post man continues through the lane and screens for the strongside wing (on the right side). At the same time, the weakside wing sets a back screen, and the point guard goes behind him and either cuts to the basket or into the corner.

If the high-post player still has the ball and the low-post player has gone through the lane to screen the strongside wing, then the weakside wing comes up so he is parallel to the foul line. He can set a back screen for the point guard, who either cuts to the basket for a possible return pass and layup or fades to the corner. The post man can either shoot a jump shot or drive to the left side of the lane, which is now cleared out. His other options are to pass to the low-post player or the strongside wing cutting off the low post. A third option is to pass to the point guard if he has faded to the opposite corner, and then cut down the lane for a return pass on a give and go. If he doesn't get the ball back, he can then set up on the low post.

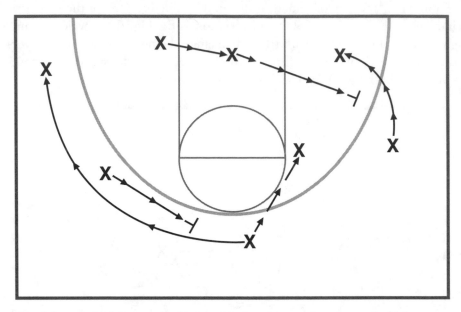

Here's how the high/low motion begins with the point guard passing to the high post.

If the high post throws to the corner and cuts to the basket, the strongside wing would then break up to the high post. You would then have a wing playing the high post and the original low-post player on the strongside wing. The original high-post player is now in the low post, while the original point guard is now on the weakside wing, and the original weakside wing is at the top of the key playing the point guard.

Nobody is standing still, and all the players are moving into different positions as the offense stays in constant motion.

More Options

Okay, let's reset the formation and look at some options. This time, instead of throwing the ball to the high post, the point guard can look for the weakside wing to cut to back door to the basket if he's overplayed. If he passes to the weakside wing without the cut, the point guard can then screen for the strongside wing or cut off the post to the basket. So, he is again following one of the general rules—to pass and screen away from the ball, or pass and cut to the basket.

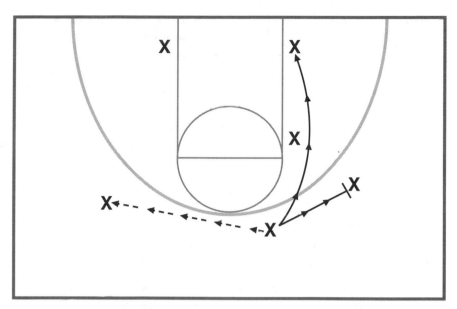

Following the general rules of the offense, the point guard passes to the weakside and screens away from the ball.

If the point guard cuts to the basket after passing to the weakside wing and doesn't get a return pass, he clears out into the left corner. Now a side triangle has been formed with the weakside wing, the point guard, and the high-post player on the same side of the floor. If the point guard breaks to the corner as described, the high post can step out above the post to receive a pass from the weakside wing, who then turns and screens down for the point guard.

Another option once the weakside wing has the ball is for the high-post man not to step out but instead to move down and screen for the low post. At this point, you can have a post exchange. The low post can come up to the foul line to receive a pass and perhaps shoot, or he can pass it back to the original high-post man, who went down low and now can pivot from the low post and catch the ball in the paint.

The final option from the original set is for the point guard to pass to the strongside wing, who is on the same side as the high post. As soon as the wing catches the ball, he has the option to drive the baseline, if it's open. If he's picked up by a defender, there should be an open low-post man on the opposite side to whom he can pass. If the high-post defender has come down to guard the low post, he can throw the ball back to the high post.

If the high-post man doesn't get the ball, he can come down and set a diagonal screen for the low-post man who breaks up from the opposite side. He should set this screen in the middle of the three-second area two steps inside the foul line. When the low

Quick Tips

When setting a down screen, the screener's back should be toward the ball. However, when setting a back screen, the screener's back should be toward the basket.

post cuts off his left shoulder coming up, the high-post man can plant his right foot and spin, sealing his man by posting up the defender in front of the basket. The wing now has the option of throwing to the low or high post, who are both on the same side. The two players on the weakside, away from the ball, continually exchange positions and set screens. That way, the high post can quickly reverse the ball to the weakside.

What About the Side Triangle?

After the initial move in the high/low passing series, you may have a side triangle on the right side of the floor with the two post players and the wing. In this scenario, players can run a side triangle offense or continue to run the motion.

The side triangle features exchanges between the two posts and the wing. If the wing has the ball facing the two posts, he has the option of passing to the player in the high post. As the high-post player receives the ball, the wing screens down for the low post. If the high post cannot get open for the pass, he can go down and screen for the low post, who can come up behind him to get the ball. As this is happening, the two players on the weakside keep exchanging. Players in the triangle always have to be ready to reverse the ball to the weakside; then they can set up the triangle again or run the motion offense from that side.

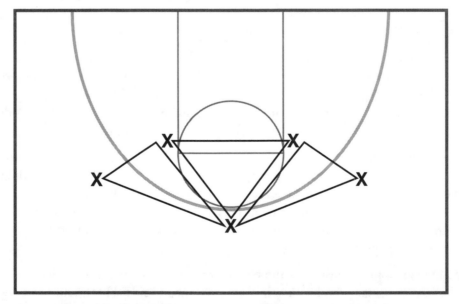

The side triangle features two post players and a wing on the same side of the court.

Running It as Box High or Box Low (Shell)

In both the box high and the box low (shell) formations, players are simply passing and replacing, and cutting and replacing. If you are running box high and the high post receives the ball, the other four players screen for each other, setting a screen on each side and making a back-door cut if they are overplayed.

With the box high offense, a wing cannot drive the baseline without some help because there is no low post. Usually a player drives to the outside with this offense. The team has to keep the four boxes (positions) filled. The post man can break to the basket whenever he feels he can get open. When the ball is on the wing, for example, the post man can try to beat his defender to the basket. If the post man passes to the wing and cuts to the basket, the wing man can't drive because the post player is now in the way. Once a player goes through in this offense and doesn't get the ball down low, he then goes to the opposite side. You almost have a kind of clocklike rotation. Everybody bumps a spot, with the one constant being the high post.

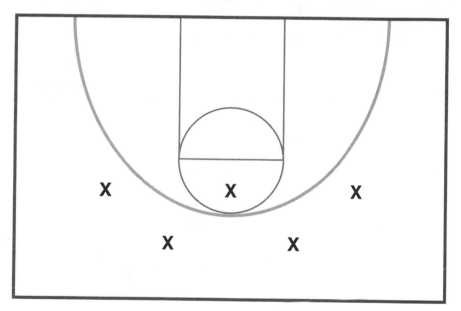

The box high variation begins with one player on the high post and the others forming a box around him.

For example, if the guard up top has the ball and can't pass it to the wing, he can dribble it in that direction and affect the exchange that way. This type of offense is suited for a team that's small and quick, and looking to get people one on one with speed mismatches. As with any of the variations of the offense, the high post can come out and screen the wing above the key to set up the pick and roll.

The difference in the shell, or low box, is that a player is constantly in the low post. It can be the same player if you have a big kid on your team who plays the position exceptionally well, or you can interchange as with the box high. Either way, these are continuity offenses in which you are replacing people in all the sets. Although the players keep repeating themselves, to a degree, it isn't exact repetition, like a weave. Players should stay within the general rules while trying to continually create openings. Once there is an opening, a player must take advantage of it by driving to the basket or shooting.

Why These Are Great Youth Basketball Offenses

These motion offenses with their variations work well for all age groups. They keep players moving and thinking, force everyone to know all the positions, and allow players to sharpen their passing, screening, and cutting. And, of course, everyone learns to take advantage of openings by trying to score. While the general rules call for four passes, you should give your players the latitude to take an open shot, even if it is there immediately and the requisite passes haven't been made. But without the opening, the crisp passes combined with movement and screening should open someone up for a good shot.

Did You Know?

In the movie *Hoosiers*, which is about a high school basketball team in the early 1950s, the coach also emphasizes four passes before a shot is taken. In fact, when he is teaching the offense, he insists on it. It is a form of the motion offense used a half-century ago, which shows how basic this offense has been to basketball. In addition, by making four passes, the players learn patience, keeping their emotions in check and not just running down the court and shooting immediately.

The one skill that is not emphasized in the context of this offense is dribbling. In all the offensive variations, dribbling should be kept to a minimum. The dribble can be used to go to the basket or create a better passing lane, but no one player should take off to dribble all over the floor. Dribbling can be used to get a player out of trouble, to reset the floor, to drive, or to take the place of passing when a pass cannot be made. Players should use their dribbling skills when bringing the ball upcourt, in fast-break situations, for breaking a defensive press, and in other special situations. But dribbling simply should not be a major part of the motion offense.

Coaches should continually go over all the options for the offense in practice. Answer the questions. Walk through the various options, then jog through them, and finally run through them. Also, remember that defense will sometimes dictate which options will work and which won't. Do everything you can to make sure your players are ready, by having them practice with defensive players guarding them.

Finally, give positive reinforcement and don't give up on your slower players. If you keep at it long enough, you'll find that most players will "get it" and enjoy it. These offenses don't feature a star system or showcase just one or two players. That's why they are a perfect way to introduce the game and the things that have to be done at the offensive end of the floor.

The Least You Need to Know

- ◆ The motion or passing offense is an excellent way to show young players the entire offensive game.

- ◆ Teach your players the general rules of the offense, as well as the rules to play the perimeter and the post.

- ◆ Use whichever variation of the motion offense—the triangle, box high, or box low—you feel best suits the talents of your individual players.

- ◆ Remind your players that the dribble is the last option in this offense and that anyone who tries to dribble around the court will disrupt the entire offense.

- ◆ Always post the one cardinal rule of the motion offense for everyone to see: DO NOT STAND STILL!

Chapter 16

Types of Defenses

In This Chapter

- Zone versus man-to-man
- Teaching the man-to-man defense
- Dealing with matchups
- Types of zone defenses

Now it's on to defense, something many young players might not want to hear about at first. In their first experiences with basketball, most kids just want to put the ball in the hoop. That's the initial challenge and the fun. The hero is the player making that last-second shot and getting carried off the court on the shoulders of his teammates. Defense? Ugh. Defense is boring. Defense isn't fun. Defense doesn't make heroes. Defense is all work with no rewards. These are some of the common views of young players—and older players as well. One of the first things a coach must do when he greets a new team is to point out the importance of defense. Though it's not glamorous in the traditional sense of the word, good defense can simply win a lot of basketball games.

In this chapter, we talk about the basic defenses used in basketball. There are just two: the man-to-man defense and the zone defense. However, there are variations of both. Some are discussed here, and others are covered in Chapter 18, on defensive strategies. Often, the type of defense a team uses depends on matchups—the individual abilities of your players versus the opponent's players. On a few occasions a zone defense might be your best bet, but most times at this level of the game your team will do better using the man-to-man defense, because it provides young players with an overall concept of the defensive game. Here, we outline the best ways to teach and set up the basic defenses, as well as suggest ways to decide upon the best defense to use under various circumstances.

Let's Talk Defense

Both of the basic defenses have been used in basketball for many, many years. In the *man-to-man defense*, a player is assigned to guard an opposing player and simply stays with him, no matter where he goes on the court. In the *zone defense*, a player is assigned to guard an area on the court and covers any player who enters that area. No secrets there. For years, many teams at the youth level, high school level, and even college level used the zone defense. It was an easier defense to learn, and it made it possible for teams to effectively clog the middle of the floor near the basket. If an offensive team didn't have proficient outside shooters, they often had difficulty *breaking* the zone.

Coaching Corner

Although many of these rules have been touched upon previously, they are listed together here. It might not be a bad idea to print out this list and either post it on the bulletin board or give a copy to each player as a reminder of the basics of defense. Here, then, are the Ten Commandments of Defense:

1. Thou shall not deviate from thy stance.
2. Keep thy nose on the ball.
3. Shoulders shall stay square unto the basket.
4. Always jump to the ball.
5. See the ball; see the man.
6. Never leave thy feet.
7. Thou shall not covet thy opponent's points.
8. Thou shall not lust for blocking shots.
9. Never giveth up the baseline to intruders.
10. Do unto the offensive man as he would do unto you. But do it to him first.

The style of the list may sound a bit hokey and is something of a parody, but it nevertheless represents a solid reminder about what has to be done on defense every day.

At the professional level, teams were always required to play a man-to-man defense. For years, zones were illegal in the National Basketball Association. It was felt that the man-to-man defense created a more exciting game for spectators and that zones would hold the scores down. It was only before the 2001–2002 season that some forms of the zone defense were allowed in the NBA, although all the teams still play man-to-man most of the time. With the man-to-man defense, individual matchups are extremely important. A 6-foot, 3-inch point guard would not be assigned defensively to guard a 6-foot, 9-inch power forward. In the zone, if that 6-foot, 9-inch player came into the area assigned to the 6-foot, 3-inch man, he would have no choice but to guard him. Maybe that's why they don't play zone defense in the NBA.

These kinds of matchups don't occur too often in the youth game. In most cases, coaches have to match up players more by speed and talent levels, especially if they are playing man-to-man defense. In fact, at the youth level, coaches should look at defense as a totally integral part of the game that their players must learn and understand immediately.

Which Defense to Choose

As soon as a coach begins working with a new team, a, she will have to decide on a defense—zone or man-to-man. There are several things to consider when making this choice.

There is a near-contradiction when it comes to which defense a coach should teach his young players. The zone defense would seem to be the easier defense for young kids to understand because it simply involves being in a specific area on the court. Guard from here to here, and don't worry about the rest. With that kind of concept, you would think that the zone defense would be the first and obvious choice for a group of eight- and nine-year-olds. Not so fast. In basketball, as in other sports, things aren't always as they seem.

Therein lies the contradiction. The man-to-man defense teaches kids more about the entire defensive concept and communicating on the court. Yes, the man-to-man defense is more difficult to teach, but the feeling here is that a coach should always teach his kids the man-to-man defense first as soon as possible, even with the youngest age level. With the zone defense, kids sometimes find themselves standing around. With the man-to-man defense, everyone is always involved at all times, especially against teams using a motion offense. No one stands still. And if the offensive players aren't standing still, then the defensive players aren't standing still. Defenders have to hustle and communicate, fight off screens, and learn how to switch and double-team.

At the older levels, a coach may find a reason to use a zone; at that point, it is fine, as long as the players also know the principles of the man-to-man defense. That way, they will be ready if their coach decides to switch defenses or if they play for a team with another coach. So the suggestion here is for young players to learn the man-to-man defense first and then the zone defense. The man-to-man defense forces players to focus more; once they learn it, they can also transfer that ability to focus to the zone defense.

Hoop Lingo

Some terms are used when discussing the man-to-man defense that everyone should know. Again, these are not ordinary terms that you'll hear on television, but as a coach, they become an important part of your job.

◆ **Ballside or strongside:** The half of the court that the ball is on.

◆ **Helpside or weakside:** The half of the court that the ball is *not* on.

◆ **Team rotation:** Every time help is given, the entire team must react and move into position to take away the most dangerous passes in order of priority. Once a switch is made, in most cases, everyone should be ready to rotate one position.

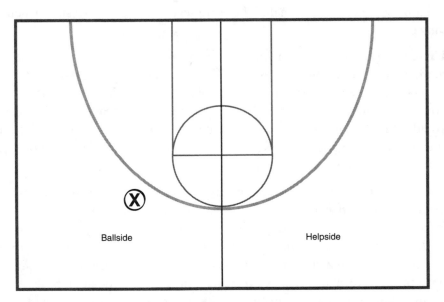

Ballside is the half of the court where the ball is located. Helpside or weakside is the other half. One pass can change it.

Man-to-Man Defensive Matchups

The man-to-man defense can be played as aggressively and tightly as the situation merits. What determines how the defense is played is speed and ability—whether the players on your team are faster or slower than your opponents. If your team has more team speed, your players can be more aggressive and play their opponents tighter. Your defenders can harass their offensive counterparts and disrupt their offense. If your team is slower, you have to give the offensive players more space, trying to deny the ball and clog the passing lanes.

Matchups are also extremely important with this defense. As a coach, you have to be able to size up the opposition and then assign your players accordingly. If you have had a chance to watch the opposition play previously, you'll know what to do going in. If you haven't seen them before, you might have to make adjustments after the game begins. Here are some general rules to follow:

◆ Always have your quickest defender on the other team's primary ball handler, regardless of size. You don't want a good ball handler to break down your defense by getting around his defender with no trouble every time he brings the ball up the court. Even if the defender is small, don't worry about the offensive player shooting over him. It's more important to stop potential dribbling dominance.

◆ You'll also want your best rebounder guarding your opponent's post man so that he is near the basket to go after the ball. If your best rebounder is occupied on the perimeter, you lose too much underneath.

◆ Your next-best defender should be on the other team's best scorer. Or, if the situation merits, you can put your best defender on the other team's best all-around player.

◆ If a defender winds up with a mismatch that he can't avoid, that defender has to concentrate on denying the ball and boxing out so that his offensive counterpart can't jump over him for an offensive rebound.

◆ Prevent better or taller players from dominating as best you can. You will need all your coaching acumen to do this, and maybe a quarter or two of experimenting to find the best defensive matchups and combinations. You may also use the halftime break to further decide upon the best matchups, and you will then have adequate time to fully explain them to your team.

Even if you are going up against a much bigger team, the man-to-man defense can be the most effective defense. Your smaller, quicker players can harass the ball on the perimeter, pick up a little sooner, and try to prevent the ball from being passed inside.

Your team will also have to work hard at boxing out and going after rebounds. You might get hurt in a couple of spots because of the size, but the man-to-man defense can still be your best bet if you feel you are physically overmatched.

Coaching Corner

A good coach must have the same instincts he hopes to instill in his players. This comes more naturally for some than for others. Either way, a coach should not only observe his players very carefully at practice sessions and in games, but he should also watch every move the opposition makes. At any point during a game, a coach might see something that could help his team and the individual players. It may be a better matchup or a weakness in the other team's defensive alignment. He might see something his team can take advantage of on offense or a way to force a team to shoot from too far out.

Principles of the Man-to-Man Defense

The primary defensive emphasis of the man-to-man defense is to focus on the ball. It is the responsibility of each defensive man to *stop the ball.* The defense must adjust to every pass and any player movement. A good man-to-man defense is never static. Players must know certain things when both defending the ball and defending off the ball. We will discuss the principles of both.

On-the-Ball Defense

When teaching your players how to defend the ball, use these guidelines:

◆ **Pressure the basketball at all times.** Maximum pressure should be applied, although a player should limit it to his ability to maintain control of the dribbler for the first three steps defensively. In other words, if the dribbler is faster then the defender, the defender has to back off a bit so he isn't beaten by those first quick steps.

◆ **Force the ball down the side.** The player with the ball must be kept out of the middle of the floor. He should be overplayed, to encourage him to dribble to the side and then be contained there. The defender should apply maximum pressure to the dribbler and try not to allow him to turn the corner on the baseline or to penetrate down the lane.

◆ **Play defense with the feet.** Players should not reach in on a defender. They should keep their feet moving and know they have help from teammates.

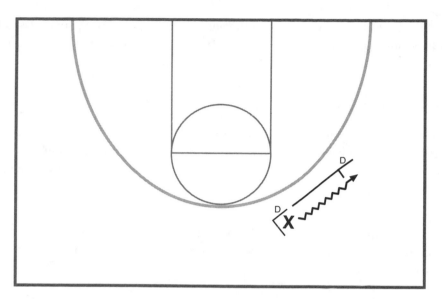

In the man-to-man defense, a defender should always try to force the ball handler to the side, protecting the middle.

◆ **Pressure the reversal pass.** Once the ball handler gives up his dribble, a defender should pressure the pass to the helpside or weakside of the court.

◆ **Jump toward the ball.** Players should force the offensive player to cut behind himself in order to maintain the ball.

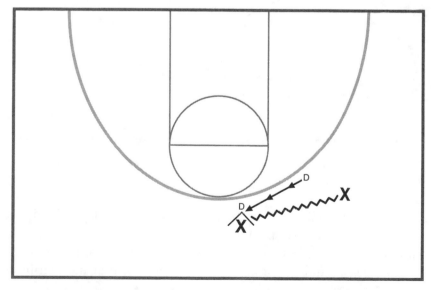

When the defender jumps toward the ball, it forces his man to cut behind him and also seals off the middle of the court.

The techniques to facilitate these maneuvers were discussed in Chapter 14, which you should review when reading this chapter. If your players master these techniques, their efforts to play man-to-man defense will be successful.

Off-the-Ball Defense

Remember, in the man-to-man defense, each player is always guarding an opponent, whether he has the ball or not. Players who are guarding opponents who do not have the ball must keep a close eye on the ball without letting their opponents elude them. They can do certain things to help the overall defense and also the player guarding the ball:

◆ **Help stop dribble penetration.** One player on each side of the ball should be close enough to stop dribble penetration before the ball handler can begin his scoring move.

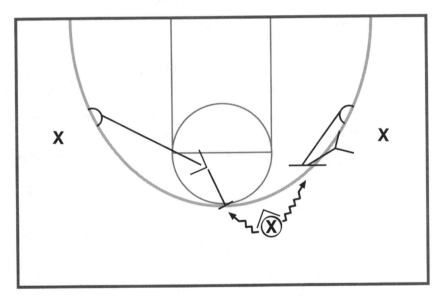

In the man-to-man defense, keep a player on each side of the ball. This shows how dribble penetration is prevented.

◆ **Help with the feet.** When helping and recovering, a player should move his feet (using the defensive slide) to get in front of the ball handler and establish a stationary position. He should never reach in. When helping, he should not turn toward the ball handler, but rather maintain his position and remain low in the defensive stance.

♦ **Talk.** Communication is essential in the man-to-man defense. Players should always let the ball handler and the rest of the team know their intentions. For example, they should let teammates know whether they are staying with their man or switching to another man.

♦ **Anticipate helping.** Players should always anticipate the defender on the ball forcing the ball handler down the side of the court. As the ball handler approaches the corner, the off-the-ball defender should anticipate the ball handler being turned toward him. If a good scorer has the ball, defenders should anticipate an attempt to drive to the basket and be prepared to help.

♦ **Deny the pass.** On the ballside of the court, the offense must be forced to go back door or be forced away from the basket to receive a pass. Once the dribble is relinquished, this becomes the first priority, and most turnovers should result from this kind of pressure.

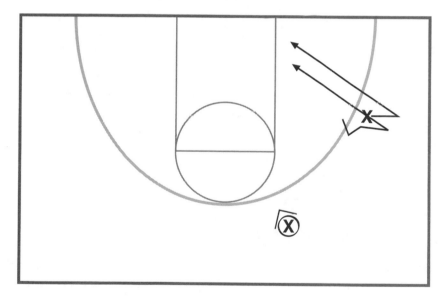

By staying in front of his man, the defender is denying the back-door cut and keeping the cutter from getting a pass.

♦ **Stay close on the back-door cut.** When denying passes, it is important for a player to stay close to his man and to turn his head toward him to watch him. This enables the defender to see his opponent cut back to the wing immediately and deny it. This is the only time when it is allowable to lose sight of the ball. This move should take only a split second, but it is necessary in order to maintain the position needed to deny passes. However, the defender must make sure he doesn't stay locked on his man to the point that he doesn't see the ball go to the other side. On a back-door cut, the defender should open to the passer as soon as possible if he loses sight of his man. In order for his man to receive a pass, the pass has to come from the passer. The defender has a chance to intercept or deflect the pass.

Once again, all the fundamental principles of guarding a man apply. As you can see, the man-to-man defense is about more than one player guarding another. The five players on the court have to work with each other, communicate, give help, and yet maintain their position so that none of the offensive players is suddenly unguarded and open for an easy shot. It takes practice and coordination.

Coaching Corner

The man-to-man defense can be set up in a couple of different ways. The basic rule of thumb is that, at the change of ball possession, the defensive players run back to the top of the key or foul line and then move out and pick up their respective offensive men at the three-point arc. This is done so that no offensive player gets behind the defense. As soon as the ball changes hands, whether it be the result of a rebound, a steal, or an out-of-bounds play, the defenders have to get back quickly. If a pass is stolen, the first thing to look for is a player breaking down the court. While the normal starting point is the three-point arc, a team can extend to the midcourt line if everyone is already back and the offensive team is bringing the ball up slowly. That way, a defensive team can exert pressure sooner, with a better chance to break up set offensive plays and make it more difficult for the attacking team to get into its offense.

More Tips on the Man-to-Man Defense

You should teach players a few more basic rules about playing man-to-man defense. For example, defenders should always be ready to rotate, to anticipate help being given on the ball, with the need for everyone to rotate their position accordingly in an attempt to take away the most dangerous offensive pass. With the defense also trying to force the back-door cut, the helpside defenders have to anticipate it and try to take the cut away. In addition, there should always be one man as the last line of defense, a defender down low who can see the entire offense. The defender in this position is responsible for lob passes and back-door cuts, and is also the last player to stop dribble penetration. Though this player also has to guard an offensive player, he has to be ready to drop off his man to stop the aforementioned offensive moves.

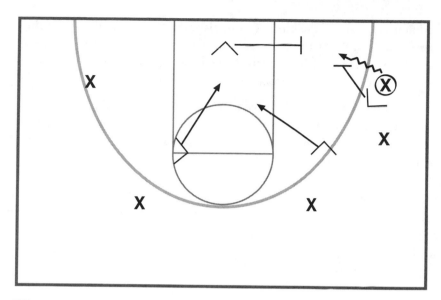

When a player has to drop off his man to cover another offensive player, everyone on the defense has to rotate so that all offensive players are still covered.

A player on post defense also has responsibilities. If the ball is in the post above the foul line, the defender should play on the outside; but when it is below the foul line, he should play on the inside. In both cases, the defender should keep a space between himself and the post man. This way, he can go over the top when necessary and reduce the chances of being sealed off. The defensive player should extend his arm and keep his head between the man and the ball. At the same time, he should keep his back foot behind the offensive man so he can quickly pivot and box out on the shot.

When defending a screener, the defensive player should stay in place if his teammate defending the ball goes over the top of the screen—in other words, in front of the screen, where he can stay with his man. However, if he starts to go behind the screen, the player defending the screener can jump out on a switch and take the ball handler while the player coming through stops and takes the screener.

Quick Tips

You can still teach the man-to-man defense to bigger, slower players. Instruct larger defenders not to go above the three-point arc, but to stay in tight to the basket. This prevents faster players from driving and setting up scoring opportunities. Bigger players are also in a better position to re-bound and block shots, which generally limits opponents to one shot.

The defensive man on the screener can also move to the high side of the screen, forcing the dribbler to veer to the outside, reverse direction, stop his dribble, or even draw a charge. If there is no switch, he can stay in that position for a second or two, and then recover and keep contact with the screener.

A man-to-man defense that is played well is exciting to watch and can be very effective. If you teach a young team to play this defense correctly, and if you have a group of hard-working, hustling players, they can give an offensive team fits. Make sure your players understand the concept of weakside and ballside. Defenders playing on the ballside should play their men straight up or should force the dribble. They should overplay a bit on the first two passes, in an attempt to disrupt the passing lanes. At the same time, the weakside defenders can drop farther off their men than normal and look to help in case the ballside defense breaks down. Once you have a team that can do all this with the man-to-man defense, then you are ready to teach your players the zone defense.

Time to Check Out the Zone

The concept of the zone defense is very simple. A defensive player is responsible for guarding an area of the court. She picks up any offensive player who comes into that area and guards that player, following to another point on the court where a teammate will pick her up. As soon as a defensive teammate comes over, the first defender releases and goes back to pick up the next person coming into her area. However, if a defender is guarding a player moving out of her area, she can't let the offensive player go if she is wide open and is a threat to score. Although players may not have to make as many split-second decisions as they do with the man-to-man defense, the zone defense still requires quickness and good basketball instincts.

There are a number of different forms of the zone defense. Each is used for a particular reason. If you set up the 2-3 zone, for example, with two players up top and the other three closer to the hoop, you'll have better rebounding and baseline defense. Yet this form of the zone doesn't defend well against the outside jumper taken from the wing or in the center at the top of the key. Conversely, having three defenders underneath makes it more difficult for the offensive players to drive and shoot out of the corners—but a team with great perimeter shooters can easily defeat the 2-3 zone, and you'll have to adjust. The adjustment is easy. You just have one of your low players rotate up top, and the zone goes from a 2-3 to a 3-2, a formation that can defend much more efficiently on the perimeter.

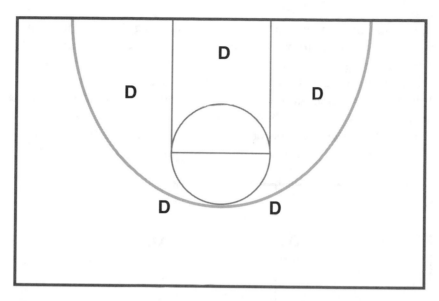

The 2-3 zone is a bit weak on perimeter defense but is strong underneath the basket.

Coaching Corner

Many people believe that youth coaches should not consider using any form of the zone defense and that the man-to-man defense is a much better defense to employ in teaching kids the game. We have said as much earlier in this chapter, stating that it is extremely important to teach even the youngest of kids to play the man-to-man defense as soon as they get on the court. However, we also feel that a coach's job is to teach the complete game of basketball, and the zone defense is part of that game. After your team has grasped the fundamentals of the man-to-man defense and has shown that it can play that defense in games, there is nothing wrong with teaching your players the basics of the zone and allowing them to use it occasionally in practice. We do feel that you should stick to the man-to-man defense in your games. However, in two situations you might consider using the zone defense in games. One is when you simply don't feel that your players can guard the five opposing players individually and that by using the man-to-man defense, your team will be beaten very badly and your players might be embarrassed. In these circumstances, the zone defense can help. The second situation occurs when a number of your players are in serious foul trouble because they are having problems guarding their opponents. By using the zone defense, they are less likely to continue fouling, and you might prevent several players from fouling out.

A 3-2 zone defense is just the opposite of the 2-3, in that the coverage becomes a little weak in the corners and in the middle, especially behind the three perimeter defenders. With this configuration, offensive players can cut into the paint pretty easily. If you want your team to protect the middle a little better, you can use the 1-2-2 zone. There is also good protection at the top of the key, but there's less range on the wings. As a coach, you may find that you have to rotate your zone a number of times to find the best configuration to contain a particular offensive team. For instance, if the outside shooters are hot at the beginning of the game, you might send a 3-2 zone against them. But if the shooters cool off later and there are a lot of rebounds up for grabs, a switch into the 2-3 would be the way to go.

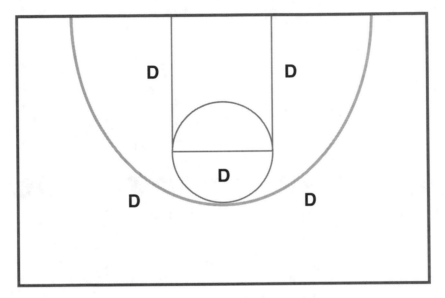

With the 3-2 zone, the perimeter is covered well, but rebounding may suffer.

A good zone will appear to operate as a single unit. All the players in the zone should keep their hands in the air and move them around, making it more difficult for the offense to pass over them. Only the player guarding the ball should be in the defensive stance. If the ball is being brought down on the right side, the entire zone shifts slightly in that direction, keeping the passing lanes tight and the players ready to pick up the ball if it moves into their area. In transition, players should retreat into the zone quickly, moving into their specified areas unless the offensive team is fast-breaking. Then, of course, players have to guard the ball and get back as quickly as they can to stop the break. If they stop it and the offense resets, they jump back quickly into the zone they have been playing.

The Box and One

One formation combines the zone defense with a touch of the man-to-man defense. Called the box and one, it is used only occasionally in special situations. The box and one is used when the offensive team has an outstanding player who can beat the zone by both shooting from the outside and driving to the hoop. If your team has an outstanding defender, you will want that player to guard the offensive star. However, if you don't want the rest of your team in a man-to-man defense, you can set up the zone box by having two players zoning the perimeter, one on each side of the top of the foul circle, and two others zoning underneath, one on each side of the foul lane. The fifth player goes man to man against the opponent's star player and follows him all over the court, as he would in the man-to-man defense.

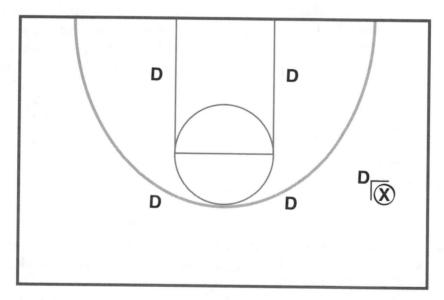

With the box and one, four players are in zone while the fifth plays the opponent's offensive star man to man.

The box and one can be an effective defense in this kind of situation, when you had planned to use a zone defense but need your star defender to stop the opposition's offensive hot shot. Since one defender is moving all over and the others are in a zone defense, communication becomes extremely important and players have to be able to help out. The box and one is the type of adjustment a coach may have to make during the course of a game if his team is in a zone defense and one player is absolutely killing it.

A Final Word

The zone defense can still be a very effective defense, and it certainly has a long history in the sport. It also has a continuing place in the game. You'll still see it used at both the high school and collegiate levels, and there is no harm in using it occasionally with your youth teams. However, allowing your teams to play the man-to-man defense is simply the better choice in most situations, especially for young players just learning the game.

> **Coaching Corner**
>
> Even if your team always plays man-to-man defense, you will undoubtedly face teams that play the zone. Therefore, your team needs to practice against various zones. This is another reason to teach the zone defense. Zone practice sessions will also enable you to evaluate your team's ability to use the zone defense in certain game situations.

Always be sure to teach the man-to-man defense first. Don't even think about zone defense until all your players not only understand the concept of the man-to-man defense and can execute it well, but also enjoy the challenge of going out as a team and realizing what a good solid man-to-man defense can do for all of them.

The Least You Need to Know

- Make sure your team understands from the beginning that playing defense is every bit as important to the success of a basketball team as playing offense.

- Always begin with the man-to-man defense, and never let your players drift into a zone defense because they want to or because they think it's easier.

- Continue to emphasize that defense takes hard work and hustle, and that players should never take it easy on defense because they are saving themselves for the offensive end of the floor.

- When you teach your players the zone, let them know that you won't be using it very often, but they should know it because they might find themselves playing it at higher levels of the game.

- As a coach, you have to watch not only your own players, but also the opposition very carefully; be prepared to make defensive adjustments at any time during a game.

Chapter 17

Offensive Strategies

In This Chapter

- ◆ Beyond the half-court offense
- ◆ The fast break
- ◆ Breaking the press
- ◆ The importance of inbounding

The majority of the time, a team's offense is based upon its half-court set. In Chapter 15, we outlined a basic motion offense based on ball movement and passing. This offense is run in the half court, which means that it doesn't begin until the point guard or another player brings the ball over the half-court line. The motion offense has a number of variations and, as suggested, is probably the best kind of offense for young players to learn and run. But sometimes during the course of a game a team has the opportunity to score, or even needs to score, without being able to set up its half-court motion offense.

In this chapter, we discuss the offensive strategies needed in situations other than the half-court offense. These include the all-important fast break, which a well-prepared team can use with stunning effectiveness; the secondary break when the fast break is slowed; a variety of inbounds plays; and last-second plays. The chapter also touches on some of the ways an offense can react to a defensive full-court press. So let's build upon that half-court foundation that has already been set.

The All-Important Fast Break

Good teams want to be able to execute a fast break, to beat their opponents down the length of the floor to get an easy basket. This is an integral part of the total offensive scheme. When a team runs a fast break well, it takes advantage of an easy opportunity to score and also makes its own opportunities by knowing how to run the break smoothly and at top speed. The fast break is fun for a team to run successfully, exciting to watch, and very effective. A team that has the ability to run the fast break gives itself a number of immediate advantages. Some of them are as follows:

◆ It can physically break down an opposing team and, in doing so, can equalize or decrease the advantages held by that team.

◆ It is a good answer to the running game of the opposing team.

◆ It can quickly detect opponents who are not in top physical condition or who cannot defend the break.

◆ It utilizes in-close shooting, usually layups or short jumpers, and almost always results in high-percentage shots.

◆ It inspires teamwork, in that it is necessary for all players to be acting as one as it develops.

◆ It utilizes fairly simple and basic mechanics, which makes it easy to teach and organize. Practice allows a team to execute it at faster and faster speed.

Although the half-court motion offense will remain the bread-and-butter of your offensive system, good teams will want to be able to fast break because it can lead to easy baskets if a team can beat its opponents down the floor. A fast break can be started after a missed shot and defensive rebound, after a steal of a pass or a dribble, after the recovery of a loose ball, on an end-line inbounds pass after a basket or free throw, on a jump ball, and occasionally after a basket, if the scoring team is caught napping. A fast break has to be run hard, but the players all must remain under control. Each player should know his responsibilities as well as those of his teammates. It is also important to recognize a good shot and to know what to do when the breaking team cannot get a good shot off the break.

Several different combinations can be run on the break, depending on how many players on the breaking team get down the court quickly and how many players on the defensive team can get back in an attempt to stop the fast break. In other words, if two offensive players are ahead of the field with one defensive player back, it's a two-on-one break. If three get out with one back, it's a three-on-one break. You can also have three-on-two and four-on-three situations and still run the break. Obviously, with more defenders back, it becomes more difficult to score.

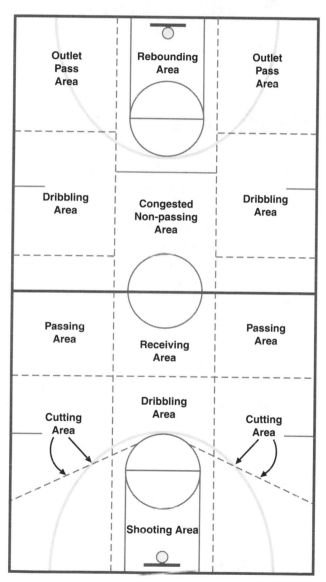

This full-court diagram shows, in general, how each area of the court is used on the fast break.

Coaching Corner

Young basketball players who enjoy the game will not only practice with their team, but also undoubtedly will practice on their own and play pickup games with their friends. In addition, they will watch other games, such as local high school games in person or college and professional games on TV. It's beneficial to teach your players *how* to watch a game. Tell them to look for specific plays or strategies each time they watch— the way players set and use screens, pass, play defense, and run the fast break. You could have them watch for just one particular thing each time. It isn't always easy to see an entire fast break develop on television, although some replays show it well. Nevertheless, watching a good team execute a fast break gives observant players a good feel for what they have to do before you teach them or after they learn it.

Player Responsibilities During a Fast Break

Let's begin with a couple of basics. First we'll check out the responsibilities of each player on the break. Remember, a fast break develops quickly and depends on speed. That means when the players release down the floor, it doesn't matter what position they normally play. While it's always best to get the ball into the hands of your best ball handler to run the break, it doesn't always happen that way. For this reason, all players should know the fundamentals of the game and should be adept at both dribbling and passing. With youth teams and players of about the same size, this shouldn't be a problem, although you will always have one or two players who have more advanced skills than the others.

The different types of fast breaks mentioned previously are run slightly differently, which we discuss shortly. But for general purposes, here are the responsibilities of all five players during a fast break:

- **Ball-handling guard.** This is the player who should be the primary receiver of the outlet pass. He looks to push the ball ahead with the pass first and the dribble second.

- **Right wing.** This player is a secondary outlet receiver on a rebound. If he gets the ball, he looks to pass it to the ball-handling guard. However, if he receives the ball over the top of the defense, he should look to take it right to the basket. If he goes to the baseline and is cut off, he should pass the ball back to the mid-post area. If he does not receive the ball by the time he reaches the baseline, he breaks back to the midpost extended area.

- **Left wing.** This player has the same responsibilities as the right wing, but he is positioned on the other side of the court.

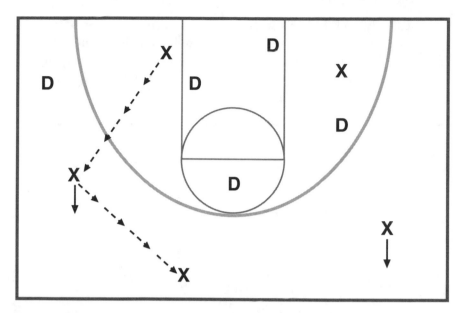

The point guard gets the outlet pass and looks to move the ball downcourt by passing first and dribbling second.

- ◆ **Trailer/low post.** The first player trailing the play (or the ball) on the break runs the lane opposite the ball-handling guard and fills the low-post ballside area. He waits until the ball-handling guard has the ball before breaking for the basket.

- ◆ **Trailer/high post.** This is the second trailer and the player who throws the ball inbounds on a made basket. He waits to see that the ball is secured and that the fast break has started. He then goes to the high-post area outside the foul line on the opposite side of the ball-handling guard.

Notice that both trailers wait to make sure the break is running. If all five players burst up the court at the same time and the ball suddenly changes hands before the break is really started, the breaking team doesn't want to be caught with no one back to play defense. During the fast break, the players on the breaking team try to stay in lanes. One is down the middle of the court, two more are down the wing areas, and the other two are down the sidelines. All the lanes converge on the basket, beginning at the foul line.

Most fast breaks begin with the outlet pass, a rebounder getting the ball on the right or left of the basket. That rebounder has to have the ability to pivot, see the entire court immediately, and then throw a quick and powerful outlet pass. In most cases, this is an overhead pass, since the rebounder should be holding the ball over his head to prevent it from being slapped away. Occasionally, he can use the bounce pass if the receiver is close by, and sometimes a baseball pass if a teammate is already far down the court.

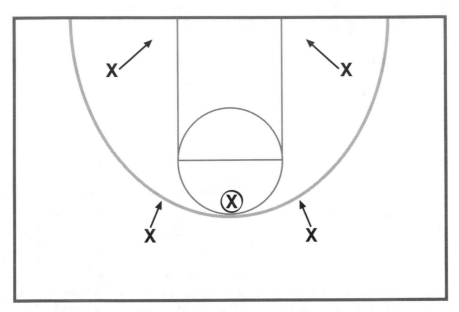

Always have two trailers hang back to make sure the break has been started successfully.

Did You Know?

When Wes Unseld joined the NBA's Baltimore Bullets for the 1968–1969 season, many wondered if the six-foot, eight-inch center out of Louisville was big enough to play center in the NBA. Everyone soon learned that Unseld was not only a fine rebounder, but brilliant at throwing quick and accurate outlet passes. This ability immediately made Baltimore a dangerous fast-breaking team and made Unseld the NBA Rookie of the Year.

On the average break, however, the outlet pass should be thrown forward and to the sideline on the rebounder's side of the court. The rebounder also has to make certain that the teammate he is passing to is someone capable of handling the ball. If it's an open big guy who doesn't dribble well in the open court, then it's probably best not to pass and to give up the chance of the break on that particular play. So the outlet passer has to make a judgment. The ideal man to throw the ball to is the point guard, or the team's best ball handler. The second-best ball handler will also suffice.

Coaching Corner

As you see from our preliminary description of the fast break, it is a play that requires quick, accurate passes as well as some slick dribbling, and everyone must be moving at top speed. It's apparent that kids in the eight- and nine-year-old age group will find this extremely difficult to do. In most cases, they simply won't have the skills at their age. However, as with all other aspects of the game, you should teach them the basic techniques of the break and walk them through it. They may not run it like 13- or 14-year-olds, but against their own age group, if they know and understand the play, they may well surprise you. In any case, players are never too young to learn.

Combinations of Breaks

Once your team gets into real action and begins experiencing the various combinations of possibilities on the court, they will certainly encounter the different forms of the fast break. This means that they must understand what to do when executing each type of break. Although the philosophy is basically the same for all fast-break situations, the technique varies slightly. The following are some pointers:

♦ **The two-on-one.** In a two-on-one situation, the ball should be passed between the two breaking offensive players until they reach the top of the key. The player who has the ball inside the foul line looks to score, unless the defender is on him. Then he makes one final pass to his teammate, who might be alongside, slightly ahead, or trailing slightly behind. The ball should be brought into the scoring area slightly to the left or right of the key. That way, the defender can take just one man, opening the other for a layup. Quick, crisp passes will keep the defender off-balance and make it difficult for him to play the ball and disrupt the break.

♦ **The three-on-one.** Now the offense has even more of an advantage, with three offensive players out on the break and just one defender back. The offense should almost always score with this kind of advantage. Here the ball handler should come straight down the middle of the court, because he'll have players cutting to the hoop on both the left and the right. Once the defender commits, the ball handler can pass to the other cutter or take a foul-line jump shot.

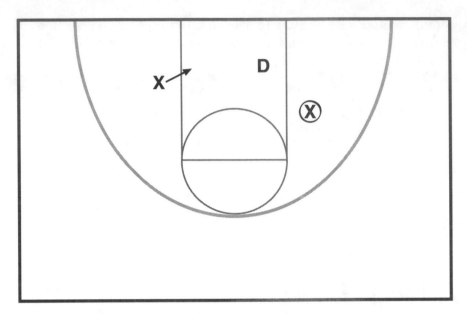

With the two-on-one break, both offensive players should pass the ball between them quickly until they reach the scoring area.

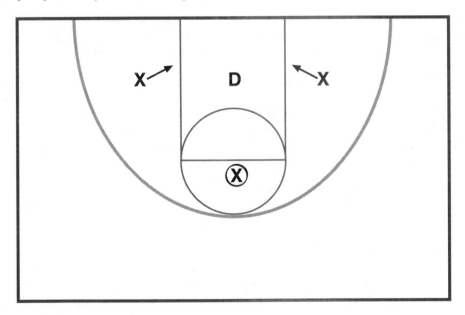

An offensive team should almost always score on the three-on-one break if players execute the play well.

◆ **The three-on-two.** Now two defenders are trying to stop the three offensive fast-breakers. The ball handler should again keep the ball in the middle of the court. Once he gets to the foul line, he has the option of passing right or left. This time, though, he should stop at the foul line for a possible return pass. If one defender picks up the player he has passed to, and the other picks up the second cutter going for the basket, the original ball handler can get the ball back for a short, uncontested jump shot. If the defender runs at him, he can pass once more to the open man. Of course, if he brings the ball down the middle and sees a chance to split the defense for a layup of his own, he can take that option as well. The worst shot a team should get on a three-on-two break is a foul-line jump shot, which is still a high-percentage shot.

◆ **The four-on-three.** This is a bit tougher because three men back can cause more havoc, obviously, than one or two defenders. The ball should come down the sideline or off the top of the key. The four breaking players should look to come down to set up in a box formation, with two players low, about 10–12 feet off the basket, and two on the wings, the foul line extended. The defense has to choose whether to have one player up top trying to guard the two wings, or two matched up with the wings and one underneath. There should be, then, an open man in the corner or at the foul line. If no one can get the ball on a quick cut to the hoop, there should be an open jumper at one of the spots—the foul line or the corner.

Coaching Corner

On both the three-on-one and the three-on-two fast breaks, the player in the middle of the floor is instructed to take the foul-line jump shot. The reason for this is that by pulling up and taking the jumper, the player still has a high-percentage shot—plus, two rebounders are already underneath to go after a possible offensive rebound. In addition, if the player drives the lane, the defender has the opportunity to step in front and draw a charge either on the shot or after the pass is released. The last thing a team wants in this situation is to be called for a charge in the middle. Under these circumstances, always make sure your player with the ball takes the jumper.

While the fast break gives the offense an immediate advantage and a chance to score quickly with a high-percentage shot, it isn't an automatic score. It takes great ball-handling skill with the execution of the play always at full speed for it to work. Unless you have your team practice the form and execution of the fast break, it just won't happen. As with so many other plays in basketball, players have to reach a point where they react automatically and know what to do without hesitation.

Work your players into the break slowly. Devise some fast-break drills to use at practice. Let them go through the basic moves unopposed at first so that they know the dynamics of the two-, three-, and four-man break. Then slowly work the defenders into the drills, at first just as a presence and then actively trying to break up the play. As mentioned earlier, it doesn't hurt to teach even very young players what it means to perform a fast break. They may not have the skills to run it at full speed, but if the situation occurs in the game, let them try. Against their own age group defending, they might just pull it off.

When the Break Doesn't Work

Sometimes your players will get out on the fast break and, for one reason or another, will not be able to complete it. Sometimes the defense will get back fast enough to disrupt the play. Perhaps a defender will slow the ball handler just enough to throw off the timing with the cutters. Or the ball will be slapped out of bounds, causing the breaking team to inbound the ball and effectively ending the break.

If the fast break doesn't work the way it is supposed to but the offensive team keeps the ball, there are two things that team can do. The first is obvious: They can slow things down until everyone is in position and start the half-court, motion offense once again. However, if your team is still moving down the court quickly and just can't get that one pass that will lead to a shot, your players can run what is called a secondary break.

Secondary Breaks

With the secondary break, the point guard brings the ball down the court to the right of the key. His two wing men are ahead of him on both sides, with two trailers behind. Because the break has been slightly disrupted, the point guard cannot get off a pass to either cutter. To keep the break alive, the wing man on the right (ballside) sets a baseline screen for the left-side wingman, and the wingman on the left (the weakside) cuts behind him (around the screen) to the opposite corner. If the lane is open, the point guard can opt to drive straight down for a hoop. But if a defender has it blocked, the play continues.

The screening wing next leaves his screening position near the baseline and moves into the foul circle to set a screen for the first trailer, who rolls off the screen down into the post. The second trailer sets a screen just outside the foul line on the left side for the ballside wing, the original screener, who now pops out and takes a pass from the point guard for a quick jump shot. The weakside wing is still in the right corner and can also try to go back door to the hoop. This almost sounds like a half-court offense, but it is run very quickly off the original break, hopefully before the defense can get set up.

Another Secondary Variation

Assume that the point guard pushes the ball up the right side of the court. The weak-side wing clears across the lane to the right corner, while the ballside wing loops around to the top of the key off staggered screens set by both trailers. If the point guard is covered, he can pass to the ballside wing as he completes his loop to the top of the key, or he can pass to the weakside wing who has cleared into the right corner. That wing can also go back door to the basket if the lane is open.

Again, both of these secondary breaks must be done quickly. If the window of opportunity closes, the point guard should just back off with the ball and allow his team to set up the motion offense once again.

> **Quick Tips**
>
> Variation plays can be run from either side of the court. Your main ball handler might be left-handed and prefer that side of the floor, or the ball might be outletted to that side. In the pattern, you may find that your shooters prefer taking their shots from the right side of the floor rather than the left.

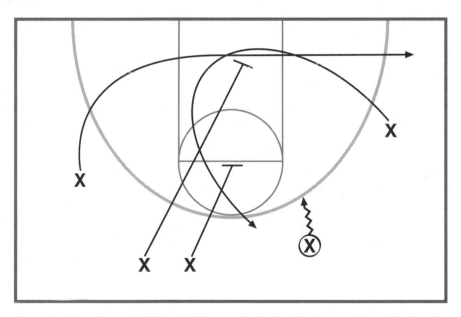

A secondary break can look like a half-court offense, but it's done quickly and before the defense can get set up.

Inbounds Plays

At first glance, it may seem just a simple, routine matter to inbound the ball following a basket or after the ball has gone out of bounds. Certainly at times during a game a player just puts the ball in play by flipping it to a teammate with absolutely no defensive pressure. But in other situations an inbounds play is extremely important. It might occur in a close game or even at the very end of the game when a team needs a basket badly. Then putting the ball in play becomes extremely important. Not only is the defense trying to stop the ball from being inbounded successfully, but they do not want the offensive team to run a play that might lead to a quick hoop.

With that in mind, the first goal of the inbounds play is simply to get the ball to a teammate successfully. If a player fails to do that, the offense can be disrupted or the ball can be turned over. The second goal is to force the defense to guard your team by running some screens and picks. The third option is to use the inbounds play to get a quick shot out of a set formation. These plays are especially important when the defense is in a full-court press or the offensive team is inbounding on the sideline in the offensive end of the court or from the baseline under the basket.

Quick Tips

On key out-of-bounds plays, it's important that the player inbounding the ball against defensive pressure is the team's best passer, the tallest player, or the best shooter. If the inbounds pass is coming from the sideline or baseline, a good shooter can inbound it and then run in behind a screen for a return pass and quick shot.

The two most common passes used on the inbounds play are the overhead pass and the bounce pass. With the overhead pass, a passer can easily get the ball over the outstretched hands of the defenders; the bounce pass can get the ball under the defense and to a player who is close by. The player defending the pass must give him 3 feet. In other words, he cannot stand any closer than 3 feet from the sideline or baseline, and at no time can he reach across the out-of-bounds line to try to get the ball.

If there is no immediate shooting opportunity, the passer should try to get the ball in the hands of the best ball handler so that he can set up the offense once again. A creative coach will certainly be able to devise his own set of inbounds plays to accommodate any situation on the court. We suggest here two or three for each key inbounding situation, just to get you started. These are tried-and-true plays that always have a good chance of working. As always, you should evaluate the players on your team and then devise the plays that you feel work best.

Full-Court Inbounds Against the Press

Normally, after a basket, the scoring team retreats on defense and the team that yielded the basket simply inbounds the ball from the baseline and starts up the court on offense. Occasionally, however, the team scoring the hoop will go into a full-court press, either zone or man-to-man, in an attempt to either get the ball back immediately or to disrupt the offense into a turnover or an errant pass. Now inbounding isn't so simple. The passer and other players must have a plan so that everyone isn't caught napping. A few rules and techniques will help break either of these pressing situations.

Against the zone, when the defense is trying to guard areas of the backcourt, the inbounds passer should get the ball to a teammate in the middle of the court, who should look to quickly kick it out to the sideline. The receiver can then look to pass up the sideline if the lane is open because there is normally less congestion there. If the initial inbounds pass is received by the point guard, he can simply break the trap with the dribble, splitting a double team and then looking to run a fast break or get the team into its half-court offense.

With the man-to-man press, the receiving team should line up with the two guards screening for each other on the foul line, and two forwards or a forward and center behind them near the half-court line. When the inbounder slaps the ball with one hand to start the play, the two guards break in opposite directions to see if one can get open for a pass. At the same time, the forward on the ballside fakes coming back to the ball and breaks long. The other forward or center (whoever it happens to be) fakes to the middle of the court and then breaks back to the foul line as a safety, in case both guards are overplayed and denied. If the forward gets the ball at the foul line, the guards can usually get open because the defenders have been denying them by staying between them, the ball, and the sideline. If they break up the middle quickly and get ahead of their defenders, they can usually get a return pass from the forward, a maneuver that will give the team the potential for a three-on-one or three-on-two fast break.

Inbounds Plays from the Sidelines

The following are inbounds plays from the sideline:

- ◆ **Option 1:** Both guards line up low outside the lane, with the point guard on the ballside (the side where the ball is being inbounded). One forward and the center should stand just outside the foul line, forming a box with the two guards. The other forward inbounds from the sideline, with his position being even with the top of the key. At the slap, the ballside forward goes down low and screens for the point guard, who sprints behind the screen and takes the pass just beyond the three-point arc. At the same time, the center goes down low and screens for the weakside guard. The inbounds passer also goes down low and joins the forward in screening for the weakside guard, who now has the option to come up on either wing as the point guard dribbles to the top of the key.

  Now the point guard can throw a quick pass to the shooting guard on whichever wing he has flashed to. At this point, the center and forward are down low on opposite posts. Whichever post is opposite the ball flashes across the lane to the opposite high post, and the ballside post player posts up his man, looking for a lob pass. The original inbounder just drops into the corner for a possible pass, and the point guard waits at the top of the key.

♦ **Option 2:** With this play, the two guards are outside the key a few feet above the foul line, with the point guard weakside. The forward and center are down low. At the slap, the 2-guard screens for the point, who fakes inside and then goes toward the ball on the wing to get the pass. After screening, the 2-guard steps out to the perimeter, and the forward (4) flashes across the lane to set up on the ballside high post. The inbounder (3) loops under the basket behind the center's (5's) screen and sets a weakside baseline screen. The point guard then passes quickly to the 2-guard, who can throw it to the inbounder (3) on the baseline for a jumper or drive, or can pass in the middle to the center, who has looped in there after setting the screen for the inbounder.

Hoop Lingo

For purposes of description and the accompanying diagrams, we will sometimes refer to players by the numeric slang names they are now called. In other words, the point guard is also **player 1**, the shooting or off-guard is **player 2**, the two forwards are **players 3** and **4**, and the center is **player 5**.

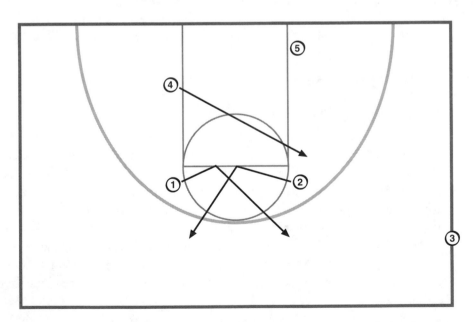

Here's the beginning of a typical sideline inbounds play. The offense is in a box formation.

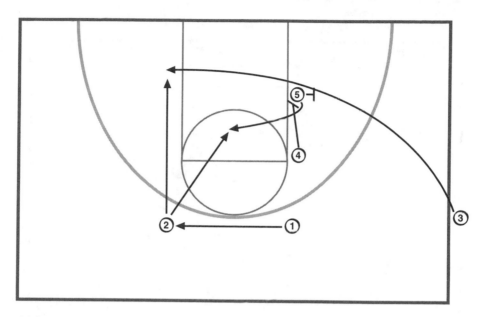

Players must make movements and cuts quickly, looking to get a man open for the shot.

Inbounds Plays from the Baseline

Following are inbounds plays from the baseline:

- ◆ **Option 1:** This one is called a *stack inbounds* play. The inbounding forward (3) is standing alongside the foul lane to make the pass. The other players line up along the same side of the lane ballside, with the center (5) in closest, then the other forward (4), and the two guards (2 and 1), the shooting guard (2) in front of the foul line, with the point guard (1) just behind it. At the slap, everyone moves quickly. The 2-guard fakes into the lane and then pops out to the wing, up from the corner. Both the 4-forward and the 5-center cross the lane and set up a double screen, and the point guard steps back across the three-point arc. The inbounds pass goes to the 2-guard, who has cut toward the corner, and that player immediately snaps a pass to the point guard, who dribbles left behind the arc. At the same time, the inbounder has run behind the double screen and is now on the weakside wing, where he can receive a pass from the point guard for a possible quick jump shot. Or, he can reverse the ball to the point guard, who can then pass to the 4-forward, who has come out to the foul line. The 4-forward can either shoot or toss a lob pass to the center (5), who moves from his screening position across the lane down low.

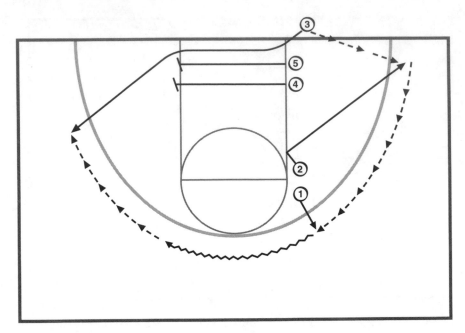

From the baseline, the team lines up in a stack formation; at the slap, everybody moves.

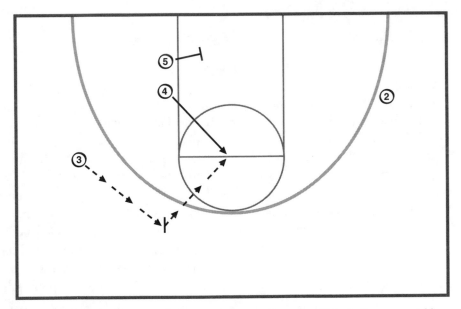

With this inbounds play, several players can be open for a shot if the ball moves quickly enough.

◆ **Option 2:** This one begins in a box formation. The inbounder (3) is in the same position over the baseline to the right of the foul lane. Players 4 and 5 set up low on each side of the lanc, while the guards set up high, alongside the foul line. The center (5) and point guard (1) are both ballside. At the slap, both low post men run up and screen for the guards. The guards then cut to their respective baselines, while the ballside post shifts over to screen for the weakside post. The ball is passed to the point guard, and then the inbounder cuts behind him and loops out to the wing, where he can get a return pass. The center (5), after screening for the point guard, moves two thirds of the way across the key and screens for the 4-forward, who goes behind the screen and then cuts to the hoop for a possible pass underneath. The 2-guard can loop back out to the wing on the weakside as a safety valve.

◆ **Option 3:** This variation begins with the same box formation. At the slap, the center (5) comcs up onto the foul line and sets a screen. The point guard comes farther across the top of the foul line and also screens, so the two are setting a *staggered screen*. The 2-guard moves around the staggered screen toward the ballside wing, where he gets the inbounds pass. Once he has made his move, the center (5) pivots and ducks into the lane, while the 4-forward also ducks into the lane. The 2-guard looks to shoot. If the center (5) doesn't get a lob pass, he posts up down low. The inbounder then loops around the 4-forward and the point guard, who is now screening inside the foul line. If the 2-guard doesn't shoot, he can throw the ball into the center on the low post and cut to the hoop, or he can swing the ball back outside to the 3-forward, who has broken up top after the inbounds pass.

Coaching Corner

During some inbounds plays late in the first half or late in the game, it is in the best interest of the defensive team to commit an immediate foul. They can't afford to give up a basket, and they may be willing to trade one point for a possible two or three at the other end. Knowing that they are going full-out to get the ball or the player, the inbounder must throw the ball to a point where, if it's deflected out of bounds, his team will either retain the ball or have time to get set up on defense. The last thing the inbounder wants to do is throw a pass that the other team can intercept and go in for a quick score. In this situation, you will want to set up a play in which the receiver of the inbounds pass is your team's best foul shooter. That way, the best-case scenario gives your team the best odds at a free-throw and time to get back on defense.

As you can see, a good inbounds play involves a great deal of coordinated movement, sharp cuts, set screens, and quick passes in search of a shot. It is the kind of effort that must be practiced—at first slowly and then at increasing speed. The object of all the plays is to get a player open for a good shot and then get that player the ball before the defense can react. That's why everyone has to move very quickly and decisively.

Last-Second Plays

Every coach must also have a couple of last-second plays, when the offense has the ball and the team needs a basket within seconds. In some instances, your team has the ball on an out-of-bounds play and needs to get that quick score. Whether the inbounds pass is under your own basket or on the sideline in the front court, you need specific plays so that your team can focus during these critical seconds. You can certainly design your own plays using the same principles presented here. As always, some rules have to be observed if you want the plays to be successful.

Last-Second Half-Court Play

If the team is in the half-court offense, the coach can send three players down low, while the point guard has the ball up top. Two of the players can screen for the third player down low, and then it's up to the point guard to get the ball to that player for a jumper behind the double screen. At the same time, the off guard can try to go back door, giving the point guard a second option if the screen doesn't work. In the worst-case scenario, if the point guard can't find an open man he'll have to take a long jumper.

Last Second Out of Bounds

There will also be instances when your team has the ball on an out of bounds play and you need to get that quick score. Whether the inbounds pass is under your own basket or on the sideline in the front court, you will once again need plays to give your team so they don't go out there guessing. As before, we will give you a couple of sample plays. You can certainly design your own plays using the same principles presented here. As always, there are some rules that have to be observed if you want the play to be successful.

Full-Court Last-Second Play

The full-court, last-second play is a tough one because it involves a long pass, a good catch, and a shot. Remember, the clock doesn't start until a player on the court receives the inbounds pass. The point guard and a forward stand on each side of the foul line, with the off guard (2) and center down court, under the other basket. At the slap, the forward breaks across the lane and sets a screen for the point guard, who cuts behind him and takes the pass as he comes across the lane. He can take only two dribbles before making his pass. The off guard and the center are on the weakside of the foul line. When they see the point guard receive the ball, the center screens for the off guard, who loops around him and takes the long pass from the point guard at the top side of the key. If there is just a second or two left, he has to pivot and take a jump shot—there is no time to drive. If there are three or four seconds, he can try to drive or look for the center rolling to the hoop for a pass. This is a difficult play to complete with just a couple of seconds remaining, because the ball has to travel the length of the court. But it can be done successfully.

A Sideline Last-Second Play

A last-second out-of-bounds play in the front court has a better chance of working because of the proximity to the basket. But because it is last-second play, everyone has to complete their roles perfectly—just to get the shot. This same basic play can be used if there are perhaps two seconds left or if there are five or seven seconds.

The setup is simple. Two players set up in the low post, one above the other, on the ballside facing the inbounder. The designated shooter (it can be a guard or forward, as long as it's your best shooter) is on the other side of the lane, opposite the two players who will set split screens. The first player is standing on the wing outside the inbounder as a safety valve.

At the slap, the shooter makes the only move. He has three options. He can run under the lower post player by the baseline for the ball. He can split the two screeners and head straight through for the ball, or he can come around the high-side screener to get the pass. If it is a last-second situation, he must turn and shoot. This is a make-or-break play; there is one chance. However, if there are five or more seconds left, other things can occur.

The inbounder should immediately run to the corner. One of the post players shifts to the other side of the lane. Now both post players are in position to get an offensive rebound and put back a missed shot. The safety-valve guard runs to the top of the key. Now the shooter can still take the shot. Or, he can pivot and drive if he sees an opening. If he takes one or two steps and draws the defense in, he can either pass to the inbounder in the corner for a shot, or flip it out to the safety-valve guard at the top of the key for the shot. Again, it's one of those bang-bang plays that requires quick movements, sharp execution, and players who aren't afraid to take the last shot.

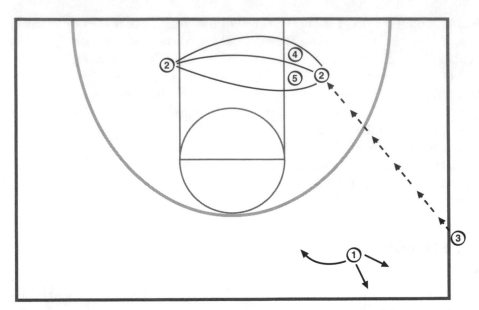

With this formation, the player designated to take the shot can take one of three routes past his screens.

A Final Word

In this chapter, we gave you basic plays that work. In fact, they are plays that have worked for coaches for a long time—plays that everyone on your team should learn, whether they are the youngest group or the oldest. All kinds of variations can be developed as you get to know your team and the abilities of the players. As always, it is best to begin with the basics.

The Least You Need to Know

- ◆ Your team must be ready to run some special offensive plays, not just your half-court offense.

- ◆ A well-run fast break can not only get your team a high-percentage shot and a quick basket, but it also can tire out your opponents and foster great teamwork among your players.

- ◆ It is necessary to know how to break a full-court press, or your team will find itself in trouble quickly.

- ◆ Having set out-of-bounds plays tailored to specific situations is another part of a complete offense.

- ◆ The last-second shot can sometimes make the difference between winning and losing. Be prepared.

18

Defensive Strategies

In This Chapter

◆ The full-court press

◆ Defensive traps

◆ Defending the fast break

◆ Stopping inbounds plays

Now we go over to the defensive side of the ball once more. This time it's defensive strategies, maneuvers you must know and teach to your team to counter some of the offensive strategies we discussed in the previous chapter. Basketball is almost like a chess game. For everything the opposing offense does, your defense must be ready to stop it. And when you go over to offense, your opponent's defense will try to do the same to your team. If the talent level is close to being equal, it comes down to preparation, knowledge, and execution. And that's where a coach can make her presence felt.

In this chapter, we give you the final pieces to the basic puzzle, discussing various defensive strategies such as the full-court press, defensive traps, ways to defend against the fast break, and how to stop various inbounds plays. It is necessary for your team to learn and understand the techniques involved with these strategies to keep an offensive/defensive balance in games. It is also important for your players to be able to make the transition from offense to defense automatically, to know exactly what to do when the ball changes hands. By adding these defensive strategies to the material already put forth, your team should be fully ready to start the new season.

The Full-Court Press

Basic defenses start from the three-point arc and go in to the basket. When you decide to have your team press full court, you lose some control from a coaching perspective because you are really relying on your players' judgment and talent for the simple reason that they will not be in a defensive set. In a pressing situation, they are guarding their opponents for a full 94 feet, the length of the court, instead of just 20 feet from the basket. You must continually evaluate the positive results of the press (steals, baskets, disruptions of your opponents' offensive flow) against the number of mistakes your team makes when pressing.

Effective presses don't always result in steals and easy baskets. A good press can wear the other team down and cause turnovers because the opponents' offensive rhythm is disrupted and because they must work extra hard to advance the ball up the floor. An offensive team with an excellent ball handler and quick, crisp passers can often break the press. Bobby Knight, the current Texas Tech coach and the former coach of Indiana University, once said that a fundamentally sound team will never be beaten by a full-court press. So there is always a great deal to think about before you ask your players to press. When they do, you must watch very carefully to see the effectiveness of the strategy and decide whether you want to continue using it in that particular game.

When Do You Order a Press?

The full-court press, or a form of it, can be used at any time to surprise the opposition, to put pressure on them, and to see if and how they can handle it. A team can try a zone or man-to-man press early to see which one is more effective. In fact, if you have any thoughts about using the press during a game, use it early to judge how well it will work. It might tell you whether to use it later during important stages of the game. If the offensive team blows through the press and scores, you may not want to use it again. If it is effective, you will have a much better idea of what you might do at crunch time, when the game is on the line.

In pressing and trapping, you also have to remember that the farther the ball has to go to reach the basket, the more time the defense has to recover. In other words, if your team traps in the backcourt and makes a mistake, the players have a chance to get back before the offensive team can take advantage of it. But a trapping mistake in the half court near the basket can often lead to a high percentage shot and a possible score.

A successful press makes it difficult for a team to advance the ball upcourt. Since a team has to get the ball over the half-court line in 10 seconds before they commit a violation, this becomes a concern when a defensive team presses. The press can also lead to traps. The best spots to trap are on the sidelines and in the corners. When a team traps in those areas, the sideline and baseline serve as an extra defensive player.

Did You Know?

In the early days of basketball, games were often played with a loose net surrounding the court. The net kept the ball from going out of bounds, but it also gave defensive players a strange advantage. If a player dribbled into the corner, it didn't take two defensive players to effect a trap. One defender could simply reach out and grab the net on both his left and right, and actually pull it over the player to "trap" him in the corner. This resulted in a jump ball!

Some Presses and Traps

Now it's time to look at some of the more popular presses and traps you may want to teach your team. We will begin with two variations of the man-to-man press.

The Run-and-Jump Defense

The run-and-jump defense can be best described as a man-to-man defense that can create many turnover possibilities. There is no set assignment after the first run and jump occurs, and any one defensive man may be guarding another offensive man. Both this defense and the run and trap that follows are considered pressing man-to-man pressure defenses.

Like other defenses, the run and jump has both strengths and weaknesses. The advantages begin with the simple fact that it gives the offense another defense to counter. It can also be used to make your opponent's best ball handler give up the ball. In addition, the run and jump can be an effective defense against teams that like to set screens for the dribbler at the point of the ball.

Weaknesses include a period of limbo when the defense is neither in man-to-man defense nor zone defense by the strictest definition of terms. Because there are no set rules, the defensive players can sometimes become confused. In addition, defensive rebounding can become a problem, and players tend to become careless in their execution of the team's basic half-court defense. With this in mind, never allow your team to forget that the half-court defense must remain solid. It all goes back to the defensive work ethic: You have to go hard 100 percent of the time.

The object of the run and jump is to get the ball out of the hands of the opposition's best ball handler. Though the defense picks up full court, players should stay as far from their men as possible without jeopardizing their ability to recover. Only the man on the ball applies pressure, trying to force the ball handler to dribble at a 45° angle, not straight up court. *If no dribble occurs and the ball stays in the air via passes, everyone should remain in a straight man-to-man defense.*

When a nearby defensive player realizes that he has a good chance of surprise, he should run at the dribbler and jump to the offensive player's outside shoulder. If the dribbler is caught by surprise, he might turn the ball over. Or he might stop his dribble and be forced to pass. He also might turn to get away from the jumper and reverse his dribble. If there is another defensive player close to the action and he sees a chance to get the ball, he can go for it.

If not, the players must rotate because the player going for the ball has left his man open. Here's where there are no iron-clad rules. Proximity and judgment must be used by all the players, and this comes with the experience of working together. The direction of the rotation is determined by the direction of the dribbler. If the dribbler is going to his left, the rotation is counterclockwise and the recovery of the man on the ball is clockwise. If the ball is dribbled to the right, the reverse pattern is used.

The three-man switch is the most typical in this defense. It's also not unusual for a second run and jump to be made before or just after the offensive team gets the ball across the half-court line. This time, four men rotate to other men; hopefully, by this time, the offense has been completely taken out of its rhythm and normal set because everyone has been forced to go at a 45° angle and has slowed down.

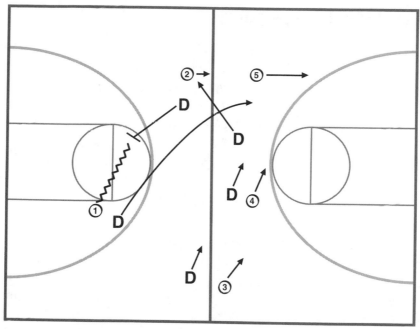

When the first jumper goes for the ball, he rotates clockwise, while all the other players rotate counterclockwise.

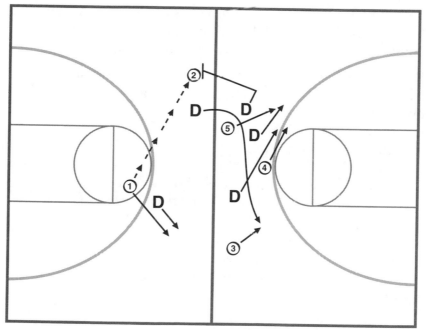

A second jump is made at the half-court line, with four players rotating to pick up new men.

Run and Jump Defensive Responsibilities

The following is a list of what each defensive player must do to make the run and jump effective.

- **Player guarding the initial ball handler (X1 in the illustration):** He plays his man tight, applying pressure in an effort to prevent the ball handler from finding an open man. He also tries to get the ball handler to put the ball on the floor. Then he attempts to keep the ball handler from slicing to the middle of the court, pressuring the ball and trying to keep his man's dribble at a 45° angle. He stays with his man until he sees in his peripheral vision the run-and-jump man attacking the dribbler. Then he enters the rotation looking for an open man.

- **Players guarding men one perimeter pass away (X2 and X3):** Their first responsibility is to prevent a pass from the ball handler to the man they're guarding. When the ball handler begins dribbling away from them, they begin giving ground in the direction of the dribble. They are still playing man-to-man defense and must always be able to get back to prevent a pass. When the ball handler begins dribbling toward them, they start thinking about the proper surprise point to initiate the run and jump. The correct point to surprise the dribbler will vary; it depends on the distance from the dribbler and the speed with which he dribbles. If the dribbler is moving fast, a player can surprise him from 15 feet away. If he's dribbling slowly, however, the defender should not leave his man until the dribbler is about 6 feet away.

- **Players guarding men two or more perimeter passes away (X4 and X5):** As with the players one perimeter pass away, the first responsibility of these two players is to prevent a pass from the ball handler to their man. They also give ground when the ball handler dribbles away from them, but they stay close enough to get back to prevent a pass to their men. When the ball handler dribbles toward them, they begin to prepare for the rotation. Again, there are no hard, fast rules; players often have to work by instinct and determine whether they have a chance to get to the ball or just pick up another man.

The run and jump may sound like a helter-skelter type of press with too much determined by chance and individual judgment. True, it is not a tightly controlled defense. But perhaps the accompanying diagrams will help you see how this can be a disruptive and sometimes effective press.

The Run and Trap

Like the run and jump, the run-and-trap defense is made to create turnover opportunities. The difference between the two is that the run and jump can be called a *jump switch*, while the run and trap is a *jump trap*. In the run and jump, players rotate in a man-to-man defense and pick up someone else's man. In the run and trap, the three men not involved in the trap rotate into zone coverage. The objective is to cover passing lanes and make steal attempts.

In the run and trap, the defender covering the ball handler plays straight-up defense and tries to turn his man to the middle of the court or to the sideline, as long as he has him moving at a 45° angle. The man who is one pass away from the ball on the weakside looks to slide off his man while still close enough to recover. When he sees that the ball handler's back is to him, he goes over to trap. Again, it is best to trap in the corners or sideline, but because the objective of the defender is to get the ball handler to turn his back via a reverse dribble, the trap can also come in the middle. It is very important that the ball handler not be able to split the defenders or get a good look over the trap. As we said, the objective is to have the ball handler turn is back to the basket and, if he can't be trapped, force him to try a cross-court pass.

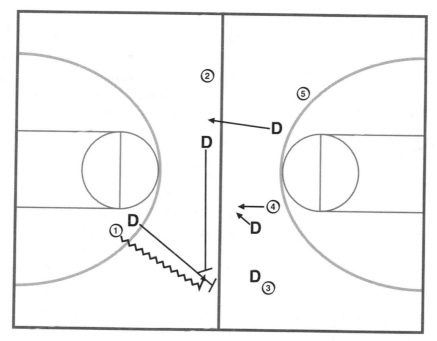

When the ball handler turns his back to the basket, a second defender slides over to trap near the sideline.

While the trap is being executed, the other three men go into zone coverage. The defensive man two passes away (X5) steps up and looks to steal the cross-court pass, while the defender one pass away ballside (X3) looks to take the penetrating sideline pass away. Many teams counter this by flashing to the high post. This pass must be stopped as well. The only pass that won't hurt the defense immediately is the long diagonal pass to the other side of the court. If the ball handler is going to try to make this pass out of the trap, he must be forced to make a high lob pass, one that will give the defense time to recover.

This is the basis of the run and trap. Once again, a great deal of quickness is required, both to make the trap and to recover if the trap doesn't work. Either way, it disrupts the offensive flow and makes the attacking team work a lot harder to get into its regular half-court offense.

The 1-3-1 Trap

This is another form of the zone press that can disrupt an offense and hopefully create havoc over the entire floor. The responsibilities of the defensive players are different from the previous presses in the most aggressive of the trapping defenses we're offering. Here are the responsibilities of each defender:

- ◆ **Point:** The defender playing the point forces the ball to the corner and traps. He can play on or off the inbounds passer and is responsible for the ball.

- ◆ **Wings:** The two wings force the pass in front of them or deny the inbounds pass. They trap in the corner or up the sideline and cover the middle when on the weakside. The wing defenders must also slow the ball down when it is passed to their side, and they must spring back when there is weakside rotation to the basket.

- ◆ **Rover:** The defender assigned to the rover position floats in the middle of the court and plays centerfield on the inbounds pass. He looks to pick off a pass out of the first trap. He also tries to slow the ball down if the trap is broken.

- ◆ **Safety:** This is the deep man on the press. He protects the basket and looks for the long pass. The safety does not leave the area of the basket unless another defender rotates back to cover this role.

Hoop Lingo

The **rover** is a term that isn't used often in basketball. But with the 1-3-1 trap, the rover is almost like a centerfielder in baseball. He plays the middle of the court, between the two wings, and looks to intercept a pass from the first trap. He can also come up and slow the ball-handler if the offensive team breaks the trap.

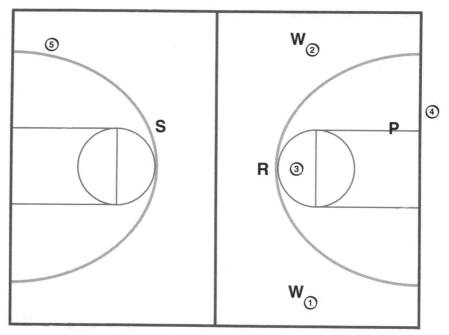

This is the basic setup for the 1-3-1 press. The point is on the ball and the safety back near the hoop.

The play can continue to develop with the 1-3-1 press at work. As with all these plays, the defenders must work together, know their roles, move quickly and decisively, and be ready to explode to the ball. And, of course, there are options depending on how the offense reacts. The following is a list of possible scenarios:

♦ The point defender should try to force the entry pass to the ballside corner and not allow the pass to the middle of the floor. He should try to make the offense catch the ball in front of the wing men. (See the illustration of the 1-3-1 setup.) The point may play on or off the in-bounds passer. If he plays on the ball, the wings are playing behind their men, forcing them forward. If he is off the ball, the wings can deny hard. In other words, they play up close to try to deny the pass to the players they are guarding. (See the following defensive setup illustration.)

Quick Tips

When coaches begin teaching defense, they always put an emphasis on moving quickly, stopping, and changing direction. The basic defensive drills are geared to this, and in defenses such as the press and trap, the early lessons pay off. A good pressing and trapping team has players who can move quickly, change direction, and beat the offensive players to a spot on the court. And that's where all the hard work and drills really pay off.

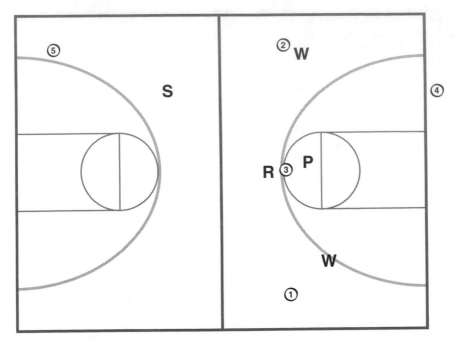

The defensive setup of the 1-3-1 press changes when the point guard plays off the inbounds passer.

◆ If the entry pass goes to the corner, the point and the ballside wing can go to trap. The weakside wing slides to cover the middle, while the rover looks to cut off the pass up the sideline. The safety continues to cover deep. (See the trap attempt in the entry pass corner in the following illustration.)

◆ Defenders should try to force a lob or bounce pass. These are slower passes and are easier to steal or deflect. The defenders should also try to force the ball handler to turn his back to midcourt. However, the defenders should *never* allow the ball handler to split a trap or go up the sideline. Players must remember to never leave their feet or foul when trapping. The man trapping should position himself directly between the ball and the man he is leaving to help force a lob or bounce pass.

◆ The defender should keep pressure on a pass back to the inbounder. Because this is not a penetrating pass, it does not hurt the pressing effort. The point should slide back to the ball handler with the wings returning to match up. Then, once again, the point should force the ball out of the middle. (See the point slide over the wings and come up to cover their men in the second following illustration.)

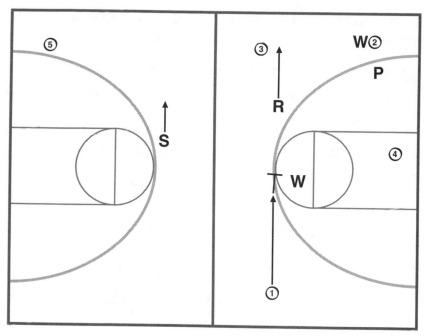

If the entry pass goes to the corner, the ballside wing and point can attempt the trap.

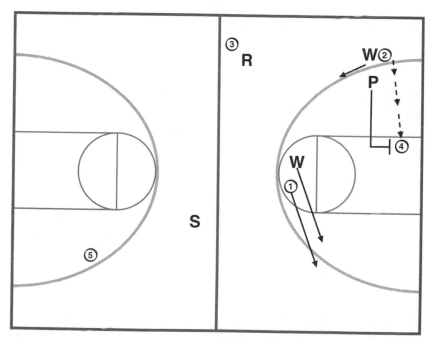

If the ball is passed back to the inbounder, the point slides over and the wings come up to cover their men.

- If there is a cross-court pass, the wing must slow the ball handler so the point can recover to trap. (See the following illustration.)

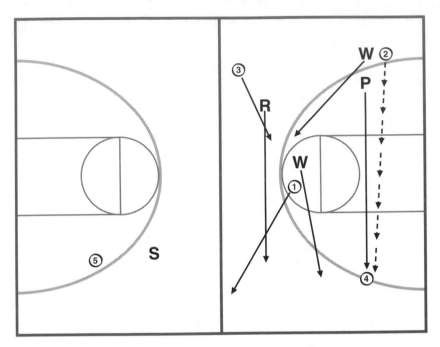

On the cross-court pass, the wing slows the ball handler as the point comes over to trap.

- The safety position covers any offensive player breaking long. The weakside wing looks to cover anyone breaking toward the middle, while the rover looks to guard the sideline pass. (See the illustration that shows coverage of player responsibility.)

- If the ball passes a defender, he must get back down the middle of the court. The weakside wing must sprint back in the rotation to help cover the basket area or move into the middle if the safety does not release for a steal.

- If the offense beats the initial trap, the defense should continue to force the ball up the sideline. In this case, the rover steps up to slow the ball handler and looks to trap with the wing. Everyone else must get back and rotate, as well as stay below the line of the ball.

- Remember, a press can be successful without steals. Other benefits of the 1-3-1 are turnovers, bad shots, and the opportunity to force the offense out of its normal rhythm.

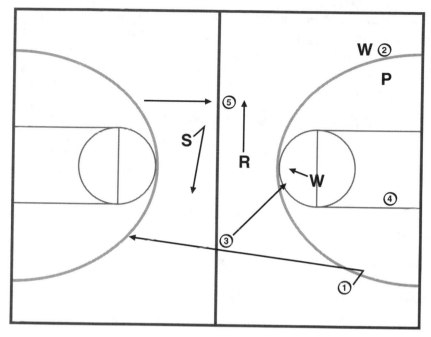

This diagram shows coverage responsibility as everyone works together.

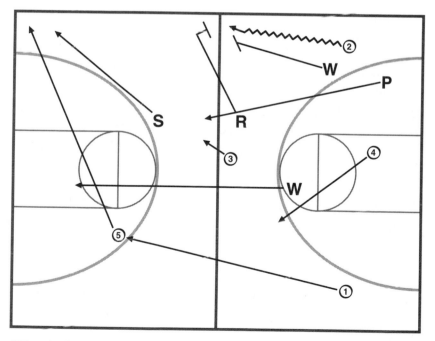

When the first trap is beaten, everyone gets back and rotates, yet the defense still looks to trap again.

This has been a very complete description of the 1-3-1 press or trap. As you can see, it is aggressive and disruptive to offenses, and it is the kind of maneuver kids should be able to learn and execute. We have already discussed forcing the dribbler and over-playing opponents. Now it's a matter of learning how to trap and rotate while protecting all areas of the court. Next, let's take a look at a second trapping press.

Coaching Corner

Presses and traps take not only practice, but a great deal of coordination between the defensive players on the floor. It's one thing to diagram the movements of these defenses, and another to walk the players through them. But just as when you are teaching the motion offense, it would benefit your players to actually watch these defensive formations in action. If you can find a tape where a team is using the press or 1-3-1 trap, show it to your team. Point out what each player must do. Stop or slow the tape to make your points, and then run it at regular speed so players can get a feel for the movement and coordination between the defensive players. This kind of demonstration will hopefully allow your players to get an instinctive feel for the press and trap before or during the time you are teaching it, and it can accelerate the learning process.

The 2-2-1 Press

The 2-2-1 is more of a delay press, an effort to slow the ball up, but it can still be an effective way to take the offensive team out of its rhythm. The two guards begin on each side of the foul line, with the two wings behind them inside the half-court line and a safety already in the front court, where she can move either backward or forward, depending on the situation.

In general, the defender on the ball plays straight up in a man-to-man defense. The other players, however, drop into a zone coverage, looking to take away the passing lanes or to double-team (trap). If no offensive player is in a defender's area, she should drop to the middle and look to cut off any players slashing to the middle. The player guarding the ball should always pressure the ball, containing the ball handler and not allowing her to get past. The deep players in the zone look for the long pass. If the ball gets behind a defender, she should look to run back and double-team. If the ball is passed away from a defender, she should drop back and seal the middle of the floor.

Quick Tips

Always remind your players that the ability to anticipate is the key ingredient in any type of press. Players should always be looking to get a hand on the ball and should know that a deflection of any kind can lead to a steal.

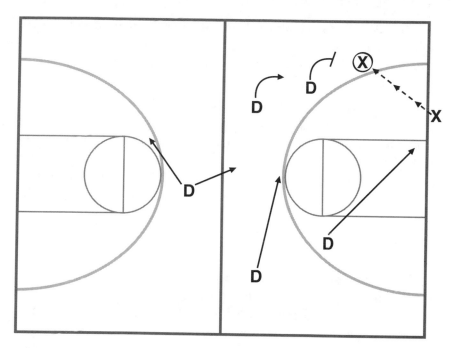

This is the initial set in the 2-2-1 press. Notice the top two defenders (1 and 2) getting ready to trap in the corner.

Here is what the various players are responsible for, beginning with the initial setup shown in the 2-2-1 press illustration. These are just basic responsibilities at the outset of the press. Players also must do additional things as the play develops or if the press is broken:

♦ Player 1, usually a wing or forward, should allow the pass to the corner if she is on the ballside and should try to make the receiver go as deep as possible to get the ball. Once the ball is inbounded, she should contain the receiver and not allow her to blow past to the middle with the dribble. If the receiver starts to dribble, player 1 should prevent her from advancing to allow player 2 to come over for a double-team. The defender should not allow the receiver to beat her up the sideline. If the offense inbounds on the opposite side, player 1 should exchange roles with player 2.

♦ Player 2, which can be the point guard, off guard, or wing, must prevent the pass from being inbounded on her side of the floor and also should try to prevent a return pass to the inbounder by stepping into the lane. She should also look to double-team the player guarded by player 1. The best time to double-team is just after the ball handler has committed to her dribble. If the ball handler dribbles away from her, player 2 should look to double-team immediately; if the ball handler dribbles toward her, she should *not* let the player split between herself and player 1. Remember, one of the objectives of this defense is to slow the ball down.

♦ Player 3, the point or off guard, is responsible for the area behind player 1, from the center line to the key area on the ballside of the court. She has to prevent a penetrating pass in her area and try to intercept or deflect any lob or slow pass. If the ball is caught in her area, she must cover the receiver using man-to-man defensive principles. If the ball handler should get by player 1, she must look to slow her down and then try to work a double-team with player 1, who is trailing the ball.

♦ Player 4, a wing, forward, or point guard, is responsible for the middle of the floor to her left as she faces the inbounder, and also for the area from her side of the center line to the foul line or deeper if player 2 is pulled over. As soon as the ball is inbounded to the opposite corner, she becomes responsible for the middle of the floor, the area between the foul circle and the center circle. When the ball is in player 1's area, she should be aware of a third player being brought back to receive a pass and should try to force this player to catch the pass below the foul line extended, or try to intercept the pass.

♦ Player 5, the center or a forward, must get to midcourt or deeper as soon as she can and should keep talking to the people in front of her. She should play up as far as possible without allowing herself to be beaten long and should always drift to the ballside of the floor. Then she should look for the long pass or a lob and also should look to guard the basket first if the press is beaten. In one situation, player 5 will rush up to try to trap on the sideline by the half-court line. If this happens, player 3 must come back immediately to take her place.

Quick Tips

If you are dealing with young kids (or even older age groups), your best bet is to keep the defense consistent. If you plan to use a man-to-man full-court press, use the run and jump. If you will use a form of the zone press, you might want your team to drop back into a zone defense after coming out of the press. This is another way to work a zone defense into your game plan. That doesn't mean that in nonpressing situations you can't go back to the man-to-man defense. No matter what press you use, try to keep it basic, but show your team the value of a pressing defense and how it pressures the other team to turn over the ball.

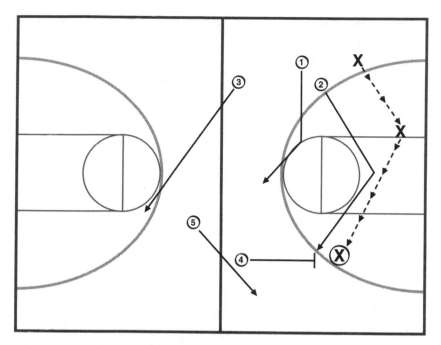

If the deep cover (player 5) comes up to help trap, player 3 must immediate rotate to cover the basket area.

You should be able to see how the 2-2-1 can slow the offense. Though the defenders are looking to trap, they also keep the court well covered. This is just another option that a team can use to disrupt an offense, especially an offense that is very effective in the half-court.

Defending the Fast Break

There are some basic rules for defending against the other team's fast break. It's nothing complex—just a matter of a team knowing how to execute and the players knowing where to go and then go there quickly. However, we have just outlined one basic way to stop the fast break, and that is to press. If your team can get into its pressing formation very quickly, it should be able to harass the outlet pass and maybe double-team or trap the receiver.

If you don't feel that your team is ready to do that, just instruct your players that on a missed shot they must get back quickly. In fact, if you are playing a breaking team, make sure you have two players start back immediately after the shot is taken. You may lose a little rebounding underneath, but you will be protected against the long pass and anyone breaking out on the dribble.

Your team can do yet another thing. If your opponent has a point guard who always gets the ball to start the break, you can jam him. In other words, as soon as the ball is rebounded, you send a player—usually the defender who is guarding him—to come up right alongside him and keep him from getting the outlet pass from the rebounder. There's no need to steal the ball—unless, of course, this can be done without committing fouls. Just by keeping the point from getting the ball and bursting out on the dribble, you've stopped the break by taking away the opponent's best ball handler. If he manages to get the ball, just have the defender back off and guard him man to man. If the defender has kept the point guard from getting the ball for just a few extra seconds, that effectively kills the fast break because the rest of the team can get back on defense in those few seconds.

Quick Tips _____

Here are a couple of additional quick tips on slowing or stopping the fast break:

- ◆ Have your bigger players retreat immediately to the paint and not worry about the ball. They can match up from that point.
- ◆ You can also have one designated player involved in the slowing-down process and tell everyone else to get back quickly.
- ◆ Finally, tell your players that they can retreat backward looking at the ball if they are fast enough, or they can turn and sprint.

Remember, in most instances, everyone should be able to run or sprint faster than the ball handler can dribble.

Defending Against Inbounds Plays

In the last chapter, we described a number of different inbounds plays, all designed to get the ball in play under changing circumstances. Now we look at it from a defensive standpoint, where the instructions aren't quite as complex. The offense might line up in different kinds of inbounding formations, such as the stack and the box, and the defense can only react to what is in front of them and guard the offensive players, no matter what the formation is. However, some general rules apply to defending all the different inbounds plays. As is the case in other phases of the game, it often comes down to execution. If the offense executes quicker and smoother, it may well prevail. If the defense does its job without being faked or fooled, it can put up a real roadblock for the offense.

Since most inbounds plays involve setting a variety of screens, defenders have to start by trying to fight through the screens. There also has to be a great deal of defensive communication. For example, when the screener's man is about to step out, the defense has to be ready to switch.

When the ball is being inbounded from the baseline at the offensive end, it's almost like an inverted play. The ball is coming from behind the basket, yet all the rules for defending screens are still in affect, with the most important being switching and communication. Defenders must always see the man and the ball. If a defender loses track of either, he will be in trouble. If you know which way your opponents want to pass the ball, you can have your defender who's on the ball stand in that passing lane to force the pass in an opposite direction. Remember, a defender must give the inbounds passer 3 feet clearance, but he can still stand in or jump to the passing lane. Defenders should always keep their hands up, but if the inbounder drops the ball to his waist, he's looking to throw a bounce pass and a defender should drop his hand on that side.

Quick Tips

It's really not difficult to practice defending the inbounds pass. You can do it at the same time you're practicing your inbounding techniques. As you decide upon the plays you want to use for inbounding in each specific situation and your players begin to understand them, throw the defense in to see who executes the best. That way, your offense is learning to make quick moves and crisp passes, while your defense is fighting through screens, switching, communicating, and trying to stop the play. Everyone benefits.

Defensive strategies play just as important a role in shaping a basketball team as do offensive game plans. As mentioned earlier, be sure to tell your players from day one that you expect the same kind of effort on defense that they are willing to give on offense. And, as a coach, make sure that *you* spend as much time teaching and practicing defense as you do offense. Of course, if you have a team that is more advanced on one side of the ball than the other, then you have to spend more time with the weaker phase of the game.

You might find that we haven't covered all the possible contingencies and circumstances of defense and defensive strategies. We have provided what we feel is a solid defensive base for young teams and young players. The skills and techniques discussed here are the same that are used at all levels of the game, right into the professional ranks.

The Least You Need to Know

◆ The objective of a full-court press is to trap, look for steals, and slow the offense from getting into its half-court rhythm.

◆ Be consistent when you press. If you use a zone press, have your team drop back to a zone defense. If the press is man-to-man, the basic defense should be man-to-man also. This is very important with the younger age groups, to avoid unnecessary confusion on defense.

◆ In a game, try a couple of presses early to see how the other team reacts to them. That way, you'll have a better idea whether to use the press again at crunch time.

◆ Slowing the ball handler and guarding against the long pass are the best ways to stop a fast break. Even a delay of just a few seconds will effectively stop the break.

◆ Fighting through screens, switching, and communicating are the keys to containing special inbounding plays devised by the offense.

Chapter **19**

Coaching a Game

In This Chapter

- ◆ Organizing the game
- ◆ Setting up the bench
- ◆ Timeouts and strategies
- ◆ Dealing with the players

It's finally game time. You may not have had as much practice time with your team as you would have liked, but when it's time to play, it's time to play. With your team going into real competition for the first time, you have to make the transition from a teaching coach to a game coach. That means being just as organized and consistent as you have been in practice since day one. You must prepare your team ahead of time and set parameters for the game itself, including organizing the bench, setting signals, deciding on strategies, thinking in terms of timeouts, and looking for ways to continue to teach without interference from players' families and friends.

In this final chapter, we talk to you, the coach, about working a game with young players. There should be no need to remind you that you are not a win-at-all-costs coach. That philosophy has no place in youth basketball.

Nor do you have to be Red Auerbach, Dean Smith, Pat Riley, John Wooden, or any of the other all-time great college and professional coaches. You are there to see that your players have fun, compete, and utilize all the skills and strategies you have taught them—including showing good sportsmanship and working together as a team. If you can do all that, consider yourself a success no matter how many games your team wins.

Know the League Parameters

You should always know everything about the facility at which the game is taking place. Does it have a place for the players to change into uniforms and shower after the game? Do the coaches have any responsibilities for setting up the gym, turning on lights, pulling out bleachers, or even sweeping the floor after the game? Depending on the league and level of competition, you may well be responsible for some of these things. Also ensure that someone is responsible for making sure the referees are at the game. Then you have to begin looking after your players.

Getting Them There Safely and on Time

Always make sure that your players arrive early to game facilities. Emphasize that they should not be fearful of being early. In fact, suggest they be at the gym 15 or 20 minutes before the designated arrival time. Of course, the coach should be early as well because nothing happens until you arrive. And you certainly can't expect your players to be on time if you're not.

Quick Tips _____

In the old days, athletes were supposed to be considered tough if they didn't take in fluids during practice or games. That theory, of course, is now ancient history. Fluids are very important, especially with sports played in the heat and with players perspiring freely during games. Instead of having a table with individual cups of fluid, you should encourage each player to bring his or her own bottle with water or an electrolyte-replacement drink such as Gatorade. The squirt-top bottle is best because there will be less spillage and no one will have to share the same open bottle, which can be a health concern. Of course, you should discourage high-sugar and caffeinated drinks such as soda. They aren't appropriate.

By getting there early, you can check on your players—make sure everyone is healthy and no one seems to be ill or has an injury you didn't know about. Being early also gives you a chance to talk to individual players before you speak with everyone as a team. If your team travels together, they should all meet at a common point, but if they aren't going to the facility as a team, make sure that each player has transportation. If you have to arrange car-pooling with several parents, do so. If you are in a cold-weather climate and are playing in a winter league, remind parents to make sure the players have enough warm clothing and something on their heads, since they will be perspiring and then showering before going out in the cold.

Setting Up the Bench

It may sound silly to say that you must set up the bench. After all, a bench is just a bench—a place for the players and coach to sit. Probably some coaches don't even think about the way the bench is set up, but you should. Some coaches prefer to be at the end of the bench, while others would rather sit in the middle with players on both sides. With the younger kids, we're recommending that you always sit in the middle of the bench. That way, as you evaluate and talk to the kids who are on the bench, you can talk to all of them at the same time. If you're at one end, the kids at the other end will have difficulty hearing you.

If you sit in the middle of the bench with players on each side, you'll have an easier time communicating with them during the game.

Timeouts, Halftime, and Afterward

During the game, there is nothing wrong with pointing out the positive things that are happening on the court. Remember, at this level you are always teaching, and when someone on the court does something right or does it very well—whether on your team or your opponent's—let your bench players know about it. By pointing out things that are happening on the court, you are not only giving your kids additional instruction, you also are keeping them involved in the game. You don't want them looking into the stands or waving to friends and family. If they know you are watching closely, they will watch as well.

What About Timeouts?

You also have to decide where you want players during timeouts. If the game has been going at a hectic pace, you might want the players on the court to sit on the bench during a timeout and the players on the bench to stand. That will give your players a breather before they resume play. No matter how you arrange timeouts, you should definitely insist upon one thing: During a timeout, all the players should focus on you, look directly at you, and listen. Some kids tend to look into the stands during timeouts, especially if family members and friends are calling to them.

During a timeout, let the players who are in the game sit down and ask the players on the bench to stand up.

You also have to be careful with your timeouts. Check league rules and see how many are allowed in each half; then save at least one timeout going into the last minute of the half and the last minute of the game. However, if you are being blown out and your team is being beaten badly, there is no reason to save your timeouts. In fact, you might use them to stop the offensive momentum of your opponent, to break up a scoring run, and to try to get your team back on track. Judicious use of timeouts is yet another important part of the game that too many beginning coaches neglect.

Halftime

How you use your halftime depends on the amount of time you have. In any case, it is limited, so you once again must be well organized. You should use the first two or three minutes to allow the players to get a drink, use the restrooms, if needed, and calm down a bit from the action on the court. If the team is winning, the kids will probably be pretty excited. If they're losing, they may be down on themselves. Think about what you want to say beforehand, make some notes, if necessary, and then be concise. Make your points in the order of importance. If adjusting the defense is the most important thing, talk about that first. If kids are taking bad shots, address that next, until you're finished. Then, just before the team returns to the court, mention that most important thing once more so it is once again fresh in everyone's mind.

Coaching Corner

At halftime, there is usually not enough time to address individual players one by one. Talk to an individual only if it is a matter of extreme importance. If you want to address a few small things to a couple of your players, a better time to do it is when they begin to warm up for the second half. You can then grab one or two of your players and speak to them quickly. As with everything else, be consistent. If you are concise, a player will always know what you want if you call her over during warm-ups, and she'll respond immediately.

After the Game

At the end of a game, make sure your players shake hands with their opponents. In fact, your league may mandate that the players shake hands. You must also establish some kind of evaluation process for the game the team just completed. Again, there are two ways to do this. You can go into the locker room and talk to your players before they take showers and change, or you can just say, "Good game, we'll discuss it at our next practice."

We recommend the second approach, for several reasons. When the game is over, players all react differently, even the youngest kids. The emotions can range from being heartbroken to being extremely happy after the same game ends. So just make a couple of quick remarks, ask them to digest what happened out on the court, and tell them you will discuss it at the next practice. Most parents will evaluate and discuss the game with their children. For this reason as well, it's better if you don't say anything after the game. If you haven't said anything, there's nothing that parents can call you about when everyone is fired up and claim you shouldn't have said something to their child, or that you should have done something differently.

For example, if one player throws the ball away three times, there may be a parent who feels he shouldn't have been in the game. You might be upset for a different reason—that the receiver wasn't where he was supposed to be when the pass arrived. By limiting what you say after the game, you can avoid much of the parental discussion with the kids about the game itself. Finally, you probably can use the time to sit back and review the game in your mind. After you have done this, you can give your team a better evaluation.

Coaching Corner

Many coaches today have someone videotaping their games, even when they are working with eight- and nine-year-olds. If you aren't taping, you should seriously think about doing it. A tape is a valuable teaching tool, a visual learning tool for everybody, even the young kids. As a coach, your instincts might tell you what to say, but the tape will confirm it one way or the other. If emotions are high because your team lost a game, you might say something you shouldn't say. If you look at the tapes, even if your instincts were right, you'll be more in control when you finally address the problem(s). Again, if you don't talk to players after a game but wait to view the tape, no tales can be brought home to the parents.

More Gametime Advice

Although winning is not absolutely the most important thing when you coach, you should always have your players try to win the game. That's still the overall objective, although everyone should obviously be aware that no team wins all of them. However, before you even start the season, you have to deal with an ethical question in your own mind. If you have decided to give equal playing time to all your kids, you must keep that commitment and try to win under those conditions. Again, it's all part of being consistent. If you promise equal playing time and then suddenly play only your best players in a close game because you want to win, you will lose some credibility and respect in the eyes of your players. Your best bet is probably to tell your players that, in basketball, like other sports, nothing is a 100 percent certainty all the time, but you will try to get everyone in the game.

As discussed previously, always use the first half to try your full-court presses once or twice in order to see how the opposition reacts to them. Then, if you find that you need the press in the second half or late in the game, you'll know how your opponents will react. If you are committed to playing everyone, use your weaker players mainly in the second and third quarters, and always integrate them with better players. And always try to make sure that no single player is ever embarrassed on the court. In other words, don't put your second-string players against the opponents' first-string players, even if you are winning by several points. Always have a more experienced and skilled player on the court to help less skilled players feel more confident.

Coaching Corner

There are a few reasons to remove a player from the game outside of the regular rotation. You can remove a player if she's not following instructions or if her on-court behavior is unacceptable. Poor sportsmanship can include arguing with officials, taunting opponents, and berating teammates. That player needs time on the bench and should be talked to before the next game.

Also, if you see that a player is winded, is very tired, or seems to be injured slightly, pull her out. Never take a chance with an injury. If the player insists that she can return but you aren't sure, don't put her back in until she is checked by an athletic trainer or doctor.

Communicating Plays

Coaches should always have some ways to communicate both offensive and defensive plays from the bench during a game. Usually these are single code words or simple phrases. For example, if you call out "Red defense, red defense," that might mean you want your team to go into a full-court press after the next basket. If the noise level is high, you might have hand signals, even if you can get the attention of only a single player. Then he can communicate it to the rest of the team.

As a coach, you should not be reluctant to change things if your team is losing or is simply not playing well. You might want to change defensive assignments if you are in a man-to-man defense and your defender cannot keep up with the opponent's point guard. If your team isn't hitting its outside shots, you might want to double up in the low post and try scoring more from the inside. That's the value of having a number of plays and variations on both offense and defense.

If You Have an Assistant

Many coaches of young kids work alone. There is nothing wrong with this. But some might have an assistant, or helper, who has worked with some of the players during practices and who decides to sit on the bench during games. If you have an assistant, you should give her specific duties. She can keep track of timeouts, chart the number of personal fouls on each of your players as well as the opposition, and keep a possession chart.

In addition, the assistant can chart both the offense and the defense. By halftime, she might tell you that the team has scored out of the triangle one out of every three times, but has scored from the shell only one of five times. This will help you make a judgment on which form of the motion offense to use in the second half and the fourth quarter. Your assistant can also keep track of the defense you are using and try to spot any holes in it. In addition, she can keep the bench organized and help with substitutions.

Substitutions

Pulling a kid out of the game can sometimes be a delicate matter. If your philosophy is to play everyone, you may have to take a player out who is having a great game. When you do this, tell him immediately how well he is playing and that he will be back in shortly. Explain that the player you sent into the game needs the experience and by giving it to him, if only for a few minutes, he will be better prepared to help the team when he is really needed.

If you pull a kid out who is having a terrible game, missing shots, not communicating, and committing turnovers, you have to use immediate positive reinforcement. Tell him not to get down on himself, that even the greatest players have bad games from time to time. Tell him to relax, keep his head in the game, and then get him back in there before the game ends. Never allow a player who is trying hard but having a bad game to feel he is being penalized for not playing well. Coaches sometimes have to walk a fine line during games, but if you are honest and keep the lines of communication open, your players should understand why you make the moves you are making.

A Word About the Jump Ball

Up to now, we have not made mention of the jump ball. At one time the jump ball played a major role in almost every basketball game. In fact, in the early days of the college game, there was a jump ball at center court after each and every basket.

So, it was important for teams to have a good jumper and set plays once the ref tossed the ball in the air. However, the jump ball is of much less importance today.

Most leagues today have the alternating possession rule. The first held ball goes to one team, and the second goes to the other team. These situations always resulted in jump balls in the old days. Today there is a jump ball at the beginning of the game and at the start of overtime. That's it. Even at the start of the second half, possession is determined by the alternating possession rule.

If you have a good leaper who wins the majority of jump balls, you can devise plays in which he taps it back or forward to a teammate who is posting up or cutting. If the other team has the advantage, you can concede the tap if it's directed backward because then your team will have plenty of time to get back on defense.

Wear the Label of Coach Proudly

Coaching youth sports is not something that should be taken lightly. Working with young kids of any age is a major responsibility, especially today when many kids find the pressures of playing well and winning to be overwhelming. As mentioned earlier, some 75 percent of young athletes are quitting team sports for good by the time they reach the age of 13. That's a very daunting statistic, and it should tell you all over again that you have undertaken a very important job.

You are teaching a sport that should be a fun-filled and healthy experience, a sport that fosters good sportsmanship, teamwork, individual skills, and camaraderie. As the coach, you are the leader, the one who sets the example for the entire tone of the team.

Hopefully, this book will serve as a guide to a successful coaching career and will help you develop healthy and happy players who will totally enjoy playing for you as they learn the game. We have tried to talk about the entire basketball experience without becoming overly technical. The advice we have dispensed here transcends the basketball court because coaching in recent years has become more than jump shots and full-court presses. The coach must provide an environment that makes players feel good about themselves and about being part of a team. He must not subject them to undue pressures and must not raise the bar of expectations too high.

Teach players the game, make it fun, show them how to compete, and to try to win without making it a must. Respect every single player you coach. Do that, and you should feel proud every time one of your players or a parent walks up to you and says "Hi, Coach!"

Coaching should be an enjoyable and rewarding experience for both you and your players.

The Least You Need to Know

◆ Coaching in a game is simply an extension of everything you have taught your team in practice.

◆ Be organized in every aspect of the game, from checking out your responsibilities at the facility where your team is playing to making sure your players are on time and dressed appropriately.

◆ Be sure to have your bench organized the way you want it and to keep the players focused on you during timeouts, not on their family and friends in the stands.

◆ Don't discuss the game immediately after it ends. Think about what you want to say; view a videotape, if it is available; and talk about it at the next practice.

◆ Do your job to the best of your ability and treat your players with respect, and you will be proud to be called Coach.

Glossary

air ball   A shot that completely misses both the rim and backboard.

alternate possession   A rule instituted to replace many former jump-ball situations. After the ball is tied up, it is awarded to each team alternately, with the first possession to one team and the next to the other team.

assist   A pass that leads directly to a basket. The passer is awarded an assist.

back-door   A maneuver in which an offensive player cuts behind his defender to the basket in order to receive a pass.

backcourt   The defensive half of the basketball court. As soon as the ball changes hands, the backcourt becomes the frontcourt, and vice versa.

ballside   The half of the court in which the basketball is located. Also called strongside.

bank shot   A shot that hits the backboard before going into the basket.

baseball pass   Usually a long downcourt pass thrown with one hand using a motion similar to that used in throwing a baseball.

blocking   Body contact that impedes the movement of an opposing player in such a way that the other player cannot stop or change direction to avoid it. It results in a personal foul.

bounce pass   A pass thrown with the intention of having the ball bounce once before reaching the receiver.

box-and-one defense   A combination defense in which four defenders play zone and the fifth covers an exceptional offensive player man-to-man.

boxing out   A player positions himself between an opponent and the basket so that he will have a better chance of grabbing a rebound than the opponent who is "boxed out" behind him.

carrying   A violation in which the ball handler allows the ball to rest in palm of his hand momentarily during his dribbling. Also called palming.

charging   A personal foul committed when a player runs into an opponent who has already established a stationary position and is not moving.

charity stripe   A slang term for the foul line.

chest pass   A pass pushed straight out from chest level that goes directly to the receiver without bouncing.

crossover dribble   A dribbling maneuver in which a player switches the ball from one hand to the other by bouncing it across the front of his body, usually done so that he can change direction quickly.

cutter   An offensive player who makes a sudden and quick move toward the basket.

defensive slide   A sideway shuffle that requires great quickness, enabling a defender to keep up with an offensive player and be ready to move quickly in any direction.

defensive stance   A position used as a starting point by all defenders. The player stays low, with the knees bent, feet spread, and hands out, ready to move quickly.

double dribble   A violation caused when a player dribbles, stops, and then dribbles again, or when he dribbles the ball with both hands.

double-team   A maneuver created when two defensive players converge to guard one offensive player.

downtown   A slang expression used to describe a long three-point shot.

dribbling   The act of moving up or down the basketball court while bouncing the ball repeatedly with either hand.

drive   A fast, hard move to the basket by an offensive player with the ball.

dunk   The act of an older, taller player jumping high enough to throw the ball through the basket when his hand or hands release it from above the rim.

fast break   The act of the offensive team or several members of the offensive team moving from the defensive end of the court to the opposite basket very quickly and before the defensive team has time to set up.

fced   A slang term describing a pass from an offensive player to a teammate who is open for a shot.

field goal   A successful basket worth either two or three points. This is not a free throw.

flagrant foul   An unnecessarily hard or rough foul deemed too harsh for the situation by the referee. It can result in a bonus free throw.

foul   An infraction of the rules resulting in a penalty and charged against both the individual and the team committing the foul.

foul out   A term used to describe the disqualification of a player exceeding the allotted number of personal fouls. This is five through the college level and six in the pros.

free throw   A shot taken unopposed from the foul line as a penalty for an infraction of the rules committed upon a player. Also called a foul shot.

frontcourt   The offensive half of the basketball court.

give and go   A play in which a player passes to a teammate and immediately cuts around his defender to the basket, looking for a return pass.

goaltending   A violation in which a tall player who can jump very high alters the trajectory of a shot that is already heading downward toward the basket. Goaltending also occurs when either an offensive or a defensive player touches the ball when it is in an imaginary cylinder extending upward from the rim.

gunner   A slang term for a player who shoots the ball almost every time it comes into his hands and often ignores teammates open for a better shot.

help and recover   A situation in which a defensive player leaves his man to help a teammate defend, and then quickly gets back to continue to cover his original opponent.

helpside   The half of the court in which the ball is not located. Also called the weakside.

high post   An offensive position near either side of the free-throw line, but outside the free-throw lane.

hoop   A slang term for the basket or, in its plural form, for the game itself.

inbounds play An offensive play that begins with the ball being passed in from a sideline or either baseline.

intentional foul A foul committed by a player for no apparent reason other than to give his team a technical advantage that could result from fouling at that point in the game.

key The area at each end of the court that is marked by the free-throw circle and free-throw lane. Years ago, when the 6-foot-wide lane widened to the 12-foot-wide foul circle, the area resembled a keyhole. Today the lane is also 12 feet wide except in the NBA, where it is 16 feet wide.

lob pass A high, arching pass designed to go directly over the head of one or more defensive players to reach an offensive player who is behind them.

low post An offensive position near the basket on either side of the free-throw lane.

man-to-man defense A form of defense in which each defender is responsible for a particular offensive player and defends that player wherever he goes on the court.

mismatch A situation in which a small player winds up guarding a much larger or taller player. It is usually the result of a defensive switch.

outlet pass A quick, crisp pass made to a teammate by a player who has grabbed a defensive rebound.

overplay To play an offensive man to one side in an attempt to force the dribble in a particular direction or to deny that player the reception of a pass.

passing lane An imaginary line between the player with the ball and a potential pass receiver.

pivot The act of a player turning his body while holding the ball, without picking up or moving the foot he has designated as his pivot foot. It can also be used as a slang term for the area designated as the high or low post.

pivot play The name for an offensive play that begins when the ball is thrown to a player in the high post with his back to the basket.

rebound A shot that doesn't go in the basket but that bounces off the rim becomes a rebound, a free ball that any player on either team can grab.

screen A legal maneuver in which a player positions himself in the path of a defender and does not move, in an attempt to allow a teammate to lose that defender and get open for a shot. Also called a pick.

shooting touch A term to describe a shooter's feel for shooting the ball softly, so that it tends to bounce around the rim with a better chance of going in the basket.

shot clock   In most leagues, this is a clock that tells the offensive team how much time remains before it must shoot the ball.

steps   A slang term for a traveling violation, which occurs when a player takes too many steps without dribbling, when a player moves his pivot foot while holding the ball, or when a player takes more than two steps after catching a pass. Also called walking or traveling.

swish   A term used for a shot that goes through the basket and touches only the net, not the rim.

switch   A defensive maneuver in which teammates take each other's men, usually because it's necessary to keep one of the offensive players from getting open. Switches often occur when the offensive team is setting a screen or a pick. The defensive players attempt to prevent the open shot by switching the offensive players they are defending.

technical foul   A foul called on a player or nonplayer (such as a player on the bench or the coach) that does not involve ordinary contact with an opponent. It can be called for unsportsmanlike conduct, such as arguing or taunting, on a player or coach.

three-point play   A play in which an offensive player scores a basket while being fouled and then hits a free throw.

three-point shot   A basket made from behind the three-point arc on the court. Also called a trey.

tip-in   A score that results from tapping a missed shot back into the basket without gaining full possession of the ball.

trap   A defensive maneuver that occurs when two or more defensive players surround the offensive player with the ball and prevent him from dribbling, shooting, or passing.

traveling   A violation that occurs when a player takes too many steps without dribbling, moves his pivot foot while holding the ball, or takes more than two steps after catching a pass. Also called walking or steps.

triple-threat position   The position assumed by an offensive player upon taking possession of the ball. The ball is usually held close to the hip on the shooting side, a position from which the player can dribble, shoot, or pass the basketball.

violation   An infraction of the rules, usually resulting in the loss of the ball and change of possession.

zone defense   A defense in which each player is responsible for an area of the court rather than for a specific offensive player.

Index

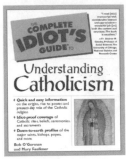

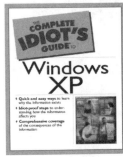